The Palgrave Macmillan Series in International Political Communication

Series Editor

Philip Seib
University of Southern California, USA

Aim of the Series
From democratization to terrorism, economic development to conflict resolution, global political dynamics are affected by the increasing pervasiveness and influence of communication media. This series examines the participants and their tools, their strategies and their impact.

More information about this series at
http://www.springer.com/series/14418

Fatima El-Issawi

Arab National Media and Political Change

Recording the Transition

Fatima El-Issawi
University of Essex, UK
London School of Economics
London, UK

The Palgrave Macmillan Series in International Political Communication
ISBN 978-1-137-53215-2 (hardcover)   ISBN 978-1-349-70915-1 (eBook)
ISBN 978-1-349-70917-5 (softcover)
DOI 10.1057/978-1-349-70915-1

Library of Congress Control Number: 2016957634

© The Editor(s) (if applicable) and The Author(s) 2016, First softcover printing 2018
This work is subject to copyright. All rights are solely and exclusively licensed by the Publisher, whether the whole or part of the material is concerned, specifically the rights of translation, reprinting, reuse of illustrations, recitation, broadcasting, reproduction on microfilms or in any other physical way, and transmission or information storage and retrieval, electronic adaptation, computer software, or by similar or dissimilar methodology now known or hereafter developed.
The use of general descriptive names, registered names, trademarks, service marks, etc. in this publication does not imply, even in the absence of a specific statement, that such names are exempt from the relevant protective laws and regulations and therefore free for general use. The publisher, the authors and the editors are safe to assume that the advice and information in this book are believed to be true and accurate at the date of publication. Neither the publisher nor the authors or the editors give a warranty, express or implied, with respect to the material contained herein or for any errors or omissions that may have been made.

Cover illustration: © igor terekhov / Alamy Stock Photo

Printed on acid-free paper

This Palgrave Macmillan imprint is published by Springer Nature
The registered company is Nature America Inc. New York

Contents

Introduction	1
Regulatory Media Reform: The Legacy of the Past and Burdens in the Present	13
Watchdogs and Patriots: How Arab Journalists Define Professionalism in Daily Practice	47
The Media Elite: Moderators or Preachers of the Public Opinion?	71
State Media: A Public Service?	99
Journalists Versus Activists? Traditional Journalists and Cyber-Activism	129
Ratings Are Votes: Media and Democratization	153

Conclusions	181
Selected Bibliography	191
Index	195

Introduction

Driving through the crowded streets of Cairo in the summer of 2012, my taxi driver could not hide his excitement while pointing to large posters featuring stars of talk shows, the lengthy televised broadcasts which keep Egyptians in front of the small screen each evening, watching live heated political debates. This was the year-long rule of the Muslim Brotherhood, when media and politics acquired an unprecedented dynamism, boosted by an equally strong antagonism. It was customary for coffee shops to display large television screens for their customers to watch the debates. An entrenched taboo, that of critiquing the president, had fallen: On his satirical show *el Bernameg*, Bassem Youssef broke audience records mocking the president, an unprecedented action in the Egyptian media landscape. Other taboos were shaken, but not strongly enough to fully erode them. Cairo by night had a different flavour than in years past; it buzzed with raging political debates that monopolised the small screen. As the TV anchor Reem Maged told me, under the former regime, "This is a nation where the only topic they could debate was football matches". A year later, the only buzzing to be heard was the blunt propaganda in praise of the military-backed regime. The debate was over.

In the aftermath of the uprisings that shook the Arab world in 2010, the power of digital activism in triggering political change has been the subject of extensive debate, policy discussions, and academic research.[1]

Much less interest has been dedicated to traditional media and its impact on framing the complex political changes in the Arab world, despite its crucial impact in shaping the values, beliefs, and identity of Arab audiences post-uprisings[2] and the primacy of television as a major source of news for Arab audiences, for both politics and entertainment.[3] Stigmatized for decades as nothing more than a tool for dispersing the regime's misinformation, national media in the so-called Arab Spring countries rose to prominence post-uprising(s) to become the main provider of information on national affairs to an audience avidly debating national politics. These audiences wanted to view the political upheaval through the eyes of their own national media, instead of the pan-Arab satellite TV channels they had previously depended upon. The immediate aftermath of the uprisings saw the chaotic outbreak of hundreds of new media enterprises, from media conglomerations to small personal projects, all locked in fervent competition to win a say in the new political arena.

The revival of national media post-uprising(s) triggered unrealistically high expectations for a "new era" of national media, evolving from a platform for blunt propaganda to a professional and credible provider of information for national audiences. However, the "awakenings" of this industry, which had been mismanaged and manipulated for decades, were handicapped by endemic challenges such as a lack of uniform professional standards; repressive regulatory frameworks and out-dated structures; issues of self-regulation and editorial standards; excessive political and ideological bias; blurred distinctions between opinions, rumours, and facts; and influence and pressure from the state and media owners alike, just to name a few.[4] Early hopes that this industry could play an effective, positive role in sustaining the fragile democratization processes faded, with political polarization taking the national media hostage. Journalists adopted an extremely antagonistic tone and enthusiastically played the roles of activist or preacher. Post-uprising, the political transition to democracy has oscillated wildly, the path lined on both sides with many trammels and beset with outbursts of autocracy and violence. The challenges are tremendous.

The role of media in democratic change, particularly its impact on promoting or stifling the fragile and often tumultuous democratization process, was and remains the object of much academic and policy analysis.[5] In the wake of the so-called "Third Wave" of democratization in the 1970s, encompassing southern Europe, Latin America, and parts of East and Southeast Asia, the transition to democracy of Eastern European states, and the move from apartheid to democracy in South Africa, the media was indeed instrumental in countering hegemonic discourse in some cases; but in others, it was less effective. Interest in the role of media in consolidating tenuous transitions to a democratic order finds its roots in the liberal conception of freedom of the press as one of the cornerstones of a healthy democracy.[6] Celebrated as a chief feature of the Western liberal model, the "watchdog" role of media in monitoring and redressing a regime's wrongdoing is difficult to implement in a previously closed and heavily manipulated media industry. While media played a major role in fostering legitimacy for new democratic institutions transitioning away from authoritarian rule, it at times assumed an inhibiting role, actively consolidating the status quo and delegitimizing democratic change.

While most scholarly work on the relationship between media and democracy is grounded in a Western context, the experience of the recent political change under the aegis of the so-called Arab Spring presents an invaluable opportunity to extend the comparative analysis of media systems and democratization to the Arab context, with the aim of analysing whether the existing literature on the relationship between media and democratization is corroborated or contested by these new democratic experiments. In so doing, this study adopts an inclusive conception of democracy, going beyond the election of competent elites to recognize the importance of civic cultures that embed democratic practices in all of life's facets.[7]

This book summarises the main findings of a large volume of field research I conducted in Tunisia, Egypt, and Libya between 2012 and 2015 with journalists from print and broadcast media.[8] My chief aspiration is to provide original narratives of the political transformations in the so-called Arab Spring countries as told by the lived experiences of the journalists reporting on them. By engaging with journalists' narratives and perceptions of political and media democratization, the book aims to provide a comparative analysis of media and political transitions unfolding in fluid and fast-moving environments, while taking into consideration the particularities of the former regimes and national contexts.

This book aspires to answer key questions on the relationship between traditional media and political change in the context of tumultuous Arab transitions to democracy. In so doing, it aspires to fill gaps of knowledge surrounding the complex and multi-layered interplay between media and politics in the context of Arab transitions to democracy, and the impact national media brings to this process, a topic which is still largely under-researched. Based on the extant international scholarly work on media and democratization, we seek to complement and extend the discussion beyond the Western context. The aim of this analysis is twofold: Firstly, it analyses the interplay between national media and political actors to understand to what extent media is contributing to fostering or impeding the fragile political transformations. Secondly, the study dissects dynamics of transformations within traditional newsrooms themselves during their difficult evolution towards embracing open and professional practices.

The notion of media "systems" has been fairly criticized for failing to accommodate changes in the media industry in the globalized world following the digital revolution that transcended the boundaries of nation-states and conventional mass media. This research pays special attention to the interactions between old and new media in the lived experiences of traditional journalists, working with notions of "media space" or "media landscape" whereby the connections between media institutions, technologies, and practices are better reflected.[9]

Based on extensive empirical research, the analysis adopts an original and unexplored perspective, investigating the specific pathways developed by Arab media in transition and unearthing media practices and values in detail. By engaging with a fluid media landscape as it adapts to the uncertainties of the transition, the study aims to draw a profile of the news community and journalists' understanding of their profession, their perceptions of political and media democratization, and their identity as active agents in this process, with specific research on distinct groups within these larger communities—such as the talk show hosts in Egypt.[10] The research was conducted with traditional journalists, those who work in institutional media where production follows editorial processes defined by the institution, as opposed to the unstructured forms of free expression favoured by cyber-activists. The notion of traditional media encompasses print and broadcast media outlets, but also new websites where the process of production follows internal institutional mechanisms. National media are defined as those media outlets that are governed by national rules and regulations on media, and target national audiences as opposed to pan-Arab media outlets that target audiences across regional borders.

The empirical research applies a thematic analysis[11] of semi-structured interviews with journalists using the following topic guide:

- Journalists' understanding of professional journalism and their relationship to their news sources
- Regulatory reforms in the media sector

- The process of institutionalization of media outlets and newsrooms
- The process of identity change for journalists
- Censorship and self-censorship
- Shifting dynamics developed between media and the political sphere
- Media funding schemes and their impact on media production

Prior to field visits, which were conducted in various phases of political transitions in each country covered by the study, a list of contacts was built through meticulous monitoring of the media in order to guarantee that the samples provided an accurate and balanced representation of this industry. Indicators such as age, gender, media genre, and position within the institutional hierarchy were taken into consideration in building samples of around 50 journalists in each country, in addition to other stakeholders such as media owners, union representatives, and media experts. While following the topic guide, the interviews were focused on the personal stories of journalists, allowing them to reflect on their professional journey while referring to practical examples from their own career and daily practice. In addition to qualitative interviews, the analysis used data from sustained media monitoring that followed relevant developments such as the reform of media regulations, and media debates around topics such as editorial independence, media funding, and the future of state media. This monitoring informed case studies used in various chapters. All the interviews were originally conducted in Arabic. The quotes as they appear have been translated into English.

Chapter 2 presents the main features of the media regulatory reform in Tunisia, Libya, and Egypt, along with a comparative analysis of the trends and challenges of media reform. Topics include media funding and ownership regulation, coercive legal dispositions, and attempts to liberate national media from the grip of Ministries of Information. Special attention is paid to the privatization of the national media, often celebrated as the pathway to liberate media practices from governments' grip (while excessive privatization is criticized as potentially leading to a fragmented and fractious media landscape). The free-market approach to media liberalization has arguably three central flaws: it excludes broad social interests, leads to a concentration of media ownership, and promotes cultural uniformity.[12] In a transitional context, different political forces and religious, and ethnic or sectarian groups often aim to control the national media, leading to a lack of genuine independence and a reduction of the public interest in order to serve partisan, religious, or ethnic interests.[13]

Chapter 3 reflects on how Arab journalists define professional journalism in relation to their sources, the representation of diverse point of views, and media activism.[14] It reflects on the complexity of journalists' own perceptions of their roles and identities, and how these perceptions are shaped and constrained by cultural and political factors. The chapter provides a comparative analysis of journalists' experiences of professionalism, taking into consideration international experiences and current academic literature on the subject.[15] With the relative and informal opening of the media and political spheres post-uprising(s), traditional journalists were faced with the challenge of reviewing their entrenched self-censorship habits and dubious relations with political actors. The continuous swing between reverential, radical, and monitory models in reporting politics shows the difficulty of reconciling old and new habits, that is, what journalists were used to doing and the new models introduced by professional training and audiences' changing expectations. The internal resistance to change within newsrooms is best reflected by the return of the "patriotic" journalist ideal in opposition to the Western "watchdog" model, with the latter being negatively painted by journalists as a denial of so-called "patriotic duty".[16]

Chapter 4 maps the forms of interactions and collusions between journalists and political actors. The political role of journalists during these transitions is particularly important, due to the re-fragmentation of the political sphere in the aftermath of regimes' fall.[17] The excessive political engagement of journalists caught in the "ideological crossfire"[18] post-uprising(s) is to be expected, given the media's transition from a closed to an open and professional institution. Players in the political system often use public communication to "mediate their respective positions and reach or break agreements".[19] In such contexts, the role of journalists as intermediaries is crucial.

Existing research on the role played by Arab traditional media as agents of political change largely focuses on pan-Arab satellite television channels, but there is little consensus on the effectiveness of these networks in fostering real change in this region.[20] This chapter concentrates on the national media, previously used by regimes primarily as a platform for propaganda, and their role in the sweeping political changes in the region. The post-uprising(s) phase witnessed an expanded function for talk show hosts willing to employ their personal agency to support various ideological agendas and political camps.[21] Egyptian talk show moderators were particularly vocal and prominent. The chapter also investigates the complex interplay between these media stars and the political agents, drawing on data from field interviews in Egypt and media monitoring, as well as existing international scholarly analysis on media elites.[22] While the role of Egyptian talk shows was pivotal in disseminating information to the masses before the events of January 201, post-uprising, these shows became the main platform for political lobbying in service of conflicting ideological camps and interests, adopting a heightened, emotionally charged tone. After the military coup, these shows transformed into a platform for incitement and antagonism, to the extent that they featured blunt calls for social exclusion and physical eradication of political opponents.

Chapter 5 pays special attention to the thorny process of reforming state media, from a redundant and stale structure to a provider of quality public-service information. For a short time post-uprising(s), state media journalists managed to include diversity and fair representation into their practices. Major progress was achieved, including newsrooms' rebellion against the official communiqué they were accustomed to using as a primary (often only) source when covering highly polemic events. Many media outlets adopted a larger scope of field, reporting not only on national events, but also on the daily needs and problems of local citizens. The chapter dissects the handicaps that have obstructed state media reform: practices of self–censorship, interdependence with the political sphere, and the state media's seemingly immutable identity as guardians of the regime. The combination of professional training and relative independence from executive powers has so far helped sustain the state media reform in Tunisia. However, this success remains highly fragile, as Tunisia still lacks the inclusive new structures that would protect this reform from changing political tides.[23]

New forms of political activism by traditional journalists and the interactions between old and new media in traditional newsrooms are the subjects of analysis in Chap. 6. In journalism studies, the notion of professionalism is deeply connected to the normative roles of the liberal and social-responsibility models.[24] New journalistic practices, such as citizen or grassroots journalism, challenge the traditional notions of professionalism and threaten "the jurisdictional claims of professionals".[25] Despite this, cyber-activist and citizen journalists proved increasingly effective, especially in breaking news on polemic events, when traditional media were not able or willing to report on them, even after the regime lost control over traditional media. This chapter looks into the use of social media by traditional journalists to network with other producers and connect with their audiences, but also to access news and information. Specifically we consider the growing trend among journalists to adopt a personal, emotional style that mimics that of bloggers, thus leading to a blurred identity, that is, at once journalist and activist. Divisions within the journalistic community, impacted by both the inclusion of citizen journalists in traditional newsrooms and the adoption of bloggers' engaged style in reporting on highly divisive political developments, are meticulously described in the chapter, along with reflections on traditional journalists' experiences and perceptions of their relationship to the blogosphere.

Chapter 7 analyses and questions the role of traditional Arab journalists as agents of democratic change in the particularly arduous and unpredictable transition from autocracy. Solidly linked to both political setbacks and successes, media democratization is itself a major factor in shaping the outcome of the transition. As Voltmer argues, "transitions to democracy are social experiments that affect virtually all aspects of a society".[26] The fall of national media into antagonism and its excessive use to incite political adversity have been a tough blow to this process. In Egypt, excessive media antagonism led to creation of a public opinion supportive of repressive measures and the suppression of rights and press freedoms. The persistent characterization of political adversaries as "others"—dangerous enemies that needed to be eradicated from within—exacerbated the antagonism of these transitions and in some cases, led to a relapse into autocracy.[27] While reflecting on existing literature on the role of media as an agent to support democratic change,[28] the chapter attempts to complement it by drawing on specific examples from Arab journalists' experiences.

Beyond its academic and policy contribution, the book aspires to present an important advocacy tool, providing original insight for regulatory reforms in the countries studied, as well as media development programmes in the region, based on assessment by journalists themselves of their roles and needs. Most importantly, this book is the story of the journalists' itinerary in reporting knotty political transformations while coping with the dramatic implications for their lives as citizens. It is the story of the journalists' struggle for professional legitimacy and independence amid a surge of repressive measures against freedom of expression and civil liberties in the name of fighting terrorism and preserving national security as well as raging violence. According to a local NGO in Cairo, the Arabic Network for Human Rights Information, to date at least 60 Egyptian journalists have been put behind bars for doing their job, a record number.[29]

Some of them were arrested at their offices, and their current whereabouts are kept secret by security services.[30] This book is also the story of these political transformations and public debates, narrated through the eyes of professional journalists.

Finally, this book is about Arab journalism, but it is meant to be itself a journalistic work as much as an academic one. In recording the experiences of these journalists, I was continuously navigating between the dual roles of journalist and academic. For long years, I was, like them, in the region reporting on complex political developments in a fluid and unsafe environment as a correspondent for international media organizations. Some of their daily challenges are the same as what other journalists encounter as they struggle for independence anywhere in the world; other challenges are unique to them. This book aspires, most of all, to convey their voice.

Notes

1. See Nezar AlSayyad and Muna Guvenc, "Virtual Uprisings: On the Interaction of New Social Media, Traditional Media Coverage and Urban Space during the 'Arab Spring'," Urban Studies (2013); Asef Bayat, Life as Politics: How Ordinary People Change the Middle East (US: Stanford University Press, 2013); Simon Cottle, "Media and the Arab Uprisings of 2011: Research Notes," Journalism 5 (2011); Christos A. Frangonikolopoulos and Ioannis Chapsos, "Explaining the Role and the Impact of the Social Media in the Arab Spring," GMJ: Mediterranean Edition 1 (2012).
2. See Walid El Hamamsy and Mounira Soliman, Popular Culture in the Middle East and North Africa: A Postcolonial Outlook (New York: Routledge, 2013).
3. Arab Media Outlook, "Arab Media: Exposure and Transition," *Dubai Press Club*, Dubai, (2012); *Asda' A Burson-Marsteller*, "Arab Youth Survey 2012," May 2, 2012, accessed September 2014, http://asdaabm.com/content.php?menu=research&page=69.
4. Naomi Sakr, Transformations in Egyptian Journalism (London: I.B. Tauris, 2013).
5. Vicky Randall, "The Media and Democratization in the Third World," Third World Quarterly, 3 (1993); Thomas Skidmore (ed.), Television, Politics and the Transition to Democracy in Latin America (Baltimore, MD: Johns Hopkins University Press, 1993); Silvio Waisbord, "The Mass Media and Consolidation of Democracy in South America," Research in Political Sociology 7 (1995); Katrin Voltmer, The Media in Transitional Democracies (Cambridge: Polity, 2013).

6. Fred S. Siebert, Wilbur Schramm and Theodore Peterson, Four Theories of the Press (Urbana, IL: University of Illinois Press, 1956).
7. Peter Dahlgren, Media and Political Engagement: Citizens, Communication and Democracy (Cambridge: Cambridge University Press, 2009).
8. The project "Arab Revolutions: Media Revolutions" was funded by Open Society Foundations and conducted field research in Tunisia, Libya and Egypt with traditional journalists of national media on the link between democratization and media as well as national media democratization.
9. See Terry Flew and Silvio Waisbord, "The Ongoing Significance of National Media Systems in the Context of Media Globalization," Media, Culture & Society (2015): 1–17.
10. See Fatima El Issawi, "Egyptian Media Under Transition: In the Name of the Regime…In the Name of the People?," POLIS, London School of Economics, March 2014; Sahar Khamis, "The Transformative Egyptian Media Landscape: Changes, Challenges and Comparative Perspectives," International Journal of Communications 5 (2011).
11. Greg Guest, Kathleen MacQueen and Emily Namey, Applied Thematic Analysis (Los Angeles, CA: SAGE, 2012).
12. James Curran, "Rethinking the Media as a Public Sphere," in Communication and Citizenship: Journalism and the Public Sphere, ed. P. Dahlgren and C. Sparks (London: Routledge, 1991), 47.
13. See Silvio Waisbord, "Latin America," in Public Sentinel: News Media & Governance Reform, ed. Pippa Norris (Washington, DC: The World Bank, 2010).
14. Hussain Amin, "Freedom as a Value in Arab Media: Perceptions and Attitudes among Journalists," Political Communication 2 (2002); Nayla Hamdy, "Arab Investigative Journalism Practice," Journal of Arab & Muslim Media Research 1 (2013).
15. Clifford G. Christians and others, Normative Theories of the Media, Journalism in Democratic Societies (Urbana: University of Illinois Press, 2009); Remy Rieffel, Que sont les médias? [What are the Media?] (Paris: Gallimard, 2005).
16. Fatima El Issawi and Bart Cammaerts, "Shifting Journalistic Roles in Democratic Transitions: Lessons from Egypt," Journalism 17, no. 5 (2016).
17. Chantal Mouffe and Ernesto Laclau, Hegemony and Socialist Strategy: Towards a Radical Democratic Politics (London: Verso, 1985), 127.
18. James Curran, 'Rethinking the Media as a Public Sphere".
19. Paolo Mancini, "The Public Sphere and the Use of News in a 'Coalition' System of Government," in Communication and Citizenship: Journalism and the Public Sphere, ed. Peter Dahlgren and Colin Sparks (London: Routledge, 1991), 142.

20. Muhammad I. Ayish, "Political Communication on Arab World Television: Evolving Patterns," Political Communication 2 (2002); Kai Hafez, "Arab Satellite Broadcasting," Real Arab World 1 (2006).
21. Fatima El-Issawi, "In Post-Revolution Egypt, Talk Shows Redefine the Political Landscape," *Foreign Policy*, October 10, 2013, accessed November 10, 2015, http://foreignpolicy.com/2012/10/10/in-post-revolution-egypt-talk-shows-redefine-the-political-landscape/.
22. Remy Rieffel, L'elite des journalistes: Les herauts de l'information [Journalists' Elite] (Paris: Sociologie D'Aujourd'hui, 1984); Serge Halimi, Les nouveaux chiens de garde [The New Watchdogs] (Paris: Liber-Raisons D'Agir, 1997).
23. Larbi Chouikha, La difficile transformation des medias [The Difficult Transformation of Media] (Tunis: Finzi, 2015).
24. Silvio Waisbord, Reinventing Professionalism: Journalism and News in Global Perspective (Cambridge: Polity Press, 2013).
25. Seth C. Lewis, "The Tension between Professional Control and Open Participation," Information, Communication & Society 6 (2012): 850.
26. Katrin Voltmer, "The Mass Media and the Dynamics of Political Communication in Processes of Democratization: An Introduction," in Mass Media and Political Communication in New Democracies, ed. Katrin Voltmer (London: Routledge, 2006), 1.
27. Chantal Mouffe, On the Political (London: Routledge, 2005).
28. See Daniel Hallin and Paolo Mancini, Comparing Media Systems: Three Models of Media and Politics (NY: Cambridge University Press, 2004); James Franck Hollifield and Calvin C. Jillson (ed.), Pathways to Democracy. The Political Economy of Democratic Transitions (London: Routledge, 2000); Vicky Randall, "The Media and Democratization in the Third World," Third World Quarterly 3 (1992); Thomas Skidmore (ed.), Television, Politics and the Transition to Democracy in Latin America (Baltimore, MD: Johns Hopkins University Press, 1993).
29. See a list prepared and released by the Arabic Network of Human Rights Information detailing names of Egyptian journalists behind bars as of July 2015, http://anhri.net/?p=146255.
30. *Committee to Protect Journalists*, "Egypt Arrests Three Journalists in Five Days, Whereabouts of Two Unknown," October 26, 2015, accessed November 10, 2015, https://cpj.org/2015/10/egypt-arrests-three-journalists-in-five-days-where.php.

Regulatory Media Reform: The Legacy of the Past and Burdens in the Present

Historically throughout the Arab world, national governments have used repressive laws to muzzle the national media and implement a culture of self–censorship. Regimes have used their Ministries of Information to ensure that media content is not infringing on entrenched red lines and to preserve their ability to enforce predetermined narratives and autocratic practices.

The processes of media reform launched post-uprising(s) were attempts to abolish repressive features in the regulatory framework. This goal has not been met, as a heavy arsenal of restrictive legal dispositions persists that make professional journalistic practices practically impossible. Attempts to abolish Ministries of Information have been generally unsuccessful, with new regimes opting for the reinstatement of these ministries as a "necessary measure" to discipline the chaotic media landscape that prevailed in the aftermath of the old regimes' fall.

In this chapter, I will present an overview of the main features of the media industries in Tunisia, Libya, and Egypt, looking at commonalities and particularities in these landscapes. I will analyze the major features of media reform and the main handicaps that threaten its successes. I will also present principal amendments and changes within the regulatory framework governing national media, both state-run and private. (It is important to note that a later chapter will deal in detail with state-run media and the reform of this media sector.)

© The Author(s) 2016
F. El-Issawi, *Arab National Media and Political Change*,
The Palgrave Macmillan Series in International Political
Communication, DOI 10.1057/978-1-349-70915-1_2

I. Tunisian Media Reform: An Example To Follow?

Media reform in Tunisia can be considered the most advanced in terms of moving to an open and diversified media landscape. However, this reform process remains very fragile—basic features of the plan still need to be approved by the new, largely conservative parliament, the first elected after the political transition post-uprising. Many doubt the new electorate's willingness to embrace progress and their sympathy towards these reforms. Journalists and media outlets continue to face physical and verbal attacks and legal intimidation, raising questions regarding the effectiveness of this process. New legal dispositions prescribed by anti-terror laws threaten to impose additional restrictions on independent reporting.

a. Old Media: The Same Old Story

The media industry in Tunisia has undergone drastic changes since the Jasmine revolution of 2011, moving away from a unilateral narrative toeing the regime's line to a diversified landscape reflecting the dynamism of the new political and social scene. A comprehensive legal and institutional reform process was launched immediately after the uprising with the aim of removing the repressive features of the old media system and introducing liberal ones. The Tunisian media was known as being among the most heavily censored media industries in the Arab world. As such, it was managed and controlled by a number of governmental bodies that insured media content adhered closely to the official discourse. Taking a "carrot and stick" approach, the government used advertisement and public subsidies as efficient control mechanisms, rewarding those outlets that were reverential and sanctioning those that were critical, thus jeopardizing the survival of independent media projects.[1]

In its bid to present an image of reform, the Ben Ali regime allowed the introduction of private broadcast media in its later years, in what was perceived internally and internationally as a cosmetic attempt to modernise national media. The audio-visual sector, previously under heavy government control, was opened up to private broadcasters, leading to the launch of two private television channels[2] and ten radio stations. The nature of the ownership of this private media sector, tied to the regime through friendship, family, or de facto nepotism, meant that its media content was as reverential as that provided by state media. The prohibition of private broadcast media from tackling politics made their impact on public opinion essentially null and void. According to a World Bank report released in May 2014, Tunis-based radio and TV stations, in addition to newspapers and magazines, were at least part-owned by a member of the Ben Ali family.[3] In regard to print media, the regime tolerated private presses but imposed several restrictions that hindered their viability, such as depriving them of advertisements coming from public administrations.

State and private media alike had to abide by editorial rules set by the regime, especially the prohibition of tackling the inner affairs of the Ben Ali family and topics such as corruption, the wealth disparity, or poverty. The Ministry of Communications held overall responsibility for the management of Tunisian media, while the Ministry of Interior was responsible for approving applications for new print publications. Neither Ministry released clear criteria or made any attempt to justify their decisions. The system of license provision for private broadcast was equally inconsistent and overrun by nepotism.[4] The approval or rejection of a license application was linked to politics without due process of any kind.

A major player in this landscape was the Agency for External Communication, created in 1990 as part of the Ministry of Communications. The agency was responsible for distributing the advertising revenues from public administrations—fundamental for the economic viability of various media outlets—to these organizations. The agency was also tasked with encouraging international media outlets to publish friendly and positive reports on the regime by sponsoring journalistic trips to Tunisia or even paying direct remunerations for such publications.[5] One of the most prominent beneficiaries of these trips was the former French Minister of Foreign and European Affairs, Michèle Alliot-Marie. She was forced to step down after the French press published the news of her Christmas holiday to Tunisia while the uprising was raging.[6]

Another important player, The Tunisian Internet Agency[7] (rebranded now as *Attounissiya* Internet) was responsible for policing online content, effectively blocking online pages containing any content that could annoy the regime or question its practices. After the revolution, access to the internet became uncensored; as a result, the agency has struggled to redefine its identity. Recently, the agency's management has frequently spoken out against attempts to return to an era of internet filtering.[8] For instance, the agency resisted calls for imposing a blanket ban on access to pornographic websites, a ban that was overruled by Tunisia's highest court.[9] The management of radio and television signal distribution was the jurisdiction of the National Broadcasting Corporation or *Office National de Télédiffusion* (ONT).

It was the regime's control instrument, operating in part by restricting access to the frequencies that enabled transmissions of broadcast content.[10] It is currently under the oversight of the new broadcast regulator (HAICA) and has assumed a purely technical function.

The fall of the Ben Ali regime was followed by an immediate suspension of the functions of most of these bodies. The Ministry of Communications that used to oversee the sector[11] was abolished, and the previously powerful Agency for External Communications was largely stripped of its prerogatives. However, no comprehensive restructuring of the former media system and its main agents was implemented.

The end of the previously rigidly regulated and monotone industry unleashed a long-repressed and eager appetite for publishing. According to the National Authority for the Reform of Information and Communication (INRIC), the body that was tasked by the first interim government with overseeing the reform of the media, as of November 2011, a total of 228 new Tunisian print publications had sprung up post-uprising,.[12] Since then, a large number of these publications have simply vanished. There are today a dozen dailies and around 30 periodicals, in addition to roughly 30 public TV and radio stations, and around 10 private television stations.[13] Print publications formerly owned by the ruling party[14] and which used to act as a platform for disseminating its ideology and narratives, were shut down, and their staffs merged into the state owned media. The Prime Minister's office confiscated those outlets that once belonged to the Ben Ali family and nominated "judicial administrators" to oversee their new management. The ownership situation and future of these outlets remains unclear. The Prime Minister's office also created a special unit for managing relations with national and international media, including granting accreditations for foreign correspondents, and dissolved the Agency for External Communications in January 2014, merging its staff and resources with that of the Prime Minister.[15] However, there are no clear rules on the distribution of public advertising revenues.

b. Regulatory Reforms: The Struggle for Legitimacy

The regulatory reform of Tunisian media focused primarily on abolishing the repressive legal features governing the media and setting the basis for a liberal and modern new legal framework. However, the process was hampered by a lack of support from politicians and fading enthusiasm from journalists. In the aftermath of the revolution, a consultative non-statutory body called the National Authority for Reform of Information and Communication (INRIC) was formed and entrusted with leading the media reform.[16] Composed of media professionals and legal experts and led by the internationally renowned Tunisian journalist Kamel Labidi, the new authority worked under the remit of the High Authority for the Achievement of the Revolutionary Objectives (*Haute instance pour la réalisation des objectifs de la revolution, de la réforme politique et de la transition démocratique*). The latter body was tasked with laying the foundations for the new republic—a function that was terminated in October 2011 when the Constituent Assembly was elected. The new body was charged with "proposing reforms for the information and communication sectors with consideration of international criteria on freedom of expression".[17]

These authorities produced three essential decrees; the first of these was the rewriting of the Press Code. The old Press Code (Law 32–1975), which had been amended four times in recent history—in 1988, 1993, 2001, and 2006—was heavily restrictive.[18] Physical and financial penalties were imposed on journalists for threatening "internal and external state security" and "public order", pursuant to vaguely worded legal dispositions. The Ministry of Interior applied these penalties arbitrarily and directed them mostly against those expressing political dissent. Defamation was treated as a criminal offense with prison terms imposed for "defamatory" speech expressed against public officials, the president, state institutions, foreign heads of state and foreign diplomats, and religious groups.[19] The length of defamation sentences depended on the official status of the defamed.

The new Press Code (Decree 115–2011 of November 2, 2011) guarantees "freedom of exchanging, publishing, and receiving news and views of all kinds". It recognizes some of most important and basic media rights, such as journalists' access to information, the confidentiality of sources, and journalists' protection against physical or economic threats as a result of exercising these rights, expressing opinions, or disseminating information. The new code abolishes all forms of licensing for print publications, replacing the old licensing process with a notification procedure before the judiciary. The decree imposes transparency on funding, ownership, editorial management, and circulation of these publications. Furthermore, it adopts anti-monopoly measures, such as prohibiting any single individual from owning two political publications that exceed 30% of the overall daily circulation of similar publications at the national level. The majority of prison sentences, including those for defamation and slander, have been abolished in favour of fines, with imprisonment reserved for a very limited number of offenses. Among those offenses are endorsing terrorism or war crimes, incitement to religious or racial hatred, disseminating ideas about racial discrimination, and publishing information related to legal cases of rape against minors.[20] In its final report, INRIC stated that these restrictions would be "limited to what it is necessary to satisfy a legitimate interest and according to the required measures in a democratic society".[21] Most importantly, the new text stipulates a unified sentence for defamation, regardless of the status of the defamed person.

A second decree (Decree 41–2011 dated May 26, 2011), allows journalists unprecedented access to governmental documents, a matter that was strictly denied under the former regime. The new decree obliges governmental bodies to facilitate access by journalists and the public to these documents. If a public administration refuses to disclose documents, it can be sued and held accountable.[22] However, this decree was criticized for its many exceptions, which threaten to transform it into a cosmetic guarantee.

The third decree, (Decree number 116–2011 dated November 2, 2011), guarantees freedom for the broadcast sector and establishes an independent regulator—the High Independent Authority for Audiovisual Communication, *Haute Authorit eIndependante de le Communication Audiovisuelle* or HAICA—tasked with overseeing the broadcast industry. Some restrictions were imposed on this newborn freedom, mostly the obligation to respect privacy, religious practice, the protection of children, and public health. The old restrictions related to the "protection of public order" and "national security" were not abolished, but were limited to special cases. According to former HAICA member Riad Ferjani, the definition of what can be considered a violation of national security was limited to few well-defined cases, namely, the dissemination of hate speech and direct calls for infighting, thus following the definitions of such crimes in international treaties ratified by Tunisia.[23]

Based on the decree establishing the new regulatory body, HAICA is composed of nine members representing various sectors in society.[24] This participatory structure aims to bring together journalists, media owners, and representatives of the political power, and the judiciary system, in order to guarantee inclusive representation and thereby avoid any political manipulation. This is crucial, since HAICA exercises significant regulatory, consultative, and judicial powers, including approving new operating licenses, producing license specifications (*cahiers de charge*) for public broadcasting outlets, and ensuring the plurality of the media's output, especially in political programs and during electoral campaigns. Most importantly, the independent body is empowered to sanction offenses committed by media outlets with gradually increasing penalties, ranging from infringement notices to fines and ultimately to the suspension or even withdrawal of operating licenses in extreme cases. The authority enjoys a binding say in all related law proposals as well as in the nomination of the heads of public broadcasters. It is considered "a tribunal of first instance," which is to say, all its decisions on imposing sanctions can be appealed through the judicial system.[25]

While Decree 41 was endorsed immediately, Decrees 115 and 116 proposed by INRIC were enforced by the government only in October 2012 after being approved by the Constituent Assembly. Ultimately the INRIC's team resigned, citing the continuous delays in implementing their dispositions, especially establishing a broadcast regulator, as an attempt by the *Ennahda*-led governing coalition to revert to old practices of media manipulation and evidence of a general lack of political will to support media reform.[26]

c. HAICA and Independence from Politics

The new broadcast regulator is a fragile body facing several challenges, chief among which is asserting its legitimacy in the eyes of the public and the new political powers that be. Although enshrined in laws, the birth of this independent body was continuously delayed and became a wrestling match between the *Ennahda*-led government and the secularist opposition.[27] The HAICA was finally endorsed by the government and effectively born in May 2013. The government and its opposition also battled over granting the new regulator an executive power, via a biding say on the appointment of high-ranking managers in state broadcasting media, a process previously used by the regime to assert control over state media. The government continuously resisted giving up this prerogative, although the new regulator legally holds exclusive right over the nomination to these posts. For instance, the *Ennahda*-led government—popularly called the Troika government[28]—appointed five directors of public radio stations without consulting HAICA in August 2013.[29] The government's nomination of a new head of state-owned television in August 2012 who is considered to be close to *Ennahda,* as well as the nomination of new director for the state-owned *Essabah* publishing house who was accused of formerly being a member of security forces, sparked an uproar in the journalistic community.[30]

Another crucial battlefield for HAICA is the right to enforce its laws and regulations regarding content as they pertain to privately owned broadcasters. HAICA's efforts to hold private broadcasters accountable has brought them into conflict with media barons vying to expand their influence over politics and economics; as a result, private media owners have frequently accused the regulator of attempting to inhibit media freedom. Providing a solution to the chaos reigning in media landscape that prevailed in the aftermath of the regime's fall is another thorny challenge for the new regulator. Eight "pirate" television stations and ten "pirate" radio stations sprang up post-uprising, benefiting from the lawless environment of the times. HAICA urged the owners of these stations to adhere to the licensing process and formally apply, threatening to halt their operations otherwise.[31] In addition, HAICA has to determine the status of those channels which received licenses under the former regime, as well as those who received provisional licenses based on the recommendations of INRIC,[32] many of which did not start operations.

Much of HAICA's legitimacy has come from its being acknowledged in the country's new constitution.[33] Attempts to reduce the far-reaching powers of this body, transforming it into little more than an advisory committee, have failed by virtue of campaigns launched by civil society groups and the media community.[34] The new constitution explicitly recognized the new regulator but changed the manner in which its members are chosen, stipulating they will be elected by the parliament, thus sparking valid fears for the body's independence and its potential misuse for political purposes. According to Article 125 of the new constitution, all independent constitutional bodies "are elected by the People's Assembly to which they present their annual report and before which they are responsible. They are elected by qualified majority". Article 127 of the constitution clearly sets the prerogatives of HAICA, entrusting it with "the regulation and the development of the audiovisual sector. It seeks to ensure freedom of expression and information, the right of access to information and the establishment of a pluralistic and impartial media landscape. The authority enjoys a regulatory power in its area of competence and must be consulted for bills related to its area of competence". According to the same article, HAICA is composed of nine members who should be "independent, neutral, competent, experienced and with integrity". They should perform their duties "for a single term of six years with one-third of the body's members renewed every two years".[35]

The constitutional reforms stipulating an election process were largely criticized by the National Union for Tunisian Journalists. The professional syndicate particularly condemned the new composition of this body and the lack of input from the professional community. Many fear that HAICA's transformation into an elected body will make it subject to under-the-table deals between political parties.[36] The new regulatory body has yet to prove that it can exercise its functions in the face of interference aiming to undermine its independence.[37] In the press sector, self-regulation is uniformly gaining popularity despite extreme political and media polarization. The National Union for Tunisian Journalists announced its plans to establish a national council for journalists which will assume an ethical role. One major task for this body would be to set a procedure for reviewing readers' complaints, as well as the adoption of an ethical code for print journalists. Despite its obvious importance and popularity, this project is yet to be implemented.

The relation between the independent body and the current secular government is as troublesome as it used to be with *Ennahda*-led governing coalition. The recent government intervention to sack two senior executives from Tunisian state television sparked wide criticism and was slammed by the head of the Tunisian national journalists' syndicate Naji Baghouri as "an arbitrary government intervention" and a "war on media". The government's decision to sack the tow executive and to replace them in breach of HAICA's constitutional rights took the decision after the TV channel broadcasted a picture of the severed head of a teenager beheaded by Islamists, sparking public outcry although the picture did not clearly show the severed head.[38]

d. Legal Uncertainty and Anti-Terror Laws

The media reform in Tunisia was largely successful in dismantling most of the oppressive features of the former media system and in introducing new liberal features. Many have praised the new constitution adopted by the former Constituent Assembly on January 2014 as a major step towards enhancing freedom of expression. Article 31 of the new constitution guarantees freedoms of opinion, thought, expression, and media and publication without prior censorship. Article 32 guarantees the right to information and the right of access to information and communication networks.[39]

However, daily practices and governmental policies are not consistent with these guarantees. The judiciary system uses double standards in dealing with legal cases against journalists, applying both the new press code and the old repressive penal code. The frequent application of prison sentences in legal cases pursuant to the penal code is transforming the judiciary into the government's main tool to quell freedom of the press. Effective liberalization of Tunisia's media sector will not be achieved without a comprehensive judicial review of all texts dealing with journalists' offences, including the penal code.[40] Legal cases targeting journalists on various grounds have become daily practice in Tunis. In addition to restrictions applied historically in the name of safeguarding national security, journalists also face new restrictions introduced post-uprising, manifested mainly in accusations of violating Islamic values. Among the many journalists facing these charges is Nabil Karoui, the director general of the privately owned Nessma TV station, which aired the French-Iranian film *Persepolis* including a scene depicting the main character talking to God. The lawsuit, which was filed by more than 140 lawyers, accused Karoui and two of his employees of complicity in airing a foreign film that would disturb public order and undermine public morality. In May 2012 Karoui was ultimately fined around $1,500.[41]

Lately, pressure and intimidation have intensified. TV camera operator Mourad Meherzi was arrested on charges including promoting a conspiracy to commit violence against government officials for filming an egg being thrown at a government minister in August 2013. Meherzi, if convicted, could face a possible seven-year prison sentence.[42] In July 2015 Nour Edine Mbarki, the editor-in-chief of the privately owned news website *Akher Khabar Online*, was accused of complicity in the Sousse terrorist attack that killed at least 39 people, pursuant to the old anti-terror law.[43] The only evidence of his complicity was Mbarki's publishing of a photograph depicting a car that purportedly transported the gunman. In addition to legal intimidation, journalists also face abuse at the hands of law enforcement agencies and police; increasing incidents of attacks against reporters criticizing security forces have prompted Reporters Without Borders to urge the government to take action.[44]

The gains of the Jasmine revolution in opening up the media and political spheres are threatened by governmental policies and decisions aimed at curbing media freedom. The government's withdrawal of a freedom of information bill that was meant to replace Decree 41was widely criticized by media freedom groups.[45] The bill was finally ratified by the parliament in March 2016, a development that was considered a victory for the Tunisian civil society especially that many exceptions on citizens' right to access information were abolished. A highly controversial draft law was approved by the Council of Ministers in April 2015 granting additional powers and protection to the security forces by banning any criticism against them. The draft law criminalizes any criticism of the country's security forces and would impose a two-year jail term for those convicted of the offense; a ten-year jail term is imposed for acquisition or use of any security secret.[46] The draft law is yet to be endorsed by the parliament.

The new anti-terror law adopted by the Tunisian parliament in 24 July 2015 sparked outcry from rights groups.[47] According to Saloua Ghazouani, Director of ARTICLE 19 Tunisia, the main concern over this law is its broad and ill-defined provisions granting immunity to security forces, which could be interpreted as putting government employees above scrutiny and thus restricting freedom of expression and media.[48] The law also includes articles that prohibit praising or condoning terrorism and inciting terror; broad interpretation of these articles could result in penalizing all street movements, protests, and civil society groups' activities. In addition, the law allows extended incommunicado detention and weakens due process guarantees, such as allowing the police to interrogate a suspect without a lawyer for 15 days. The new adopted bill is fomenting fears of a resurgence of police state repression: it was implemented to replace a law adopted in 2003 under Ben Ali's regime, a law under which about 3,000 people, many of whom were political dissidents, were tried on terrorism charges based on confessions extracted under torture.[49] Aside from these individual measures, the future of media reform remains uncertain. The newly elected parliament is expected to vote on the decree laws 115 and 116; they can decide to adopt, amend, or reject them. According to Kamel Labidi, the current parliament is not particularity sensitive to the need for a professional and independent media industry.[50]

II. Egypt: Polarization and Counter-Revolution Media

Since Egypt won independence from the United Kingdom in 1952, the country's media has been largely state-owned. The nationalization of the press in 1956 created a heavy apparatus of state-owned media with the sole mission of voicing the regime's message. The re-introduction of private media in late seventies helped diversify the media content, but failed to challenge existing taboos. National media remains governed by a set of heavily bureaucratic bodies tasked with not only organizing but also controlling the media content and operations.

a. Old Media: Centralised Control

The national press was put under the oversight of the Supreme Press Council at the Council's inception in 1975. As stated in article 67 of the Press Law of 1996, the Council oversees the printed press "in order to ensure its freedom and independence and the exercise of its powers in the framework of the basic components of the society".[51] According to the same law, the council is presided over by the head of the Shura Council, the upper chamber of the Egyptian parliament, and composed of the directors of state-owned publishing houses, the editors-in-chief of state-owned and partisan newspapers, the chair of the journalists' syndicate, and other syndicate members, academics, legal experts, and public figures appointed by the Shura Council. The Supreme Press Council was responsible for granting licenses to new publications; it did so according to opaque process lacking both clarity and consistency, as obtaining a newspaper license is defined simply as a "special privilege" under Article 49 of the current Press Law.[52] After the military takeover in July 2013, the Supreme Press Council was dissolved, and interim President Adly Mansour decided to establish a new Supreme Press Council formed by himself and made up of 15 members. The new board will be comprised of the head of the journalists' syndicate as well as media professors, writers, lawmakers, and prominent public figures. The new Supreme Press Council is expected to serve until the election of a new parliament for the country.[53] A proposal by few parliament's members for a new law granting President Sisi the right to form himself the Supreme Press Council in waiting for the adoption of a new press code, has sparked the uproar of the media community.

As to the broadcast sector, the state-owned Egyptian Radio and Television Union (ERTU), established in 1970, is governed by the 1979 Law 13—amended by Law 223 of 1989—defining its overall mandate as the fulfillment of the "mission statement of the audio-visual media and broadcasting services […] in compliance with overall public policy and widely acknowledged professional standards and criteria."[54] In practice, ERTU exercises a monopoly over all terrestrial domestic broadcast and is used as a governmental arm.[55] The head of this heavy structure was originally appointed by the Minister of Information, and then later by the president himself after the abolishment of the Ministry. The Ministry of Information, created in 1952, historically exerted powerful control over the media and was considered one of the most powerful political tools of the regime. After being abolished post-uprising in February 2011, the Ministry of Information was reinstated in July 2011. The Brotherhood government defended the reinstatement by arguing the move was aimed simply to prepare the ground for the Ministry's eventual, permanent abolishment. The Ministry was abolished again in June 2014, but the action was not accompanied by any clear vision for reorganizing the media sector.[56]

b. Privatization: Monopoly, Anyone?

The policies of relative political and economic openness under the late President Anwar Sadat (1976) allowed the reintroduction of private media. The party-owned media contributed to challenging the regime's narratives while bearing a strong ideological tone. The reintroduction of the privately owned press—called the independent press—in 2004 was a major step in widening the scope of public debate and diversifying media content. The independent press introduced a "newsy" format and content, favouring coverage of the everyday problems of ordinary citizens in opposition to the state-owned media's excessive focus on governmental activities.

The launch of private satellite TV ventures aimed to counter the popularity of the influential pan-Arab satellite TV stations.[57] Egypt was the first Arab country to launch a satellite TV channel—the Egyptian Space Channel (ESC)—on Arabsat in 1990. The Egyptian satellite, Nilesat, launched in 1996, was established as a joint public-private company operating Egyptian satellites. As of 2013, it broadcasts around 700 TV channels, and over 100 digital radio channels.[58] The post-uprising era witnessed a boom in the creation of private national media outlets, especially television stations. However, the licensing system remained obscure. The new TV channels close to the Brotherhood, launched post-uprising, were shut down immediately after the military coup.[59]

Several legal restrictions on the funding and operations of the new private media limited its ability to provide counter-narratives to the official discourse. The Press Authority Law No. 148 of 1980 limited private press ownership to legal entities and political parties. Newspapers could be privately owned on the condition that they would "take the form of cooperatives owned exclusively by Egyptians, with no one person owning more than ten per cent of the overall capital" (Article 52).[60] While these restrictions sought to prevent a monopoly, in practice they transformed private media ownership into a club for wealthy businessmen through so-called "nominal shares": small shares owned by relatives, friends, and connections of the wealthy businessman who maintain overall control on the editorial and business operations of the outlet. The obscurity of the licensing process leads to large media "empires" owned by businessmen wealthy enough to amass television stations, print media, and online media outlets. The vacuum of regulation for private media is obstructing its development beyond the model of media empires.

Private satellite television stations broadcast from the Media Public Free Zone in Nasr City, a suburb of Cairo; they respond to the quasi-governmental General Authority for Investment (GAFI).[61] While they do not submit to ERTU law, they must obtain a broadcasting license from GAFI, and the strong link between GAFI and the government limits its ability to function independently from political dictates. Furthermore, these licenses are considered business projects and don't provide any specific guidelines related to media operations. Thus, the private broadcasting sector lacks a clear framework for regulating diversity, fairness of representation, systems for allocating frequencies, and the rules for election coverage.[62] This opaque legal framework has been used as a tool for intimidation when the influential private TV stations dare to venture beyond the agreed-upon topics they can cover. The licenses of private broadcasters allow them to provide a general service, with no specific authorization to broadcast news; many bypass these restrictions by providing news in their popular talk show slots but face the danger that their license can be revoked or their programmes halted with no due process. In addition, these private ventures are dependent on the satellite companies that distribute their signals, and which are largely under the government's control.[63] In the radio sector, the state exercises a near monopoly, restricting most of the FM frequencies to state broadcasters. The Egyptian Radio Spectrum Allocation Chart, which is responsible for the allocation of the frequency spectrum, provides most of their frequencies to ERTU stations only.[64]

c. The Legal Arsenal

The regulatory system governing national Egyptian media did not witness major change post-uprising. While freedom of expression and media were guaranteed in the pre-uprising constitution, several laws in addition to the Press Code prescribed numerous restrictions, thus making the margin of manoeuvre for professional journalistic practices very narrow. These laws include the Press Law 156 of 1960; the Press Authority Law 148 of 1980; the Journalists' Syndicate Law 76 of 1970; chapter 14 of the Egyptian Penal Code related to publishing crimes; the Press Law 93 of 1995 (commonly called the Press Assassination Law); the Press Law 96 of 1996; and finally the Law 147 of 2006 amending some related articles contained in the penal code.⁶⁵ In addition to these laws that specifically address the media in Egypt, the 1958/162 Emergency Law authorizes the banning of publications and the trial of civilians, including journalists, before military courts. The law, abolished under President Sadat, was reintroduced following his assassination in 1981,⁶⁶ and then lifted again in May 2012.⁶⁷ Since then, it has been reinstated by military-backed governments at various occasions in the name of national security and combatting terrorism.⁶⁸

Just as in Tunisia, defamation of officials is treated as criminal offense, in breach of international standards; this is a powerful tool used by authorities to suppress and silence dissidents. Several legal provisions impose lengthy prison terms together with hefty fines for journalists convicted of libel and other ill-defined publications crimes. Prison sentences of up to five years are imposed for offences such as criticizing a foreign head of state or publication of material that constitutes "an attack against the dignity and honour of individuals "or an "outrage of the reputation of families."⁶⁹ Article 179 of the penal code imposes a prison term of up to three years for insulting the president; this article was used by authorities to silence the opposition, labelling political dissent as personal defamation. Article 184 imposes restrictions on media coverage of topics related to the parliament, the army, the courts, and other public authorities. Article 186 provides protection for judiciary and public officials from criticism; those accused of "insulting" or "humiliating" these officials face prison sentences of 6 months or more.⁷⁰ Article 21 of the Press Law prohibits statements that address the "demeanour of a public servant, prosecution personnel, or public employees, unless such dealing is closely related to their duties and responsibilities, and is aimed at realizing the public interest." Any breach of these dispositions can be punished by prison terms of up to one year and/or a fine.⁷¹ Other infractions journalists can be imprisoned for include intrusion into citizens' private lives, attacking religious faith, or accepting donations from foreign organizations.⁷²

The lack of professional protection for journalists aggravates the fragility of their working conditions. The Journalists' Syndicate Law (1970) prohibits a journalist from working if he/she is not registered with the syndicate. Similarly it is forbidden for any media outlet to hire a journalist not registered with the syndicate.⁷³ Nevertheless, a large number of journalists in Egypt are not registered due to the tough requirements regarding years of experience and scope of publications, making this membership a privilege available to very few.⁷⁴ The syndicate is also not open to broadcast journalists. These restrictions are largely viewed as a tool to exclude critical journalists and to buy the obedience of journalists members by the provision of special dispensations such as subsidies products, travels, flats, etc.

d. The Constitution in Theory and Practice

In the aftermath of the uprising, the interim constitution adopted by the Supreme Council of the Armed Force (SCAF—the Constitutional Declaration[75]) guaranteed media freedom and freedom of expression. Media censorship was not totally abolished, as it can be applied in exceptional cases such as during "national emergency or time of war".[76] Under the Brotherhood's administration, the 2012 constitution was adopted in a referendum, preserving this duality between articles that protect freedom of expression and others that co-opt it. The constitution provides for freedom of opinion and access to information in Articles 45–49. However, opposing legal provisions, such as Article 44, which prohibits "the insulting of prophets", largely negate these freedoms. This is in addition to the restrictions contained in various legal documents, especially the penal code.[77] Some important progress was achieved, mainly allowing individuals to launch new publications by notification in replacement of the former licensing process (Article 49). The 2012 constitution provided for the formation of independent Councils tasked with overseeing private and state-owned media (Articles 215 and 216). However, the formulation of these articles sparked controversy; the allusion to safeguarding "society's constructive traditions and customs" was denounced as a tool to prohibit coverage of certain topics in the name of religion.[78]

A new constitution, adopted by popular referendum in January 2014, has much of the same duality. On one hand, it recognizes the freedom of expression and thought (Article 65) and the freedom of the press and audio-visual and electronic media (Article 70). It grants all Egyptian legal and natural persons the right to own private media in all platforms (Article 70). The constitution recognizes the obligation of public bodies to disclose information and documents. It prohibits censorship of media outlets, as well as repressive sanctions against journalists for "offences" resulting from the exercise of their profession; on the other hand, however, it does allow censorship "in war time and general mobilization". Journalists convicted of "crimes of incitement to violence, discrimination among citizens, or attacks on individuals' honor" (Article 71) can receive repressive sentences. The launch of new audio-visual and electronic media will be regulated "according to the law" that will define "the procedures of the establishment and the ownership" of these media outlets (Article 70). The fact these sanctions are left to be defined later by "the law" without further detail leaves room for restrictive practices.

Furthermore, Article 204 of the constitution permits prosecution before military courts for "crimes that represent a direct assault on … the documents of the armed forces and their military secrets". The lack of clarity on the definition and scope of a "direct assault" allows for variable interpretations. In October 2014, President Abdel Fattah al-Sisi issued a decree placing all "public and vital facilities" under military jurisdiction for two years, thus paving the way for further military trials of civilians including journalists.[79] Article 31 of the constitution considers cyber space to be "an essential part of the economy and the national security", allowing potential restrictions on online media in the name of security and economic interests.[80]

Pursuant to Article 72 of the new constitution, the state committed to the "independence" of state-owned media in order to make sure the media content is "neutral and reflective of all opinions and political and intellectual trends and social interests". However, there is no clarification on how this independence would be implemented practically, and the current conditions of the state media are far from matching these criteria. The constitution establishes three independent Councils to oversee the media sector. Formed under Article 211, the Supreme Council for the Regulation of Media is an independent entity entrusted to "regulate the affairs of audio and visual media and regulate the printed and digital press, and other media means". The Council is responsible for guaranteeing and protecting media freedom, independence, plurality, and neutrality, which it does by monitoring the media outlets' sources of funding, and ensuring media organizations abide by professional standards and "the requirements of national security".[81] A second body, the National Press Organization, is entrusted with managing and developing the assets of print state institutions as well as ensuring its modernization, independence, and neutrality (Article 212). The National Media Organization is responsible for managing state broadcast and electronic media in order to ensure its independence and neutrality, as well as its economic viability (Article 213).[82]

Despite these definitions, the formation of these councils is unclear, left to be defined by "the law" with no further indications. The power granted to these councils contradicts international standards of self-regulation for print media. The vague allusion to the obligation to "respect the requirements of national security" paves the way for political control with the aim to restrict media content. The independence of these bodies is solidly linked to their structure—how members are nominated, how the organizations are funded, and what their prerogatives are and how they implement them. Debates on these crucial questions continue with no resolution in sight.[83] The establishment of these bodies became a subject of competition between two different committees: the first composed of 50 members, mainly journalists and representatives of professional media bodies, and the second formed by the Prime Minister with no input from the media community.[84] The first panel recently presented a law project "for the organization of the press and the media", as well as a second project proposing the abolishment of all prison sentences for journalists for offences related to their profession. The second project did, however, maintain optional prison sentences for offences such as incitement to discrimination and defamation, granting the judge in such cases the choice between imposing a prison sentence or a fine.[85] These are still law projects yet to be ratified or rejected.

The rise of the military-backed regime has nullified any progress within the constitution, as Egypt has seen an unprecedented crackdown on media and civil liberties. Security forces have perpetrated extrajudicial killings, torture, and arbitrary mass arrests, while civilians are being tried before military courts. The regime has openly restricted freedoms of expression, association, and peaceful assembly.[86] According to the Egyptian Center for Economic and Social Rights, there are as many as 41,000 prisoners currently held in Egypt with no legal due process; most are members of the Muslim Brotherhood or secular and leftist activists expressing political dissent.[87] According to a prison census conducted by the Committee to Protect Journalists on June 1, 2015, at least 18 of the 41,000 Egyptians behind bars are journalists,[88] most of them accused of affiliation with the banned Muslim Brotherhood. According to a local NGO, the Arabic Network for Human Rights Information, there are to date at least 60 Egyptian journalists behind bars for doing their job.[89] The campaign by the authorities targeting critical media has included not only journalists' arrests, but also temporary detention of staff, confiscation of production equipment, and the blocking of pan-Arab TV channels by the Egyptian satellite operator Nilesat. The only members of the media community left alone are those fuelling a populist media narrative glorifying the regime. The continuous intimidation of critical journalists was recently condemned by the Secretary General of the United Nations and human rights watchdogs after the arrest of investigative journalist Hossam Bahgat and his interrogation about an article he wrote on the trial of 26 military officers accused of plotting a coup against the government of President Abdel Fattah el-Sisi. Bahgat was released after the international campaign decrying his arrest.[90]

The Egyptian anti-terror bill approved by President Abdel Fatah el-Sisi in August 2015 represents further major setbacks to the rights and freedoms enshrined in the new constitution. The bill flagrantly contradicts the country's constitution, imposing hefty fines (up to about $50,000) for publishing or spreading "false" reports on attacks or security operations against armed groups.[91] It allows a "proportionate" use of force for police and security forces "in performing their duties" and seeks prison sentences for those found guilty of "inciting, or prepared to incite, directly or indirectly, a terrorist act".[92] This includes "promoting ideas that call for violence" and creating or using websites that spread such ideas. Most importantly, journalists have to stick to the official narration related to any "terrorist" attack or they can face fines (Article 33).

The vast scope of this law threatens to prevent any possible independent reporting on military operations, thus granting security forces a free hand in conducting these operations without transparency or accountability. Egypt's journalists' syndicate condemned the new anti-terror law, arguing "it is confiscating journalists' rights to access information from its various sources by limiting it to one side" of the story, and stressing the bill is putting the press under the "direct oversight" of the executive power.[93] Their concerns are not unfounded: media reports stating that dozens of troops had been killed in a Sinai attack in June 2015 aroused the fury of the military, which had issued an official death toll of 21 soldiers killed during the operation.[94] On September 2015, three journalists working for the al-Jazeera English network were sentenced by an Egyptian court to three years in prison for airing so-called "false news" based on their coverage on the aftermath of the coup; the sentence was internationally condemned as politically motivated, aimed at quelling independent reporting.[95]

III. Libyan Media Reform: A Process in Limbo

The Libyan media enjoyed unprecedented openness in the immediate aftermath of the 2011 uprising that overthrew the Gaddafi regime. Yet the reform of the national media sector was beset by diverse and complex problems, some stemming from the legacy of the former regime and others mirroring the challenges of the country's political transition. Most importantly, this reform lacked real vision. The heightened political transition, rife with violence and divisions, forced media staff to adopt new forms of self-censorship. The polarization of the new media landscape and its use as a prominent platform for political propaganda stalled the development of a professional and independent national media.[96] The lack of clarity regarding what values the media should adopt, and what the identity of the post-Gaddafi media should be, has undermined this already chaotic process.

a. The Gaddafi Media: A Propaganda Machine

National media under Gaddafi was exclusively state-owned and heavily censored. Media outlets had to avoid publishing any material that could be deemed offensive, particularly to Islam, national security, territorial integrity, and Qaddafi himself.[97] However, in describing their practices, journalists interviewed considered these legal restrictions less worrisome than the habits of self-censorship, the regime's control, and the interference of security services.

While this chapter will not deal with the structure of the former state media, it is worth noting the brief and failed attempt of media liberalization under Gaddafi's regime. In the 2000s, the regime yielded to international pressure and allowed a controlled opening of national media. This coincides with the end of United Nations sanctions on Libya in 2003 and the regime's adoption of limited top-down economic liberalization. Human rights watchdogs were allowed in the country for the first time in 2004[98] and the Internet was introduced in 2001.[99]

The "Al Gad" project, launched by Gaddafi's son Saif al-Islam Gaddafi, was a major attempt towards the liberalization of national media. Launched in the mid-2000s, the media reforms were one component of a comprehensive project that sought to rebrand the face of the regime and to engage its opponents through an alleged state reform initiative. The ambitious media reforms provided journalists with a much more open environment, in which censorship was limited to the crucial features of the regime: mainly the person of Gaddafi, national security, and territorial unity. The project was composed of a main TV channel, *al-Libiyya*; two newspapers, *Oea* and *Quryna*; and a news agency, Libya Press. However, the media's newfound freedom allowed by the junior Gaddafi was short-lived: it buckled under the pressure of internal battles between old and new regime's guards. The so-called media openness was a mere façade.[100] Although largely cosmetic, the project did introduce a new and modern editorial style, allowing journalists to experience first-hand professional journalism as well as providing them with training opportunities. As expressed by Mahmood al-Sharkasy, a Libyan TV talk show host, "we learned for the first time about something called professional skills"[101] through the training provided by the project.

b. Media Reform: An Aborted Initiative

The national media, used for decades as a simple publisher of the regime's communications, managed to open to diverse views and embed a 'newsy' output, becoming—for a brief period at least—a true provider of information. However, the legacy of the old regime is extremely heavy; the outbreak of civil war dividing the country into eastern and western regions,[102] and the fall of Tripoli into the hands of Islamic militias has forced many media outlets to halt operations, transforming those that remain into mouthpieces of the forces in control on the ground. Despite the formation of a unity government, or Government of National Accord, which is operating from the capital since April 2016, the conditions on the ground are still very volatile.

Freedom of expression and freedom of the press were recognized by Libya's Interim Constitutional Declaration, which was adopted post-uprising. Although Article 13 of the Constitutional Declaration endorses "freedom of opinion for individuals and groups, freedom of communication, liberty of press, printing, publication and mass media", the charter does not explicitly abolish censorship or acknowledge explicitly the right to seek, receive, and impart information and ideas.[103] According to the government's Decision 7 of December 2011, the new state media apparatus is limited to one official state television station, one official radio station, and one official newspaper.[104]

A 47 member Constitutional Drafting Assembly, elected with the task of drafting a new Libyan constitution according to Libya's interim constitution, is still struggling to deliver a new constitution for the country. The special commission which is convening since April 2014 in the eastern city of Bayda is coping with particularly difficult security conditions. The commission was originally intended to have 60 members, but security concerns hampered the elections of members for certain areas such as the city of Derna and several other areas in the south.[105] Nevertheless, the Drafting Assembly managed in April 2016 to reach a consensus on a draft constitution that will be submitted to a vote by the parliament.

The Committee for Supporting and Encouraging the Press (CESP), formed to oversee the reorganization of the press sector, decided to dismantle the former state newspapers and to publish new ones, but neglected to put together a vision for these future publications. Most importantly, the journalistic community did not view the media reform as legitimate, and found itself divided between newcomers—bloggers and amateurs journalists—and the old state media staff, most of whom were not allowed back in the media scene. This reform was led by cultural figures from the Gaddafi's opposition with no link to the media profession, a major handicap according to Soad Salem, a journalist from the former state media. "Their leadership is a main reason for the failure of the process of professionalism of the new Libyan media, they know nothing about media", she argues.[106]

The media sector suffers from the lack of extensive legislation, with the recent return of repressive practices such as those treating libel and defamation as criminal offences. The decision to finally reinstate the Ministry of Information after its abolishment post-uprising reflects the government's disarray in reforming the media sector. The Libyan parliament voted to reestablish the Ministry of Information to address the legacy of the former regime and create some order in a chaotic media sector.[107] The transitional power was first in favour of the abolishment of the Ministry of Information; Decree 44 issued in May 2012 established a High Media Council that would be responsible for overseeing the media sector. The Council was tasked with reorganizing Libya's media industry—formulating regulations and laws for media, adopting a code of ethics, and granting necessary licenses for various media groups.[108] The council was given authority over the assets of state media, print and broadcast. However, the High Media Council became itself the subject of a power struggle and competition among journalists leading up to the election of a second competing Council[109] and finally to the government's decision to stall the project.[110] There are currently a few new journalists' syndicate struggling to represent the journalistic community, thus exacerbating existing divisions.

According to a Freedom House assessment of 2014, Libya declined from a partly-free to a not-free media landscape, due an increased use of Gaddafi-era penal and civil codes to bring defamation cases against journalists, as well as the imposition of new legal restrictions on any criticism of the February 2011 revolution. For instance, the amended version of Article 195 of the penal code outlaws all criticism of the revolution or insults to officials, in replication of a law which was applied under the former regime banning all acts considered as an attack against the Great Fateh Revolution (Gaddafi's coup) and its leader. Another repressive decree bans satellite television stations that broadcast views perceived to be hostile to the revolution, or aimed at destabilizing the country, or creating "discord between Libyans".[111] The resurgence of Gaddafi-era laws is a serious setback. It opens the door for a return to self-censorship practices among journalists fearing legal reprisals, in addition to the fear of retaliation at the hands of armed groups. For instance, a Tripoli court sentenced Amara al-Khitabi, the editor-in-chief of the private *Al-Umma* newspaper to five years in jail and a hefty fine for "insulting the judiciary" after he published a list of the names of 87 judges and prosecutors he claimed were corrupt. The sentence has been decried as excessively harsh.[112]

c. The New Media Landscape: Coping with Chaos

The period after the uprising witnessed an explosion of new private media outlets driven by the opportunity to publish beyond the dictates of the state. According to a Freedom House assessment of the Libyan media situation in 2014, there are currently about 50 television channels and dozens of radio stations. There are two state-sponsored dailies, the official state paper *February* and the state-sponsored *Libya*, and nearly a dozen prominent private weeklies and monthlies published in the cities of Tripoli, Benghazi, and Misrata. Although hundreds of newspapers are registered, many publish only sporadically. There are three state-owned radio stations operated by the Libyan Radio and Television Corporation along with over a dozen private stations. There are two main state-operated television stations (*Libya al-Wataniyah* and *Libya al-Rasmiya*) along with five main private television stations. Local media funded by regional councils, especially radio and TV stations, are heavily engaged in inciting discord among cities, militias, and tribes.[113]

Most of these suffer from weak structures, opaque funding, and poor sustainability. The enthusiasm of the period immediately following the uprising has faded, as the media has largely became a platform for slander, misinformation, and ideological battles. A report by the Committee to Protect Journalists ascribes this decline to warring parties' actively feeding the media misinformation to help fuel the raging violence; regardless of the reason, the mismanagement of the media at large is evident.

Tripoli newspapers are no longer published in paper form due to a strike in July 2014 by staff of the printing houses. The Commission for Support and Encouragement of the Press is divided between a commission appointed by the Tripoli government and a new entity in Baida (East) appointed by the internationally recognized government.[114] State television and radio stations are controlled and sometimes directly managed by factions and armed militias (see Chapter 5 on state media). New channels launched in the capital, such as the February Channel, Libya Panorama, Zintan Channel, Tribes Channel, and Libya 24 Channel, offer no clear information regarding their operations and funding.[115] Most private TV channels that are still broadcasting suffer from continuous reshuffling and shifts in their staff, many of whom are forced to resign for fear of retaliation.

As the new media landscape has worsened, the security situation has drastically deteriorated as well: Libya suffers from a significant dearth of reporters, as field reporting is becoming effective suicide.[116] According to Reporters Without Borders, there were 7 murders, 37 abductions, and 127 physical attacks or acts of harassment targeting journalists between the end of the revolution and October 2014. The country was ranked 137th out of 180 countries in the 2014 Reporters Without Borders press freedom index, regressing by six places compared to its ranking in the previous year.[117] Newly launched private TV and radio stations find their offices and staff frequently targeted. In Tripoli, *al-Assima* TV Channel was stormed, forcing it to stop operations; *al-Dawliya* TV Channel suffered the same fate. Both stations adopt a liberal editorial line openly allied with anti-Islamic factions. In Benghazi, media organizations supporting Islamic trends were under attack by Tobruk government forces: both the radio and website *Ajwaa al-Bilad* and Free Libya TV station were closed.[118] The UN Human Rights Council's resolution of 22 September 2014 highlighted the plight of Libyan journalists, urging Libyan authorities to conduct "impartial, speedy, thorough, independent and effective investigations into all alleged violence against journalists and media workers falling within their jurisdiction".[119]

Conclusions

Examples drawn from transitional experiences of media reform confirm the difficulty and unpredictability of opening up media systems. The emerging media systems are by nature "a complex juxtaposition of the old and the new, a compromise between an ideal vision and what is possible in a given situation, a unique conjunction between the trajectory of the past and the immediate constraints of the transition itself",[120] as rightly noted by Professor of Communications and Democracy Katrin Voltmer.

Immediately after the fall of the previously repressive regimes, Arab journalists hoped to create an independent system for regulation, with no or limited intervention from the state. Despite chaotic conditions, positive developments have been achieved: All of the new constitutions recognize the freedom of media and freedom of expression and prohibit censorship. The licensing system for printed publications finally allows for the launch of new publications owned by individuals through simple a notification process.

Yet for every step forward, there is a step back: although prison sentences for offences committed by journalists in relation to their work were mostly rescinded, they have been re-imposed through laws or the new regime's practices. Journalists continue to struggle against criminal charges of defamation and vague legal dispositions restricting media coverage for the alleged safeguarding of national security interests. In the particular case of Tunisia, where a new press code was adopted with strong positive features, the refusal of the judiciary to acknowledge this progress, which resorted to the application of dispositions from the penal code in journalists' cases, made this reform meaningless. The guarantees of media freedom granted by the Egyptian constitution were also nullified under an unprecedented campaign of media repression, implemented by the military-backed government and designed to silence dissenting voices.

The imposition of exceptional measures under the aegis of anti-terror laws is allowing a wide range of restrictions on media content, media staff, and civil liberties in general, leading to a de facto return to the repression that prevailed before the uprisings, or worse. The ongoing crackdown on media and civil liberties in Egypt reflects the danger of loose legal provisions, as they often become powerful tools to silence critical media or force journalists to self-censor. According to Article 19 of the International Covenant on Civil and Political Rights (ICCPR), restrictions on media content should be limited to protected interests, and applied only when these restrictions are necessary. These restrictions should be also proportionate and carefully designed for the unique goal of protecting citizens' interests.

The opening of the media sector to private ownership resulted in a boom of new outlets, especially in the broadcast sector, as we see in Libya. However, without an appropriate regulatory framework to organize and protect this newfound freedom, we see issues quickly emerging: new licenses for broadcasters seem to be awarded based on favouritism and allegiance to regimes, while private terrestrial private broadcasting is still prohibited in some areas, particularly in Egypt. The general enthusiasm for establishing independent regulatory bodies for national media faded as new regimes grew reluctant to give up power over state-owned media. Even when such bodies are established, without a clear vision they can still easily transform into tools of governmental control. To succeed in bringing about lasting reform, they need to be explicitly independent from the political sphere with regard to both the legal framework establishing them and the system used to appoint members. In addition to the process for choosing the members of these bodies, other factors critical to maintaining independence include fixed tenures of their members, requirements regarding their expertise in the subject matter, and the approval of the regulator's budget by the parliament instead of via executive power.[121]

The establishment of these bodies requires the political endorsement of regimes but also the support of the media community: only with them engaged in the process will the outcome be perceived as legitimate. The exception proves the rule in Libya, where attempts to establish an independent media council failed mainly due to the lack of consensus among the nation's journalists regarding the council's role and other central issues. The establishment of such bodies requires a consultation with regional and international agents, drawing on common experience and existing expertise. The relative success of the Tunisian experience emphasizes this point: the creation of the Tunisian HAICA, effectively independent from the executive power, is unprecedented in the Arab world. Yet the regulator's independence is still threatened: as the regulator will be elected by parliament, this key position is still vulnerable to political machinations. Thus, the new regulating body faces the challenge of asserting its prerogatives and gaining acceptance from the larger media community. Demand continues for the establishment of independent bodies for overseeing printed publications; however, a system of pure self-regulation could be risky, as this requires prior implementation of best practices inside newsrooms and the engagement of the media community in adopting these systems effectively. Establishing a new culture inside newsrooms is an essential first step.

Dismantling the features of old repressive media systems has proved—and still proves—a formidable task, given the legacy of these structures and the difficult task of determining what values reform should promote and how they should be implemented. New rulers' lack of political support is a major handicap to this thorny process; the success of media reform is closely linked to the success of the political transition in general. Viable democracies require an exposure to opposing views and respect for political opponents.[122] The heated political battles endemic to the political transitions taking place in the so-called Arab Spring countries, and the relapse into severe autocratic rule some are enduring, render the national media's ability to provide professional and diverse output questionable at best.

Notes

1. Fatima El Issawi, "Tunisian Media in Transition," *Carnegie Endowment for International Peace*, Washington, DC, 2012.
2. These two stations are Hannibal TV and Nessma TV.
3. *Al-Jazeera*, "Revealing Tunisia's corruption under Ben Ali," March 2014, accessed September 10, 2015, http://www.aljazeera.com/indepth/features/2014/03/revealing-tunisia-corruption-under-ben-ali-201432785825560542.html.
4. Fatima El Issawi, "Tunisian Media in Transition".
5. Ibid., 4.
6. Ibid.
7. See the website of the agency, http://www.ati.tn/en/.
8. Afef Abrougui, "The Internet is Freedom: Index Speaks to Tunisian Internet Agency Chief," *Index On Censorship*, February 3, 2012, accessed September 10, 2015, https://www.indexoncensorship.org/2012/02/tunisia-internet-moez-chakchouk/.
9. Rohan Jayasekera, "Tunisia's Press Faces Repressive Laws, Uncertain Future," *Index On Censorship*, May 2, 2013, accessed September 10, 2015, https://www.indexoncensorship.org/2013/05/tunisias-press-faces-repressive-laws-uncertain-future/.
10. Fatima El Issawi, "Tunisian Media in Transition".
11. Decision 161/2011 issued by the first Tunisian interim government.
12. *National Authority for the Reform of Information and Communication (INRIC)*, 'INRIC Final Report', April 30, 2012, p. 59, accessed September 10, 2015 (French version).
13. Interview by the author with Tunisian journalist and activist Bechir Ourda, conducted by phone from London, 10 September 2015.
14. These publications are *al Hurriya* and *Le Renouveau*.
15. *Jawhara*, "Le personnel de l'ATCE réclame sa reintegration dans la function publique," May 12, 2015, accessed September 10, 2015, http://www.jawharafm.net/fr/article/le-personnel-de-l-atce-reclame-sa-reintegration-dans-la-fonction-publique/90/8995.
16. Decree 10/2011 dated 2 March 2011.
17. Ibid.
18. The Constitution of 1959 guaranteed the freedom of expression but it was never implemented in the practice.
19. Fatima El Issawi, "Tunisian Media in Transition", 7–8.
20. Ibid., 9–10.
21. INRIC, "Final Report", 27.
22. Decree 41, 2011, dated May 26, 2011, *Le Journal Official*, May 31, 2011, 792.

23. Interview with author, Tunis, November 2014.
24. In the current structure of HAICA, members are nominated by: The president of the republic, the judiciary, the speaker of the parliament, the union of journalists and representatives of the broadcast sector.
25. Fatima El Issawi, "Tunisian Media in Transition", 10–11.
26. Rohan Jayasekera, "Tunisia's Press Faces Repressive Laws, Uncertain Future".
27. Monia Ghanmi, "Tunisia Fosters Media Pluralism," *Maghrebia*, July 7, 2011.
28. After its victory in the first elections post Ben Ali, *Ennahda* Islamic party managed to build a cohabitation with two political parties—the Congress for the Republic and Ettakatol party, of secular background. The governing coalition was popularly called the Troika.
29. *Reporters Without Borders*, "An Open Letter to the Prime Minister," August 22, 2013, accessed September 11, 2015 (French), https://rsf.org/fr/actualites/lettre-ouverte-de-rsf-au-premier-ministre-les-autorites-doivent-revenir-sur-les-nouvelles.
30. Reporters Without Borders, "State media appointments discussed at meeting with government", August 29, 2012, accessed September 08, 2016 https://rsf.org/en/news/state-media-appointments-discussed-meeting-government.
31. See *Al Araby al Jadeed*, "HAICA calls officials not to appear on pirate TV channels", June 23, 2016, accessed September 09, 2016. (Arabic) https://www.alaraby.co.uk/medianews/2016/6/23/%D8%AA%D9%88%D9%86%D8%B3-%D8%A7%D9%84%D9%87%D8%A7%D9%8A%D9%83%D8%A7-%D8%AA%D8%AF%D8%B9%D9%88-%D8%A7%D9%84%D9%85%D8%B3%D8%A4%D9%88%D9%84%D9%8A%D9%86-%D9%84%D8%B9%D8%AF%D9%85-%D8%A7%D9%84%D8%B8%D9%87%D9%88%D8%B1-%D8%B9%D9%84%D9%89-%D9%82%D9%86%D9%88%D8%A7%D8%AA-%D8%BA%D9%8A%D8%B1-%D9%85%D8%B1%D8%AE%D8%B5%D8%A9.
32. The INRIC had recommended the approval of licenses for 11 radio stations and 5 TV stations from 33 applications provided the HAICA endorses these recommendations after its establishment. Only one of these TV stations started operations.
33. On January 26, 2014, the Tunisian Constituent Assembly adopted a new constitution which was signed by the then President Monsef Marzouki.
34. Fadil Alriza, "A Tale of Two Decrees," *Foreign Policy*, June 11, 2014, accessed September 11, 2015, http://foreignpolicy.com/2014/06/11/a-tale-of-two-decrees/.
35. Articles of the new constitution related to the HAICA, http://haica.tn/%D8%B9%D9%86-%D8%A7%D9%84%D9%87%D9%8A%D8%A6%D8%A9/%D9%81%D8%B5%D9%88%D9%84-%D9%85%D9%86-%D8%A7%D9%84%D8%AF%D8%B3%D8%AA%D9%88%D8%B1/.

36. *Tunivisions.net*, "L'intance constitutionnelle de l'information: quels enjeux," March 5, 2013, accessed September 11, 2015, http://tn-news.com/portal/v4/40694104.
37. *Article 19*, "Tunisia: Independence of HAICA Should be Protected," May 2, 2014, accessed September 11, 2015, https://www.article19.org/resources.php/resource/37532/en/tunisia:-independence-of-haica-should-be-protected.
38. Nada Ramadan, "Tunisia's Journalists' Syndicate Criticises the Government's 'War on Media'," *Al Araby al Jadeed*, November 18, 2015, accessed November 30, 2015, https://www.alaraby.co.uk/english/news/2015/11/18/tunisias-journalists-syndicate-criticises-the-governments-war-on-media.
39. Tunisia's constitution of 2014, https://www.constituteproject.org/constitution/Tunisia_2014.pdf.
40. See a report by *Article 19* on Tunisia' media reform, http://www.article19.org/resources.php/resource/3081/en/tunisia:-world-press-freedom-day-highlights-lack-of-progress-on-media-reform.
41. *The Telegraph*, "Tunisian TV Mogul Fined Over 'Blasphemous' Film," May 16, 2012, accessed September 15, 2015 http://www.telegraph.co.uk/news/worldnews/africaandindianocean/tunisia/9244054/Tunisian-TV-mogul-fined-over-blasphemous-film.html.
42. *Reporters Without Borders*, "Authorities Urged to Drop All Charges against Detained TV Cameraman," August 29, 2013, accessed September 15, 2015, http://en.rsf.org/tunisia-authorities-urged-to-drop-all-29-08-2013,45120.html.
43. *Committtee to Protect Journalists*, "Tunisia Charges Editor with Complicity in Terrorist Attack," July 23, 2015, accessed September 11, 2015, https://cpj.org/2015/07/tunisia-charges-editor-with-complicity-in-terroris.php.
44. *Reporters Without Borders*, "Face aux violences policières, Reporters sans frontières appelle à lutter contre l'impunité," May 29, 2014, accessed September 10, 2015, http://fr.rsf.org/tunisie-face-aux-violences-policieres-29-05-2014,46363.html.
45. *Committtee to Protect Journalists*, "Tunisia Charges Editor with Complicity in Terrorist Attack".
46. Asma Ghribi, "A New Law Sends an Ominous Signal in Tunisia," *Foreign Policy*, May 5, 2015, accessed September 15, 2015, http://foreignpolicy.com/2015/05/05/a-new-law-sends-an-ominous-signal-in-tunisia-arab-spring-bardo-tunis/.
47. Nick Rodrigo, "Tunisia's Anti-Terror Law: Superficial Solution to a Deeper Crisis," *al-Araby al-Jadeed*, July 31, 2015, accessed September 11, 2015, http://www.alaraby.co.uk/english/comment/2015/7/31/tunisias-anti-terror-law-superficial-solution-to-a-deeper-crisis.
48. Ibid.

49. *Human Rights Watch*, "Tunisia: Flaws in Revised Counterterrorism Bill," April 8, 2015, accessed September 10, 2015, http://www.hrw.org/news/2015/04/08/tunisia-flaws-revised-counterterrorism-bill.
50. Interview with author, Tunis, June 2015.
51. See the fourth section of The Press Law 96 of 1996 published by *Al-Jazeera.net*, http://www.aljazeera.net/specialfiles/pages/bea9b266-bdbf-4f4f-8677-05671f453131.
52. Toby Mendel, "Political and Media Transitions in Egypt: A Snapshot of Media Policy and Regulatory Environment," *Internews*, 2011, accessed September 11, 2015, p. 10, http://www.internews.org/sites/default/files/resources/Internews_Egypt_MediaLawReview_Aug11.pdf.
53. *Ahram Online*, "Egypt Interim President Appoints New Board for Supreme Press Council," August 5, 2013, accessed September 11, 2015, http://english.ahram.org.eg/NewsContent/1/64/78366/Egypt/Politics-/ Egypt-interim-president-appoints-new-board-for-Sup.aspx.
54. *ERTU Law*, Law No 13 of Year 1979 on the Egyptian Radio and Television Union, 1979.
55. Rasha Allam, "Egyptian Television Broadcast Regulatory Framework: Challenges and Opportunities," *Article 19*, September 20, 2012, accessed September 11, 2015, https://www.article19.org/join-the-debate.php/80/view/.
56. Eman el Shenawi, "Egypt Axes Media Ministry: Reform or Ruse?," *al-Arabiya*, June 18, 2014, accessed September 10, 2015, http://english.alarabiya.net/en/media/television-and-radio/2014/06/18/Egypt-scraps-media-ministry-reform-or-ruse-.html.
57. Nathan Brown, "Can the Colossus be Salvaged? Egypt's State-owned Press in a Post Revolutionary Environment," *Carnegie Endowment for International Peace*, August 22, 2011.
58. See Nilesat website, http://nilesat.com.eg/nilesat_8024/press%20releases/AboutUs/CompanyProfile.aspx.
59. *Al-Jazeera*, "Egypt's Military Shuts Down News Channels," July 4, 2013, accessed November 10, 2015, http://www.aljazeera.com/news/middleeast/2013/07/2013740531685326.html.
60. Toby Mendel, "Political and Media Transitions in Egypt".
61. It is defined by law as an "autonomous" agency reporting to the Egyptian government and its chair and members are appointed by the Prime Minister.
62. Toby Mendel, "Political and Media Transitions in Egypt".
63. Ibid.
64. Ibid.
65. Amira Abdel Fattah, "Press Freedom in Egypt," *The Arabic Network for Human Rights Information*, June 2008, accessed September 11, 2015, http://anhri.net/?p=108525&lang=en.

66. *The Telegraph*, "Egypt's State of Emergency Ends after 31 Years," May 31, 2012, accessed September 15, 2015, http://www.telegraph.co.uk/news/worldnews/africaandindianocean/egypt/9303195/Egypts-state-of-emergency-ends-after-31-years.html.
67. *CNN*, "Egypt Lifts Unpopular Emergency Law," June 2, 2012, accessed September 15, 2015, http://edition.cnn.com/2012/05/31/world/africa/egypt-emergency-law/index.html.
68. Egypt declared a three-month state of emergency in October 2014 in the north and centre of the Sinai peninsula after a suicide car bombing killed 30 Egyptian soldiers.
69. See the report of Freedom House on freedom on the press in Egypt for the year 2011, http://www.freedomhouse.org/report/freedom-press/2011/egypt.
70. The law 58 01 of the year 1937 promulgating the penal code, http://hrlibrary.umn.edu/research/Egypt/criminal-code.pdf.
71. Fatima El Issawi, "Egyptian Media Under Transition: In the Name of the Regime…in the Name of the People?," *POLIS*, London School of Economics and Political Science, 2014.
72. Ibid.
73. Amira Abdel Fattah, "Press Freedom in Egypt".
74. The syndicate limits its membership to journalists who have a large breadth of published works and experience, thus putting young journalists at a disadvantage.
75. After Mubarak resignation, the Supreme Council of the Armed Forces acted as the interim government. The council suspended the 1971 constitution and organised a constitutional referendum on nine new articles to the constitution that was held on 19 March 2011. It was proclaimed by SCAF on 23 March.
76. Fatima El Issawi, "Egyptian Media Under Transition".
77. Ibid.
78. Sarah Carr and Mohamed Adam, "In the Name of Morals and Sharia, Media Freedoms may Contract," *Masress*, January, 29, 2012, accessed September 11, 2015, http://www.masress.com/en/almasryalyoumen/1347611.
79. *Human Rights Watch*, "Egypt: Unprecedented Expansion of Military Courts," November 17, 2014, accessed September 11, 2015, https://www.hrw.org/news/2014/11/17/egypt-unprecedented-expansion-military-courts.
80. The Egyptian constitution of 2014, https://www.constituteproject.org/constitution/Egypt_2014.pdf.
81. Ibid.
82. Ibid.

83. Fatima El Issawi, "Egyptian Media Under Transition".
84. Interview by author with media expert Naglaa el-Emary by phone from London, September 2015.
85. See an analysis of these draft laws by *Mada Masr* news online, http://www.madamasr.com/ar/sections/politics/%D9%81%D9%8A-%D8%A7%D9%84%D9%8A%D9%88%D9%85-%D8%A7%D9%84%D8%B9%D8%A7%D9%84%D9%85%D9%8A-%D9%84%D8%AD%D8%B1%D9%8A%D8%A9-%D8%A7%D9%84%D8%B5%D8%AD%D8%A7%D9%81%D9%8A%D8%A9-%D9%85%D8%A3%D8%B2%D9%82-%D8%A7%D9%84%D8%AA%D8%B4%D8%B1%D9%8A%D8%B9%D8%A7%D8%AA-%D8%A7%D9%84%D8%B5%D8%AD%D9%81%D9%8A%D8%A9-%D9%81%D9%8A-%D9%85%D8%B5%D8%B1.
86. See report of Human Rights Watch on right abuses in the country during 2014, http://www.hrw.org/world-report/2014/country-chapters/egypt?page=1.
87. *Human Rights Watch*, "Egypt: UN Should Condemn Worsening Abuses," November 4, 2014, accessed September 20, 2015, https://www.hrw.org/news/2014/11/04/egypt-un-should-condemn-worsening-abuses.
88. *Committee to Protect Journalists*, "Egypt's Imprisonment of Journalists is At an All-time High," June 25, 2015, accessed September 11, 2015, https://cpj.org/reports/2015/06/egypt-imprisonment-of-journalists-is-at-an-all-time-high.php.
89. See a list prepared and released by the Arabic Network of Human Rights Information detailing names of Egyptian journalists behind bars as of July 2015, http://anhri.net/?p=146255.
90. Kareem Fahim, "Egypt Extends Detention of a Journalist, Hossam Bahgat," *The New York Times*, November 9, 2015, accessed September 01, 2016, http://www.nytimes.com/2015/11/10/world/middleeast/egypt-extends-detention-of-a-journalist-hossam-bahgat.html.
91. The draft bill initially proposed a prison sentence for publishing false news but this sentence was withdrawn later and replaced by fines.
92. *Al Jazeeraa*, "Egypt Adopts Controversial Anti-Terrorism Law," August 17, 2015, accessed September 11, 2015, http://www.aljazeera.com/news/2015/08/egypt-adopts-controversial-anti-terror-law-150817042612693.html.
93. *Ahram Online*, "Egypt's journalists' syndicate says new anti-terror law will curtail press freedoms", July 05, 2015, accessed June 01, 2016, http://english.ahram.org.eg/NewsContent/1/64/134619/Egypt/Politics-/Egypts-journalists-syndicate-says-new-antiterror-l.aspx.
94. *The Guardian*, "Egypt Imposes Anti-Terror Law that Punishes 'False' Reporting of Attacks," August 17, 2015, accessed September 11, 2015, https://www.theguardian.com/world/2015/aug/17/egyptian-president-ratifies-law-to-punish-false-reporting-of-terror-attacks.

95. *The Guardian*, "Al-Jazeera Journalists Jailed for Airing 'False News', Egyptian Court Ruling Says," September 6, 2015, accessed September 11, 2015, https://www.theguardian.com/media/2015/sep/06/al-jazeera-journalists-jailed-for-airing-false-news-egyptian-court-ruling-says.
96. Fatima El Issawi, "Transitional Libyan Media: Free at Last?," *Carnegie Endowment for International Peace*, Washington, DC, 2013.
97. See the report of Freedom House of the status of the freedom of the Press in Libya in 2009, https://freedomhouse.org/report/freedom-press/2009/libya.
98. *Reporters Without Borders*, "The Birth of 'Free Media' in Eastern Libya," April 2011.
99. Fatima El Issawi, "Libya Media Transition: Heading to the Unknown," *POLIS*, London School of Economics and Political Science, 2013, 14.
100. Ibid., 20–22.
101. Ibid.
102. The country has witnessed two major military operations: the so called "Dignity" operation in the East led by General Hafter claiming to fight Islamic groups and the operation "Dawn Libya" in the West led by Islamic factions who took control over Tripoli and forced the elected parliament and government out of the capital.
103. Fatima El Issawi, "Libya Media Transition: Heading to the Unknown", 27.
104. Taher Zaroog, "The Media should be Free of Government Influences," *Reinventing the Public Sphere in Libya*, accessed September 10, 2015 www.reinventinglibya.org/lnmu.php.
105. Ayman al Warfalli, "Libya's Constitution-Drafting Body Starts Work," *Reuters*, April 21, 2014, accessed November 30, 2015, http://www.reuters.com/article/2014/04/21/us-libya-constitution-idUSBREA3K0NS20140421#1YfdA5lqfYU5aZ8M.97.
106. Interview with author conducted by phone from London, September 2015.
107. George Grant, "Libyan Media to Be Regulated by New Ministry of Information," *Libya Herald*, November 26, 2012, accessed September 10, 2015 https://www.libyaherald.com/2012/11/26/national-congress-votes-to-create-new-ministry-of-information/.
108. Fatima El Issawi, "Libya Media Transition: Heading to the Unknown".
109. A conference in Jadu in western Libya in June 2012 ended with a group of journalists electing a second Council.
110. Fatima El Issawi, "Transitional Libyan Media: Free at Last?"
111. *Amnesty International*, "Libya: Three Years on, Gaddafi-Era Laws Used to Clamp Down on Free Expression," February 13, 2014, accessed September 10, 2015, https://www.amnesty.org/en/latest/news/2014/02/libya-three-years-gaddafi-era-laws-used-clamp-down-free-expression/.

112. *Al Arabiya*, "Libya Journalist Sentenced to 5 Years Jail for Defamation," November 21, 2014, accessed September 15, 2015, http://english.alarabiya.net/en/media/print/2014/11/21/Libya-journalist-sentenced-to-5-years-jail-for-defamation.html.
113. See Freedom House report on the freedom of press in Libya in 2014, https://freedomhouse.org/report/freedom-press/2014/libya#.Ve8a_hFVhHw.
114. *Africagate News*, "The Nomination of a New Head of the Libyan Committee to for Supporting and Encouraging the Press," July 14, 2015, accessed September 11, 2015,(Arabic), http://www.afrigatenews.net/content/%D8%AA%D8%B9%D9%8A%D9%8A%D9%86-%D8%B1%D8%A6%D9%8A%D8%B3-%D8%AC%D8%AF%D9%8A%D8%AF-%D9%84%D9%87%D9%8A%D8%A6%D8%A9-%D8%AF%D8%B9%D9%85-%D9%88%D8%AA%D8%B4%D8%AC%D9%8A%D8%B9-%D8%A7%D9%84%D8%B5%D8%AD%D8%A7%D9%81%D8%A9-%D8%A7%D9%84%D9%84%D9%8A%D8%A8%D9%8A%D8%A9.
115. *Correspondents.org*, "Libyan Media: A Detailed Scene," November 25, 2014, accessed September 10, 2015, http://www.correspondents.org/ar/node/5937.
116. Fadil Aliriza, "Lack of Media Coverage Compounds Violence in Libya," *Committee to Protect Journalists*, April 27, 2015, accessed September 10, 2015, https://cpj.org/2015/04/attacks-on-the-press-lack-of-media-coverage-compounds-violence-in-libya.php.
117. *Reporters Without Borders*, "'Not Seeing News from Libya Anymore?'—RWB's New Campaign," October 23, 2014, accessed September 12, 2015, http://en.rsf.org/libye-not-seeing-news-from-libya-any-23-10-2014,47140.html.
118. Ibid.
119. *Reporters Without Borders*, "Libya Still Extremely Dangerous for Journalists," October 14, 2014, accessed September 13, 2015, http://en.rsf.org/libya-libya-still-extremely-dangerous-14-10-2014,47108.html.
120. Katrin Voltmer, Building Media Systems in the Western Balkans: Lost between Models and Realities (Sarajevo: Analitika – Center for Social Research, 2013), 17.
121. A paper by Toby Mendel, workshop's papers, Tunis, March 2015.
122. Katrin Voltmer and Mansur Lalljee, "Agree to Disagree: Respect for Political Opponents," in British Social Attitudes: The 23rd Report, ed. Alison Park, John Curtice, Katarina Thomson, MirandaPhillips, and Mark Johnson (London: Sage, 2007).

Watchdogs and Patriots: How Arab Journalists Define Professionalism in Daily Practice

In the polarized Egyptian media scene that prevailed under the Muslim Brotherhood's short-lived rule, the majority of journalists interviewed about their professional identity said simply: We are Egyptians before being journalists. For them, the main task of a "professional" journalist is to defend the country from a perceived danger to its sovereignty, rather than to provide their audiences with comprehensive fact-based storytelling encompassing different views. Similarly, journalists in Tunisia and Libya felt that taking a political stance was a necessity in their profession, especially when the identity and the future of the post-uprising political and societal systems were perceived to be at stake.

Journalists in these countries, whose role used to be limited to disseminating the regime's communiqués and policies, were empowered in the post-uprisings era. However, with this newfound freedom often translating into a chaotic expression of personal opinions, they are still not truly liberated from the "public relations" role they used to perform on the regime's behalf. For decades before the uprisings they sang the praises of regimes. Now they continue to perform the same function—only at the service of the political and ideological agendas that arose in the post-uprisings era.

With the exception of Tunisia, where some main legislation was changed, media reform has not been institutionalized. Many legal restrictions against journalists have remained in place, and often, where legislative reform existed, it was not applied in practice, allowing the repression of media staff to continue. The collective experience of practicing journalism under authoritarian regimes has prevailed, with both self-censorship habits and dubious relationships between journalists and politicians remaining strong—in defiance of calls for change. The forceful return of the ideological role of media and the ideal of the "patriotic" journalist acting in defence of the nation against external and internal "enemies", helped consolidate this resistance to change.

Theoretical Analysis

According to normative models[1] defined by the four theories of the press,[2] the nature of the press is a reflection of the nature of "the system of social control",[3] which underscores the solid link between media and politics. Although important in linking theory to journalistic practice, this analysis has been criticized for failing to accommodate both the complexities of modern media systems and the tremendous changes in the media industry following the rise of new media platforms.[4] The four "normative traditions of public communication"[5] of Christians et al.[6] define four different roles for media: monitorial (watchdog of the power sphere), facilitative (media acting as a platform for citizens' participation), radical (radical opposition media), and collaborative (reverential media). Dissection of the various roles played by journalists demonstrates not only the link between politics and media but also the impact the media has on the public—how, for instance, it supports the deliberation of diverse civil society voices through the facilitative role.

Although it has the advantage of extending beyond the Western context, this typology is problematic in many ways. The ability of Western media to provide neutral and objective content—the main pillar of the monitorial role—is doubtful.[7] In the context of political democratization, the watchdog function of the media is even more problematic, with media tending to exacerbate existing tensions. Data from this field investigation demonstrates that Arab journalists have a tendency to reject the concept of objective reporting, considering it at odds with their perceived "duty" to defend a political agenda. In the wake of the so called Arab Spring idea that media should question the political power did not translate into practice. Rather the media became a platform to disseminate accusations and slander, with media outlets, especially television, proving one of the most powerful tools of political campaigning. The main problem with these normative media models is that they try to prescribe rather than to describe the media. They are "based on how things should be rather than how thing are in reality and what are the dynamics that shape them".[8]

The three models proposed by Hallin and Mancini[9] take into consideration both the regulatory framework and behavioural patterns of journalists in (what they present as) an empirical description of media practices. The "liberal model", predominant in Anglo-Saxon countries, is market led, with neutrality and a low level of state intervention as key journalistic values. The "democratic corporatist model", predominant in Northern Europe, places great importance on the role of public service and the need to fairly represent different interests and groups. The "polarized pluralist model", favoured in Mediterranean European countries, is characterized by an intricate link between politics and media, as well as a popular partisan media that reflect ideological leanings ("political parallelism").[10] While this analysis does try to accommodate non-Western experiences, its most significant shortcoming is the limitation of these experiences to one model (the polarized pluralist model), without taking into account the vast diversity of media and political systems. It also contains an implicit normative judgment, presenting all non-Western and emerging media systems as immature and flawed compared to the efficiency of liberal and corporatist Western models.[11] The practice of "exporting" models has often lent rigidity to the thorny task of reconstructing media systems in the context of democratic transition. The internal deficiencies of emerging democracies and their media systems make implementing these imported models an impossibly difficult task,[12] since an important precondition for media reform is the ability of implemented models and norms to acquire legitimacy, being "domesticated" through integration into local values and customs.[13]

According to the social constructivist perspective, institutions are in a continuous process of definition, creation, and recreation through collective discourses and the interpretations of those applying their rules.[14] Institutions in a new environment are bound to deviate from Western models, in accordance with how they are interpreted and used by individuals within that environment.[15] Building democratic media institutions is, therefore, a long-term process that needs to be embedded in "collective deliberations" in order to gain legitimacy and sustainability.[16] As Votlmer contends, "Without this rooting in public discourse institutions remain isolated, without legitimacy and ultimately unprotected".[17] This lack of legitimacy goes a long way in explaining the troubles experienced during media reform processes in the countries of the Arab uprisings. Old and new media institutions are manipulated by both the political sphere and wealthy businessmen, and are often a favourite target for repression at the hands of new regimes and outlaw militias. However, institutions themselves also help fuel political tensions and social divisions by having dubious links to the political sphere and attempting to portray political adversaries as ultimate enemies that are in need of suppression.

Media systems reform is shaped by the structure and traditions of the old regime. The "unique types of media systems" that are generally the fruit of emerging democracies are hybrid in their nature and difficult to be labelled according to models of media in established democracies.[18] This contention is supported by the case of Egypt, where the legacy of the past, as well as entrenched habits of serving regimes within media practice, overshadowed—and then stalled—media reform efforts.[19]

I will now discuss journalists' perceptions of their professional roles insofar as they facilitate the representation of diverse views and voices in the public sphere. I will investigate how they approach and understand the notion of impartial reporting, and how they define professionalism in the context of a tumultuous political transition. This analysis is based on the living experiences and narrations of a sample of journalists interviewed in Tunisia, Egypt, and Libya.

A. Plurality, Polarization, and the Surge of Unilateral Storytelling

Media plurality is considered one of the main features of a healthy and dynamic political sphere. Under political transitions, the media's role as a "marketplace of ideas" is crucial in order to provide a platform for alternative views and to empower a vibrant civil society. However, since in a "marketplace of ideas" the presentation of arguments and counterarguments is considered a necessary exercise in order for the "truth" to emerge,[20] media plurality can also aggravate pre-existing conflicts, create new ones, and exacerbate confusion.

Plurality can be expressed in the representation of diverse views and interests within media content or by opening the media sector to a diversity of voices through commercialization of the market (external diversity). However, excessive pluralism can also be used as a weapon against the ideals of fair representation if it leads to fragmentation in the media landscape. Political forces, using the media for political gain, have the potential to turn it into a powerful tool for deepening social and political divisions. Case studies from national media in the so-called Arab Spring countries highlight the destructive effect of an extremely polarized media landscape.

The notion of a "marketplace of ideas" was accommodated by Arab journalists in the immediate aftermath of the uprisings to various degrees and in different forms according to the national context. In all three media industries covered by this research, the margin of representation of dissenting voices witnessed an unprecedented expansion in the immediate aftermath of the uprisings, to the extent that such voices were granted a platform in state media (a departure from the sector's previous unilateral content).

The (former) secretary of the Egyptian journalists' syndicate, Jamal Fahmy, interviewed after the 25 January 2011 uprising, described this unprecedented openness. Fahmy stated, "I could not even dream of walking by the national TV headquarters under Mubarak and now I am frequently solicited on its platform, so much so that I could spend a whole day there".[21] This change, although limited in time and scale, was an extraordinary improvement on the decades-long practice of using state-owned media to demonize political opponents—often by reporting only negative stories about them.

Diversification of state media content was common across all three media industries that were previously controlled by regimes, though it was particularly obvious in Libya. In both Libya and Tunisia, the pre-revolutionary media landscape was mainly state-owned. The media industry in Egypt was relatively more diversified, although red lines largely restricted the coverage of many topics, especially those related to the military. The advent of the independent press in Egypt in the early 2000s allowed some deviation from the official line, as well as some narrow representation for the regime's opponents, barring the voicing of their most radical demands. In the last years of the Mubarak regime, this relaxation extended somewhat into state-owned media, especially among those who had been perceived as tools for rebranding the regime's image. Soha el-Naqqash, a (former) anchor of State Nile TV, vividly recalls an extraordinary development in journalistic practice in this flagship TV station when journalists were finally allowed to cover the demonstrations of opposition groups and movements: "For me, covering a demonstration for the state TV was a huge change, even if we were not reporting on radical slogans against the regime in our coverage of these demonstrations".[22]

In the immediate aftermath of the uprisings, representation of diverse views was acknowledged by journalists as an expression of liberation from the grip of the regime's unilateral dictate. This diversity was at first cherished and protected by journalists as the guarantee of a new newsroom culture. Gradually though, the ability of media professionals and their organizations to tolerate this diversity and to present it as an important feature of the emerging political sphere diminished, and eventually vanished, as media practitioners reverted to partisan reporting. Once the power struggle between emerging systems of control became fierce, media professionals and their management became less and less inclined to follow what media development agencies preached as Western ideals of professional journalism. So although there was a vast expansion in diversity immediately after the uprisings, the trend for fair representation of different political actors, views, and perspectives gradually regressed and finally became limited to topics that did not generate tension between opposing camps. The return to biased storytelling in the midst of raging political and ideological battles was in line with what journalists had long practiced. The relative diversity of media content was not underpinned by any solid institutional development that would have allowed it to become sustainable within media practice.

B. The Rise of Private Media

Opening the market to private media projects enabled external media diversity, and media outlets began to present discussions of different political viewpoints. However, this diversification was in the end revealed to be illusionary. Funding of media projects tended to be strictly linked to opposing political camps, the fierce political battle provoked heated discourse, and journalists' belief in their 'duty' to defend a political ideal took them away from fact-based reporting, which, for some, amounted to a denial of their *raison d'etre*. They themselves were a part of the transformational process that would finally decide their fate, and that of their institutions. A decisive factor in the failure to maintain diversification (only recognized by a few of the journalists interviewed) was also the entrenched habit of bias, and the fear—or laziness—to push beyond it.

The experience of Ahmad Hamdy, a junior reporter for the Egyptian state-owned Nile TV, is instructive. He reflects on the difficult dynamics of internal newsrooms, post-uprising:

> *Our major problem is our editors, who still follow the old practices, such as waiting for the government to issue a communiqué before reporting on the events. The quality of reporting is very much linked to the personality of the editor of the day. There is no clear editorial policy.*[23]

Most importantly, the opening of the media market to new players and new voices did not actually lead to the acceptance of "the other" as a legitimate partner in the democratization process. In an environment of heightened political polarization, the so-called diversity propagated by media further deepened the political and social divides, rather than providing a platform for shared experiences and goals.

In Tunisia, national mainstream media was viewed as the spearhead of the campaign to preserve the secular state, disseminating negative content against Islamic groups in the face of the grassroots Islamization that allegedly occurred with the formation of the Islamic *Ennahda*-led government.[24] While the Islam-affiliated media outlets, especially in the broadcast sector, were new players in the media scene, the pre-uprising media, especially the national state television station, was accused by *Ennahda* supporters of being the new mouthpiece of the secular opposition. According to journalist Adel Thabti, state channels failed to give equal representation of different views, especially on extremely divisive topics such as the wearing of the Islamic *niqab* (full veil) on university campuses, something that was strictly forbidden under the former regime and fuelled tensions between secularists and Salafi groups.[25] He accuses state TV of purposefully failing to invite representatives of Salafi groups to explain their position.

The need for diverse representation has been consistently challenged by the need to protect an identity perceived as threatened. For instance, the head of the news services in Tunisian Nessma TV, Sofian Ben Hamida, has been less concerned with representing diverse views than with reflecting the identity of his television channel as a radical voice promoting the secular opposition against new Islamic trends. "During the elections,[26] we decided that we will be ourselves, without any censorship and without denying our values. We are a modern secular channel and we don't think that we should be apologetic about it".[27]

The channel recently changed its identity, adopting the slogan, "the TV station of the family" and beginning to open its platform to the *Ennahda* party. The Tunisian press reported on a rapprochement between the Islamic party and the owner of the TV station, Nabil Karoui, despite the station's previously having played a major role in discrediting the Islamic party and calling it a danger for Tunisian identity.[28] This alleged rapprochement is explained by the press as Karoui's reaction to his exclusion from the higher spheres of the secularist *Nidaa Tunis* party despite the support he lent during the latest presidential elections. In short, the identity of the channel is fluid—it can change depending on the interests of its owner in the political arena and the need for political standing.

In Egypt, the introduction of new players in the private broadcast sector, which included a burgeoning of pro-Islamic private media outlets, was an important post-uprising development, especially under the Brotherhood's rule. (While some of these religious channels were in fact operating pre-uprising, they had been forbidden from tackling politics and frequently had their programmes suspended by the government.) However, these TV channels were not able to attract a large viewership beyond their supporters and quite often adopted a radical tone, with some programmes openly preaching extremist views.[29] They were abruptly shut down immediately after President Mohamed Morsi's removal. These new players were not able to counterbalance the power of the prominent media empires owned by businessmen known for close ties to the Mubarak regime.

Private non-Islamic TV channels acted as the main spearhead of the opposition to the short-lived Brotherhood government, fuelling popular anger against what they presented as the new regime's failure to respond to people's needs and its dodgy regional links, which were at odds with what they perceived as the Egyptian identity. The influential private broadcast media was instrumental in pushing boundaries under the Mubarak regime by diversifying media content and allowing some representation for dissident voices. The business interests of the wealthy owners of these media outlets and their links to the regime did not hinder the development of this margin of freedom (which was extended and reduced according to circumstance).

After the January 25 uprising, national media became a powerful player in the political battle between Islamists and their opponents. While the (so-called) secular media claimed to be under attack, the new regime and its supporters accused it of spreading lies and fuelling popular anger calling for the "purification" of the media community. The "media production city" where private TV broadcasters are based was the scene of frequent Salafi-led calls to purge the media of anyone allegedly still loyal to the Mubarak regime. This reaction was also common in Tunisia where several sit-ins organized by *Ennahda* supporters took place, with participants demanding media "purification", especially the removal from state television of so-called "agents" of the Ben Ali regime. They used the popular slogan "The people want to change the media".

The rise of private media did not, however, lead to the implementation of new practices in newsrooms. The editorial policies of these media outlets could shift from one extreme to the other, depending on the current interests of media owners, who usually use these outlets as a tool to strengthen their relations with regimes. As described by Mohamed Radwan, a former journalist from al Masry al Yom private newspaper, "There is no legal framework establishing boards of trustees who will define editorial policies of these newspapers. The private press is treated as investment companies. However, we are not selling sugar; our product is contributing immensely to the formation of public opinion".[30] The post-coup degeneration of private Egyptian media into a propagandist discourse for the military regime is reflective of this sector's inability to provide an independent model where diversity and fair representation could finally be embedded.

Moreover, the survival of various forms of repression from the old regime, as well as the surge of new forms of repression, meant these new media projects were practically not able to challenge old practices. Libya is a perfect example. As the country descended into chaos, the ability of new media outlets to accommodate diverse views was gradually restricted. Media organizations and professionals were accused of providing a platform for incitement and national divisiveness. New political actors, the deteriorating security situation and hegemony of militias, and a public not accustomed to open debate—all these elements curbed Libyan media, imposing new forms of self-censorship.

The pronounced political affiliations of various media outlets consolidated the popular belief that the media fuelled factional tensions, thus forestalling any attempt to cover the crisis from a variety of sides. A good example is the coverage of infighting between militias of the cities of Misrata and Bani Walid in October 2012. Infighting was sparked by the alleged torture and killing of a Misrati rebel, believed to have been involved in the killing of Gaddafi, by militias in Bani Walid. The situation escalated dramatically. Libyan forces launched an operation against Bani Walid, leading to the deaths of at least 20 people and the wounding of more than 200.[31] In their coverage of this important crisis, most media outlets failed to report both sides of the story for fear of retaliation. The local TV stations of the two towns, located in media markets that flourished since the revolution, took the lead in the incitement campaign between the two cities. Ibrahim el-Mezwoghi, the head of *Libya al-Ahrar* TV network's Tripoli office, reflects on the difficulties of practicing professional and balanced field reporting in a climate of mounting instability: "Tribal frictions and geographical divisions make it impossible for media to claim neutrality or provide unbiased account of events. Covering news is becoming increasingly difficult. Ordinary citizens often interpret news based on tribal affiliations. Some of our correspondents were threatened and others were literally beaten".[32]

In talk show programmes, the reluctance of opposing politicians to appear together made hosting representatives of varied political currents on the same platform impossible. Being challenged on a media platform by a talk show host was often interpreted by politicians as a personal criticism, which led to aggressive reactions and threats against media staff. The experience of Mahmoud al-Sharkasy, an anchor for *al-Assema* TV station, is reflective of the impossibility of tackling a story from diverse angles, especially when it touches a sensitive topic like the hegemony of militias. "They sent me indirect threats reminding me that I have a family and children", he confided. "I am not afraid of them but I became wiser and less enthusiastic. I am now calculating risks and limiting its scope".[33]

The political engagement of new private media outlets based on the political agenda behind their funding (and with a lack of transparency about this funding), made them a favourite platform for political lobbying, at the expense of the safety of their staffs, who were often threatened or attacked.[34] With the civil war dividing the country and Tripoli in the hands of Islamic militias, the margin of manoeuvre for independent reporting in national media became minimal. Journalists again became little more than mouthpieces for those in power.[35]

C. Neutral or Engaged: The "Patriotic" Journalist

The two principles of media pluralism and media partisanship present opposing models of how the media can deal with competing views, either by allowing their inclusion or sanctioning them through exclusion. In practice, these models can develop in tandem,[36] coexisting in the same media landscape. This research demonstrates that journalists quite often shift from one model to another within daily practice, depending on the topic and current political circumstances.

The heightened political conflict of the Arab political transitions caused media professionals to oscillate between two opposite ideals: representing all sides of the debate and using media as a powerful platform for political mobilization. Overwhelmed by the unprecedentedly fast pace of political developments, journalists swung between reporting complex events and attempting to make sense of them for audiences. Excessive polarization and the fierce struggle over the state later shifted journalists from the role of mediator (who explains facts and puts them into context) to that of activist (who mobilizes audiences, encouraging them to position themselves with or against a particular ideological camp). Rather than following the liberal or the corporatist democratic models (presented by Hallin and Mancini), journalists were mostly attracted by the model of "polarized pluralism", which is often understood negatively in terms of consolidating a democratic public communication.

In established Western democracies, the two models of "journalism of information" and "journalism of opinion" coexist but assume different functions.[37] While leading national newspapers have a clear political leaning, though still providing in-depth investigative reporting, news agencies provide information customized for large audiences with no political flavour. Waisbord argues for the importance of media partisanship in times of crisis, stressing that it allows audiences to make sense of complex events, which are beyond their ability to analyse and assess without this influential mediator. Most people choose a source of information that supports their political views, and which is therefore trusted by them, when trying to make sense of conflicts that have an important impact on their life. Instead of trying to understand these extraordinary events from different points of views, as suggests the corporatist model, most people tend to be reassured by following the coverage of these events via media outlets that are in harmony with their political beliefs—and therefore biased. In emerging democracies, the protection of the fragile new democracy experiment requires both vivid partisanship for orientation and factual impartial reporting for the development of a public sphere that encourages compromise and shared visions across society.[38] As argued by Curan, the biggest danger comes when the media landscape becomes homogenous—all its arms propagating one view as an ultimate truth that is not be challenged.[39]

The fall of the previous system of control over traditional national media in the so-called Arab Spring countries affected journalists in different ways. A feeling of empowerment among journalists who were finally allowed to practice their profession was mitigated by a sense of confusion at having lost the comfort of those clear guidelines that had restricted their output. A statement by Egyptian journalist and anchor Reem Maged is reflective of this state of confusion: "We did not see something similar before. We were confused. This was a first time for us. There is nothing wrong with making mistakes".[40]

Journalists' sense of empowerment was first perceived exclusively as a challenge to politicians—an outpouring of potentially unfounded accusations and slander. A statement of the Tunisian reporter at *Realites* magazine Hanen Zbeiss reflects on the shifting balance of power between journalists and politicians: "we could finally say all we want, we could interview any political figure we want, and we could even slam any of them. We were free."[41] But this sense of empowerment was accompanied by huge challenges. Journalists had to recreate their identity: no longer a mouthpiece of the regime, but a reporter on the daily concerns of ordinary people. This was a chaotic process with no clear strategy underlying it. For Tunisian journalist Hanen Zbeiss "setting strategies was at that time a luxury, we were in a crazy situation, the country's history was changing hour after hour, we had to deliver."[42] Amira Arfawi from the Tunisian state TV recounts the chaos that prevailed immediately after the fall of the regime in the state television newsroom: "Everyone was working in his own way. There were no directives or guidance, absolutely nothing. We went to the street, talked to people. We wanted to tell our audience that things are back to normal,"[43] she said.

Tunisian journalists had to improvise in order to cope with the deluge of unprecedented political changes. In Libya, journalists' experiences demonstrate an even greater confusion. The immediate aftermath of the uprisings saw international media development agencies attempt to introduce a journalistic model inspired by Western practice. But the model's implementation was hindered by resistance from new political actors attempting to reproduce the old repressive practices for dealing with media, militias' hegemony over the country and the lack of harmony between new practices and the traditions that had been used in reporting for decades. Freelance journalist Mohamed Saghir was arrested by Gaddafi security and tortured in its prisons. He believed the situation would be better after the regime's fall—but this was not the case. Reflecting on the difficult move towards independent reporting, he noted: "Before, we used to have only one red line: Gaddafi and his family. After the liberation, we started to have hundreds of red lines. If I criticise a political party, I would receive an angry phone call. If I criticise a minister for his or her performance or decisions, I—or the media institution where I work—become labelled as troublemakers and the ministry could even refuse to deal with us. I might also risk losing my job".[44]

The breaking of taboos—or at least the most prominent ones—left journalists in a state of confusion. How were they to understand their new relationship with this changed political sphere, and how were they to deal with it? According to the Egyptian journalist Mohamed Kheir, "media staff lost their compass. Under the former regime, the relationship between the political system and the media was clear and stable, whether it was positive or negative. This solid structure no longer existed."[45]

This confusion was exacerbated by a lack of transparency from governmental officials when providing clarifications on polemic topics. Manal el-Diftar, head of news services at CBC private network, describes how the culture of media production was rooted in rumours during the short-lived Brotherhood rule:

> *Most of the information we got from the government or the presidency is a denial of non-confirmed information reported by media. If we asked about official information to elucidate the story, we get no answer. We have to always deal with unfinished stories.*[46]

D. They Need To Be Told What To Think

The fierce political polarization, mainly between secularists and Islamists,[47] transformed media into a battleground. From a state of confusion, journalists adopted strong political roles, seeing themselves as activists, advocates, and preachers of public opinion. For most interviewed journalists, neutral reporting either did not exist or was not compatible with the particular role they assigned themselves as reporters of this complex political transition.

Advocacy journalism flourished, particularly in political talk shows but also in all media forms where journalists' main function, as perceived by them, was to take a stance in the political struggle. In Egypt after the 25 January 2011 uprising, journalists' role as political activists came to prominence as private media outlets flourished. There was a growing appetite for investing in media as a platform for political lobbying. Talk shows became the most popular and vibrant arena for political debate.[48] The prominence of these debating platforms and the growing popularity of talk show "stars" was accompanied by the consolidation of two contradictory journalistic roles: the "attack-dog journalist" whose main mission was to mobilize people against ideological "enemies", even if this required dealing with misinformation, and the "lap-dog journalist", whose identity was reduced to legitimizing the political camp he or she was supporting. These opposing journalistic roles could coexist within the practice of one professional group, and sometime even within the practices of a single media professional.[49] Advocacy journalism became the prevalent journalistic model adopted by national media.

For talk show hosts, neutrality is often understood as an act of treason or a denial of their perceived responsibilities as leaders of public opinion. The blurred line between journalism and activism empowered the notion of the journalist as advocate of a "good cause". Talk show host Reem Maged is a good example of this dual identity. While the revolution was unfolding, she decided to leave the studio for Tahrir Square, where demonstrators gathered demanding the fall of the Mubarak regime. For her "this was my natural place". Under the Brotherhood rule, her daily talk show became an important platform for the defence of what she perceived as revolutionary principles. Maged has not been on screen since the military coup. Her previous criticisms of the military made her an unwanted figure after the demise of the Brotherhood. Her attempt to make a comeback and present a social magazine about leading Egyptian women was not successful, as the private TV channel, ONTV, decided to halt the magazine's production.[50]

On the opposite side of the spectrum, Tamer Amin believes in "guiding" public opinion. His role, as he conceives it, is not to report the news but to make news. In so doing, he believes he can "propose solutions to current problems, thus urging decision-makers to respond to it." He also believes his audience is not ready for objectivity: "There is a difference between the public opinion in the West and that in Arab countries. Here, they need to be told what to think. They need guidance. I try not to interfere or to express my opinion but I received phone calls from my audience; they would like me to weigh in on some issues".[51] Being one of the strongest voices in support of the military backed regime, Amin does not hide the fact he also offers his "services" for it, occasionally even delivering his guests to the police. He said in a press interview: "the interior ministry called me and told me that the journalist from the Muslim Brotherhood I was interviewing is accused in a legal case, I told them to wait for him while he leaves our studios." Asked about how this practice fits with professional standards, he simply replied, "I only follow the law of my country."[52]

Like their Egyptian counterparts, Tunisian journalists were dragged into the political struggle, especially when they were set against a backdrop of highly divisive events such as elections and political assassinations.[53] For instance, the challenge of delivering high-quality, impartial, and professional coverage of the first free general elections post-uprising, in which *Ennahda* scored high, was made harder by journalists' lack of experience and the media's bias towards certain political camps. The journalistic enthusiasm that characterized the elections of 2011 faded in the general elections of

2014[54]; the tough political struggle between Islamists and secularists was exacerbated by the demise of Islamists in Egypt and the growing popularity of the campaign against terrorism, empowering hard-liners in the two belligerent camps. The presidential race between the two candidates (Beji Caid Essebsi from the secular *Nidaa Tunis* and the interim President Moncef Marzouki believed to be supported by Islamists)[55] saw an escalation in accusations between the rivals and their popular bases, even to the extent of racist comments and slander. Media supporting the two camps reflected this tension and accentuated it. A report by the independent broadcast regulator (HAICA) on the fair representation of political parties in the coverage of the parliamentary elections campaign demonstrated that broadcast media, especially TV stations, were transformed into a platform for political polarization, with each TV station providing a platform to its political allies while denying it to the political opponent.[56]

E. Media as a Platform for Exclusion

Journalists' attraction to the polarized model is in harmony with the popularity of polarized US talk shows, a format adopted by many Arab television stations as the popular way of framing events.[57] The adoption of this format as the dominant template through which to debate politics in the post uprisings era, at a time when democratic institutions were still fragile and lacked solid legitimacy amongst public opinion, led to a further erosion of public support for the democratic process.

The rise of televised talk shows and their popularity transformed them into "political clubs" manipulated for the purpose of political lobbying. In this sense, talk shows acted as an influential platform to de-legitimize and thus to exclude the political adversary. This turned traditional media into a weapon against the successful implementation of democratic values through the building of solid democratic institutions.

According to Henri Lefebvre,[58] political contention arises when there are contradictions between discursive and material space. The denial by mainstream media of access and representation for social and political groups considered "the enemy" is instrumental in creating significant long-term social and political divides. As Martin and Miller argue, when there is contradiction between different types of spaces—the perceived, the conceived, and the lived space[59]—as well as between expectations and reality, there arises a high potential for conflicts and contentiousness in society.[60]

Egyptian media historically offered a platform for excluding opposition groups—those labelled the "enemy". The military coup in July 2013 that led to the overthrow of the Brotherhood sparked the flourishing of a new form of "patriotic" activism, in defence of the state and against alleged terrorists. The transformation of both state and private media into platforms for singing the praise of military rule and slamming its opponents (the so-called "terrorists") has consequentially demonised first the Muslim Brotherhood, and second the regime's secular critics, leading to their exclusion from both the political and media spheres. Head of ERTU Issam el-Amir reflected on this culture of exclusion, which is particularly rife within state media. Asked about the representation of the Muslim Brotherhood post-coup in state broadcasts, he stated:

> *There is a great hostility from the Egyptian people against the Muslim Brotherhood. The streets' anger against them is overwhelming. Some of our viewers are expressing opinions such as "burn them all". I asked presenters not to tolerate these expressions... We are the reflection of the streets' pulse and people's will. If we expressed views against people, they will remove us the same way they removed powerful presidents. We cannot go against people's will.*[61]

The fall of the old system of control over national media gave journalists the ability to freely express their opinions. In practice this often translated into the use of a sensational tabloid style, which became the most prominent one in the media landscape. The explosion of personal views on media platforms transformed national media into a free-for-all platform, as the former first secretary of the Egyptian journalists' union, Gamal Fahmy, described: "it became common to see a TV presenter slamming his or her management and presenting his or her resignation to the audience directly on air".[62]

The lack of debate on professional practices and editorial policies within newsrooms represented a major obstacle to enabling a genuine "newsroom revolution" in journalistic practice. Most importantly, entrenched habits of self-censorship led to a situation where journalists were fearful of using their newfound liberty and unsure of how to work beyond directives. The change in media practice was mainly reflected in new trends which allowed a relative diversity in media content as well as on-the-ground reporting about the daily lives of ordinary citizens. However, this change was neither solid nor sustainable enough to launch the process of defining (or redefining) professional standards and values in the new context. Importantly, the complex and fast-developing political transition gave the debate on media values and practices a secondary priority. The advocate role distracted journalists from the debate on editorial standards. The ability to freely express views overshadowed the need to introduce investigative reporting, a tradition yet to be embedded in newsrooms practice. According to a study on the roles favoured by Egyptian journalists conducted in 2006,[63] support for sustaining democratic values within journalistic practice is mainly understood by them in terms of encouraging debate, rather than investigating and examining the government's policies. These findings are in line with journalists' testimonies provided by this field research.

The battle to liberate editorial policies from the grip of political regimes was a particular priority for Tunisian journalists, who lobbied for the establishment of editorial boards independent from media owners and the government. Although most of these attempts did not succeed, according to Hisham Snoussi, a member of the independent Tunisian broadcast regulator HAICA,[64] they did manage to introduce a new culture within newsrooms that valued an independent editorial policy defined by journalists themselves. However, the battle for editorial independence had to be fought with a new political power reluctant to give up the prerogatives of former regimes in controlling the media content as well as with media owners who possessed a good deal of authority over media content.

Dynamism in the private media sector did not lead to revolutionary change in media practices. For instance, the fall of the old media control system in Tunisia opened the door for the launch of several pirate broadcasters—operating without a license—and numerous publications with limited staff and circulation, dubious standards, and poor working conditions. The redefinition of professional standards was not a priority for those engaged in these new projects, who were concerned rather with serving their owner's political ambitions and interests. The experiences of the commercialization of media in Latin America and post-communist countries confirm the weak impact of privatization on progress towards an independent media. Being highly politicized, media ownership by politicians or oligarchs became a strong instrument to serve their ambitions, rather than providing audiences with an independent and quality media product.[65]

Conclusion

The political and media transitions have empowered a mix of authoritarian and pluralistic practices[66] among journalists. New practices coexisted with the old without being able to challenge them. In the case of Egypt, media fell into its old habits: serving the regime and delegitimizing its opponents in the post-coup environment. This was the result not only of the crackdown on media freedoms by the new regime—including arrests of journalists and a ban of articles and publications[67]—but also (and most importantly) journalists' own perception of their role as defenders of the regime against those perceived or declared as "enemies".

Journalists could experiment with new practices, but they were not sufficiently empowered to be able to establish them as new habits. Reactions to sudden and rather chaotic changes were shaped both by existing structures and history of the media industry. Hybrid media practices were dominated by expressions of personal opinions, featuring the personality of the media practitioner as hero or leader. The struggle between the two opposing models (the obedient and the advocate/activist journalists) did not valorize independent reporting. The two models of obedience and resistance are not necessarily conflictual, since the same journalist could adopt a highly critical tone against political opponents and a highly pronounced obedient attitude towards ideological friends. The short "awakening" that shook newsrooms after the uprisings was not underpinned by solid, sustained changes that would have allowed an editorial "revolution" to take place or challenged the identity and role of the journalist as "guard of regimes". The lack of adequate professional training was another obstacle. This was true for Arab journalists as well as for those in similar transitional conditions. Lack of professional training makes journalists less able to resist pressures from media owners, government officials, or others who seek to influence reporting.[68]

The intricate link between the success of political reform and that of media reform is reflected by the political roles played by journalists in the absence or weakness of political institutions. The transformation of journalists into lobbying instruments for competing political forces blurred the line between the role of the journalist informing the public on these transitions and that of the activist shaping the nature of transitions and urging an audience to side with or against particular political and ideological camps.

The fall of the transitional processes into violence, chaos, or counter-revolutions with the return of autocratic regimes empowered the old repressive tools to muzzle media. However, media professionals and their institutions were less concerned with safeguarding the few gains they had secured than with mobilizing their audiences to support their political allies. Weak or absent professional syndicates, divisions among journalists, and fragile working conditions all hindered the media community's ability to launch a debate on professional standards and to protect advances towards political openness against the many pressures facing them, including those imposed by political allies. The transformation of national media into a platform to exclude those labelled as "dangerous" elements in society, denying them visibility, now aggravates the ongoing political antagonism and threatens to deepen social and political divisions.

Media's ability to perform independently and professionally is linked to the political environment and largely impacted by the margin of manoeuvre left for journalists to work in, fighting against pressure imposed by the new political players. For instance, Reporters Without Borders ranked Egypt second in the world for the number of journalists arrested and the fourth "biggest prison" for journalists, with 46 journalists arrested in 2014 on pretexts such as "being Muslim Brotherhood sympathizers, endangering national unity, or inciting violence or riots".[69] With the formation of a new regime that possesses a core authoritarian element,[70] any attempt by media to distance themselves from the hegemonic political environment could amount to an idle endeavour.

Notes

1. These normative models are the authoritarian, libertarian, social responsibility, and Soviet communist models.
2. Fred S. Siebert and others, Four Theories of the Press (Urbana, IL: University of Illinois Press, 1956).
3. Ibid., 1–2.
4. John Merrill and Ralph Lowenstein, Media, Messages and Men: New Perspectives in Communication (New York: Longman, 1979); Herbert Altschull, Agents of Power: The Media and Public Policy (New York: Longman, 1995); John C. Nerone (ed.), Last Rights: Revisiting Four Theories of the Press (Urbana IL: University of Illinois Press, 1995).
5. Clifford G. Christians and others, Normative Theories of the Media: Journalism in Democratic Societies (Urbana, IL: University of Illinois Press, 2009), 19.
6. These normative traditions are: corporatist, libertarian, social responsibility, and citizen participation.
7. Nico Carpentier, "Identity, Contingency and Rigidity. The (Counter-) Hegemonic Constructions of the Identity of the Media Professional,"

Journalism 6, no. 2 (2005); Robert M. Entman, "Framing Bias: Media in the Distribution of Power," Journal of Communication 57, no. 1 (2007).
8. Jennifer Ostini and Anthony Y. H. Ostini, "Beyond the Four Theories of the Press: A New Model of National Media Systems," Mass Communication and Society 5, no. 1 (2002), 45.
9. Daniel C. Hallin and Paolo Mancini, Comparing Media Systems: Three Models of Media and Politics (Cambridge: Cambridge University Press, 2004).
10. For the notion of interdependency between mass media and political parties, see Colin Seymour-Ure, The Political Impact of Mass Media (London: Constable, 1974).
11. See Katrin Voltmer, "How Far Can Media Systems Travel? Applying Hallin and Mancini's Comparative Framework Outside the Western World," in Comparing Media Systems Beyond the Western World, ed. Daniel C. Hallin and Paolo Mancini (Cambridge: Cambridge University Press, 2012).
12. See Craig L. LaMay, Exporting Press Freedom: Economic and Editorial Dilemmas in International Media Assistance (New Brunswick: Transaction Publishers, 2009).
13. Andrew Chadwick, The Hybrid Media System: Politics and Power (Oxford: Oxford University Press, 2013); Katrin Voltmer, Building Media Systems in the Western Balkans: Lost between Models and Realities, Working paper (Sarajevo: Analitika—Center for Social Research, 2013), 13.
14. John R. Searle, The Construction of Social Reality (Harmondsworth: Penguin, 1995).
15. Peter Berger and Thomas Luckmann, The Social Construction of Reality: A Treatise in the Sociology of Knowledge (Garden City: Doubleday, 1966).
16. Katrin Voltmer, "Building Media Systems in the Western Balkans: Lost between Models and Realities", 14–15.
17. Ibid., 14.
18. Katrin Voltmer, "Comparing Media Systems in New Democracies: East Meets South Meets West," Central European Journal of Communication 1 (2008): 37.
19. Fatima El Issawi, "The Role of Egyptian Media in the Coup," in IEMed Mediterranean Yearbook 2014, ed. European Institute of the Mediterranean, Barcelona, Spain, 2014.
20. John Stuart Mill, On Liberty (London: Penguin, 1859/1972).
21. Interview with author, Cairo, December 2013.
22. Ibid.
23. Fatima El Issawi, "Egyptian Media Under Transition: In the Name of the Regime…in the Name of the People?," POLIS, London School of Economics and Political Science, London, 2014, 37.

24. See Fatima El Issawi, "Transitional Libyan Media: Free at Last?," The Carnegie Papers, *Carnegie Endowment for International Peace*, Washington, DC, 2013.
25. See Suzanne Daley, "Tensions on a Campus Mirror Turbulence in a New Tunisia," *New York Times*, June 11, 2012, accessed 10 November 2015, http://www.nytimes.com/2012/06/12/world/africa/tensions-at-manouba-university-mirror-turbulence-in-tunisia.html.
26. The moderate Islamist *Ennahda* party won the country's first democratic elections after the uprising in October 2011 securing more than 41 % of the vote. See http://www.bbc.co.uk/news/world-africa-15487647.
27. Fatima El Issawi, "Transitional Libyan media: Free at Last?", 17.
28. *Webdo*, "Après Ghannouchi et Laârayedh, Nabil Karoui courtise les jeunes d'Ennahdha," June 3, 2015, accessed November 10, 2015, http://www.webdo.tn/2015/06/03/tunisie-apres-ghannouchi-et-laarayedh-nabil-karoui-courtise-les-jeunes-dennahdha/.
29. See Fatima El Issawi, "In Post-Revolution Egypt, Talk Shows Redefine the Political Landscape," *Foreign Policy*, October 10, 2012, accessed November 5, 2015, http://foreignpolicy.com/2012/10/10/in-post-revolution-egypt-talk-shows-redefine-the-political-landscape/.
30. Fatima El Issawi, "Egyptian Media Under Transition: In the Name of the Regime…in the Name of the People?", 54.
31. Chris Stephen, "Gaddafi Stronghold Bani Walid Captured by Libya Government Troops," *The Guardian*, October 24, 2012, accessed November 5, 2015, https://www.theguardian.com/world/2012/oct/24/bani-walid-captured-by-libya-government.
32. Fatima El Issawi, "Libya Media Transition: Heading to the Unknown," *POLIS*, London School of Economics and Political Science, London, 2013, 58.
33. Ibid., 44.
34. See freedom House report of the freedom of the press in Libya for the year 2014, https://freedomhouse.org/report/freedom-press/2014/libya#.VcDMxflVhHw.
35. Reda Elboum, "The Libyan Media: A Detailed Scene," *Correspondents.org*, November 25, 2014, accessed November 10, 2015, http://www.correspondents.org/ar/node/5937.
36. Katrin Voltmer, "Building Media Systems in the Western Balkans: Lost between Models and Realities".
37. Silvio Waisbord, "In Journalism We Trust? Credibility and Fragmented Journalism in Latin America," in Mass Media and Political Communication in New Democracies, ed. Katrin Voltmer (Abingdon: Routledge, 2006).
38. Katrin Voltmer, Building Media Systems in the Western Balkans: Lost between Models and Realities, 20.

39. James Curran, "Mass Media and Democracy: A Reappraisal," in Mass Media and Society, ed. James Curran and Michael Gurevitch (London; New York: E. Arnold, 1991).
40. This Statement by Reem Maged was expressed in her talk to POLIS (LSE) conference 2014 under the title of "Egyptian Media After The Uprising: Transparency in Transition Time?", See the conference webpage: http://blogs.lse.ac.uk/polis/?s=conference+2014.
41. Fatima El Issawi, "Tunisian Media in Transition," The Carnegie Papers, *Carnegie Endowment for International Peace*, Washington, DC, 1.
42. Interview with author, Tunis, December 2011.
43. Ibid.
44. Fatima El Issawi, "Libya Media Transition: Heading to the Unknown", 34.
45. Fatima El Issawi, "Egyptian Media Under Transition: In the Name of the Regime…in the Name of the People?", 70.
46. Ibid., 71.
47. The most accurate label for the first group would be non Islamist media outlets rather than secularist or liberal, some of these media outlets rejects the label of secularists.
48. See Fatima El Issawi, "In Post-Revolution Egypt, Talk Shows Redefine the Political Landscape."
49. Fatima El Issawi and Bart Cammaerts, "Shifting Journalistic Roles in Democratic Transitions: Lessons from Egypt," Journalism 17, no. 5 (2016).
50. Kahled Dawoud, "Reem Maged versus the Government," *The Atlantic Council*, May 22, 2015, accessed November 10, 2015, http://www.atlanticcouncil.org/blogs/menasource/reem-maged-versus-the-government.
51. Fatima El Issawi, "Egyptian Media Under Transition: In the Name of the Regime…in the Name of the People?", 77.
52. See an article published by the Network of Arab Media (moheet.com) containing a YouTube video in which the presenter talks about delivering his guests to the police: http://moheet.com/2015/03/24/2239387/%D8%A8%D8%A7%D9%84%D9%81%D9%8A%D8 %AF%D9%8A%D9%88-%D8%A3%D9%85%D9%8A%D9%86-%D9%8A%D8%B9%D8%AA%D8%B1%D9%81-%D8%B3%D9%84%D9%85%D8%AA-3-%D8%B6%D9%8A%D9%88%D9%81-%D9%81%D9%8A-%D8%A8.html.
53. The country witnessed three assassinations of several political figures during 2013. See http://www.independent.co.uk/news/world/africa/tunisia-shocked-by-assassinations-oppositionleaders-mohamed-brahmi-and-chokri-belaid-killed-with-the-same-gun-8733972.html.
54. The first regular parliamentary elections in the country led to the victory of the secularist party *Nidaa Tunis* (Tunisia's call) in December 2014, See https://www.theguardian.com/world/2014/dec/22/tunisia-elections-veteran-politician-beji-caid-essebsi-wins-vote.

55. *BBC*, "Tunisia election: Essebsi and Marzouki face run-off," November 25, 2014, accessed November 10, 2015, http://www.bbc.co.uk/news/world-africa-30191945.
56. See the report published by the regulatory body on their website, http://haica.tn/fr/2015/01/le-pluralisme-dans-les-medias-audiovisuels-pendant-les-elections-legislatives-et-presidentielles/.
57. Muhammad I. Ayish, Political Communication on Arab World Television: Evolving Patterns, Political Communication 19, no. 2 (2002).
58. Henri Lefebvre, The Production of Space (Cambridge, MA: Blackwell, 1991).
59. Perceived space refers to the physical or material environment, whereas conceived space is the discursive, and the intersection of these two is the lived or dominated space.
60. Martin, Deborah and Byron Miller, "Space and Contentious Politics," Mobilization: An International Journal 8 (2003).
61. Fatima El Issawi, "Egyptian Media Under Transition: In the Name of the Regime…in the Name of the People?", 50–51.
62. Fatima El Issawi and Bart Cammaerts, "Shifting journalistic roles in Democratic Transitions: Lessons from Egypt".
63. Jyotika Ramaprasad and Naila Nabil Hamdy, "Functions of Egyptian journalists. Perceived Importance and Actual Performance," The International Communication Gazette 68, no. 2 (2006).
64. Interview with author, Tunis, December 2013.
65. Katrin Voltmer, "Comparing Media Systems in New Democracies: East Meets South Meets West", 37; Silvio R. Waisbord, "The Mass Media and Consolidation of Democracy in South America," Research in Political Sociology 7 (1995).
66. Raymond Hinnebusch, "The Arab Uprisings and the Stalled Transition Process," in Mediterranean Yearbook 2014, ed. European Institute of the Mediterranean, Barcelona, Spain, 2014.
67. *Mada Masr*, "Authorities Delay Newspaper from Printing Due to Security Concerns," December 15, 2014, accessed November 10, 2015, http://www.madamasr.com/news/authorities-delay-newspaper-printing-due-security-concerns.
68. Sallie Hughes and Chappell Lawson, "The Barriers to Media Opening in Latin America," Political Communication 22, no. 1 (2005).
69. *The Guardian*, "Egypt is one of the 'biggest prisons' for journalists, says watchdog," February 23, 2016, accessed September 01, 2016. https://www.theguardian.com/world/2016/feb/23/egypt-prison-for-journalists-reporters-without-borders-letter.
70. Fatima El Issawi, "The Role of Egyptian Media in the Coup".

The Media Elite: Moderators or Preachers of the Public Opinion?

In the immediate aftermath of the Arab uprisings, many talk show hosts took advantage of their expanded freedoms by vocally supporting particular ideological agendas and political camps. The empowerment of national media post-uprising(s) was mostly reflected in the growing impact of televised talk shows, which became the preferred platform, not only to debate national politics, but also to promote ideals and political agendas. In these televised battles, all manoeuvres—including misinformation and widespread rumours—were allowed and even encouraged. In this chapter, I will investigate the complex link between these media stars and political figures, drawing on case studies and data from the field investigation conducted under the remit of my research project, while looking at the interplay between media and politics during the thorny process of political transition. The analysis will focus on Egyptian talk show hosts, who were pivotal in disseminating information to the masses before the January 25, 2011 uprising. They became a strong platform for political mobilization under the tumultuous and short-lived Brotherhood rule, and later provided legitimacy to the military-backed regime after the military coup that overthrew the Brotherhood government in July 2013.

The democratization process in Egypt has witnessed an alarming setback post-coup, with the military-backed regime committing serious violations of human rights and civil liberties; national media is again deferential, barely reporting on the regime's wrongdoings and willingly embracing an unprecedentedly blatant propaganda. This chapter will look into the role played by prominent media figures both in promoting the fragile democratization process and undermining it, leading to the relapse of the political transition into autocracy.

I. The Alliance Between the Media and the Political Elite

In his book entitled, *Les nouveaux chiens de garde* [The New Watchdogs], Serge Halimi describes the subtle and complex relationship between the political and media elites in France. The solid alliance between some 30 leading journalists and the driving forces behind France's political and economic systems encompasses three primary forms: the blackout of important information, the systematic invitation of the same guests to comment on events, and personal relations between prominent media figures and politicians at the private level. This solidarity between media "stars" and leading political actors allows them to control the industry throughout its various platforms. "For them, the sun never sets," writes Halimi.[1]

The social profile of this French media elite is carefully analysed by the French sociologist Remy Rieffel. In his book *L'Elite des journalists* [the Journalists' Elite], Rieffel describes the phenomenon of leading journalists from the printed press legitimizing new or less-established journalists in order for the latter to enjoy professional recognition and access to this privileged community. In so doing, these prominent journalists build professional "tribes" they manage and control, in the aim of asserting their leadership and professional status. In the time when the research was conducted—between 1979 and 1981—prominent opinion writers and commentators of the printed press wielded much greater influence over the public than French televised talk show hosts and news presenters, whose power would grow later. Rieffel describes the deep connivance between the members of this privileged club and the political elite, namely, deputies, senators, ministers, and high-ranking civil servants. The two elite groups share more than interests and political stances: they belong to the same social class, enjoy a similar social background, and have benefitted from the same education, attending the same schools and universities. The strong chains linking these two groups are further consolidated by a common lifestyle: The members of the political and media elites frequent the same hotels, clubs, restaurants, etc.[2] Such closeness transforms journalism into a simple intermediary between public opinion and the political sphere, leading to a blurring between the roles of journalist and politician.[3]

The British media presents similar dynamics. In his book "The Establishment: And how they get away with it", Owen Jones describes the role of media elites in legitimizing a set of neoliberal ideas, thus becoming themselves an "an integral part of the British Establishment".[4] The strong concentration of media ownership is criticized as restricting a plurality of viewpoints to be expressed onto media platforms. The media owners, wealthy businessmen and corporations, perceive their interests as colluding with conservative policies and exercise a big influence on the editorial stance of these media, by dictating the general editorial line or by appointing senior staff who share their political stance. The powerful media owners perceive their investments in media as a tool to assert their influence.[5] However, the complexity of the British media landscape, the importance given to professional values, and the ability of media producers to express and promote their political views all mean that media organizations reflect much more than the political stance dictated by the media owner.[6] The US media elite are also perceived as a main channel of support and legitimization for liberal ideals.[7] At the top of the so-called media elite sit the media barons, whose prominence is linked to their ability to provide allocative powers, and who enjoy more powerful and durable influence than the more fragmented and transient leading journalists.[8]

These "clubs" of media and political elites constitute networks of powers that connect with other networks of power, other "clubs". The interdependency between media and political elites is reciprocal. Journalists are dependent on the political elite to create the news they report, as well as to provide information or commentary on the major events of the day. However, if the political elite controls patterns of media access, the media controls access to discourse. Thus the elite depend on the media to secure their visibility. In this sense, mass media is, in itself, an institution of elite power and dominance, with obligations not only to the public but also to the political elites.[9]

The notion of political parallelism—one of the dimensions used by Hallin and Mancini to describe media systems—describes the subtle interdependency between political and mass media elites in Western established political systems.[10] In transitional environments where power struggles over the features and identity of the new regime can be overwhelming, a journalism of advocacy and partisanship often flourishes as a necessary tool for the audience to make sense of these complex conflicts; most people will rely on sources of information that support their own political views, rather than those that contradict and challenge their beliefs.[11] In post-uprising

Egypt, where political parties are weak and non-political actors—such as the military—dominate the political dynamics, this parallelism took a dynamic two-way form for a short phase before replicating old forms of dependency on the powers that be. Under the Brotherhood rule, when polarization reached an apex, the media elite actively shaped the political sphere, empowered by the new political actors' lack of legitimacy. The media elite were one of the main targets of the political polarization, frequently attacked while actively engaging in cementing this polarization. With the fall of the transition into an autocracy post-military-takeover, the media elite again became the regime's mouthpiece. The balance of power is shifting again to the benefit of the politicians; yet the media "stars" are not hiding their eagerness to serve the new masters. The case studies presented in this chapter demonstrate and confirm this thesis.

II. The "Renaissance" of the National, and Flourishing Talk Shows

The fall of political regimes as a result of popular uprisings leads to a sudden and chaotic openness of the political and media landscapes. As Laclau and Mouffe contend, the broken "chain of equivalence" between various oppositional groups post-uprising(s) can lead to a re-fragmentation of the political sphere.[12] The fall of the traditional power structure with the departure of Mubarak and the election of a Brotherhood government in Egypt reshaped the political and media landscape, while the apparatus of civil servants loyal to the former regime—called the "deep state"—remained resilient to change.[13] The launch of numerous new media outlets, as well as the raging wars of political interest groups fighting for media attention, further contributed to this fragmentation.

Unlike other Arab countries that went through a regime change, Egypt enjoyed a relatively open media landscape before the uprising, whereby dissent was tolerated when it was not breaching established taboos. The emergence of influential private broadcasters in the last decade of the regime widened the scope of political and social dissent on media platforms while keeping it under the watch of media barons, those wealthy businessmen who stood united with the political regime through shared interests. At the same time, they can also be the subjects of the regime's anger when they are perceived as not honouring their political allies' expectations. As an example, the Egyptian businessman and co-founder of *al-Masry al-Yom* newspaper Salah Diab was arrested at his house in November 2015 by a heavily armed masked police unit, a move the Interior Ministry justified by declaring that Diab was in possession of unlicensed weapons. The special unit was accompanied by a photographer who snapped photos of Diab in handcuffs, widely circulated online and disseminated by tabloid newspaper *al-Youm al-Sabee*. The businessman's lawyer, Farid al-Deeb, links Diab's arrest to *al-Masry al-Yom's* recent "rebellion" against the regime, reflected by a growing criticism and dissent expressed in the coverage of the newspaper of Sisi's policies, including reports on torture in prisons and police stations and other appalling abuses by security forces.[14]

In the immediate aftermath of the uprising, the scope of political dissent expressed on media platforms witnessed a tremendous expansion as these expressions were granted an unprecedented visibility in various programming, including state media. Religious channels—such as the Salafi-affiliated stations *al-Hafez*, *al-Omma*, and *al-Nas*—featured talk shows engaging in political debates, a subject matter forbidden under the former regime; and new private ventures launched without any clarity on their funding sources and editorial lines. These new ventures included those backed by businessmen close to the former regime[15] with large operations and an anti-Islamic agenda, as well as a few Islamic-friendly private broadcasters with much more limited operations and programming. These pro-Islamic stations, owned by businessmen close to the Brotherhood, led to an unprecedented diversification of the media landscape.[16] While the link between media funding and politics occupied a prominent position in political debates, the procedure for granting licenses to new broadcast ventures remained largely obscure and nepotistic. The new private media projects remained in the realm of the traditional model: wealthy businessmen, linked to the regime, owned large conglomerations with media operations spanning over various platforms.

The rise of national media post-uprising contributed to the regression of the influence exercised by pan-Arab satellite broadcasters, which used to provide national audiences with a window of fresh information and diverse views, as opposed to the monotone content of state-owned media. The old pan-Arab broadcasters had to change their editorial orientations in order to cope with the new competition and changes in the mood of national audiences.[17] This trend was fueled by the openness of national media in Egypt and the proliferation of new private media projects eager to invest in this field for mostly political purposes. Audiences were more interested in national crises than regional ones, the transitional process to democracy fuelling heated debates at home.

In this environment of hyper-nationalism and the glorification of the national, local talk show hosts began taking the lead from their colleagues in pan-Arab stations. National audiences' suspicion towards regional powers, especially Qatari and Saudi, manifested as resentment towards prominent broadcasters publicly regarded as representing the agendas of these powers. For instance, the closure of *Al Jazeera Mubasher Misr*, an affiliate of the Al Jazeera network based in Cairo, was understood as either an expression of the governmental pressure on Qatari media or, on the contrary, a landmark shift in the troubled Egyptian–Qatari relations. The controversial channel was accused by the Egyptian government and national media of siding with the outlawed Muslim Brotherhood in reporting the dramatic events in the country post-military coup.[18]

The particular features and history of the Egyptian media industry cemented the ability of the media elite (especially talk show hosts) to use their personal agency to support political agendas. While state-owned media are officially the sole provider of political information, news bulletins provided by the redundant and old-fashioned state-owned broadcasters are little more than the narration of governmental activities. The licenses provided to private broadcasters implicitly ban them from producing news bulletins by confining them to what the license vaguely refers to as "general" programmes. In order to counter these restrictions, talk shows became the main platform to both provide news of the day and interpret it—that is, help audiences make sense of it. In a country with one of the highest illiteracy rates in the Arab world[19] and high levels of television consumption,[20] televised talk show hosts were pivotal in providing massive audiences with simple (yet biased) interpretations of events around them. Before the uprising, they were instrumental in the dissemination of information to rural communities; post-uprising, the popularity of these TV slots reached an apogee. As scholar Marwan Kraidy argues, this was the "renaissance" of national broadcasting, terrestrial and satellite.[21]

In using their personal agency to lobby for political ideals or agendas, Egyptian talk show personalities are following in the footsteps of prominent talk show hosts of pan-Arab satellite channels, who were instrumental in opening up the public debate to political and social dissent. The pan-Arab televised talk show scene, with the lead example of *Al-Jazeera*, allowed a limited relative representation of radical oppositional forces and challenged some of the most entrenched social and religious taboos.[22] The effective impact of these shows is not a matter of consensus among scholars: some question their capacity to generate tangible change, while others celebrate what they call a new Arab public sphere enabled by these televised debates.[23]

Egyptian talk shows echo the emotionally charged and heated Arab talk show scene. The latter follows an American tradition of politically biased TV programmes in which the presenter supports a political agenda and calls upon his audience to follow him, thus adopting "liberal-commercial patterns",[24] as the dominant mode of framing events and issues in Arab television. A prominent example of these heated shows is the controversial debate programme on *Al Jazeera* called "The Opposite Direction". The passionate style adopted by the presenter Faisal al-Qassem inflames dissensions between his guests to the extent of physical confrontation. With shouting and swearing frequent occurrences in the studio, tens of millions of Arab tuned in—the sensational style used by the presenter is thought to be one of major selling points of the programme.[25]

Under the Mubarak regime, the rise of talk show slots on Egyptian TV stations was limited to a few programmes. Their main task was to consolidate the relative openness of the political sphere by providing a voice to civil society groups without reporting on their radical demands. A major production was *el Beit Beitak* ("This Home is Yours"), the flagship programme aired on state TV and produced by a private company. The programme launch was part of an attempt to revamp the image of the regime and counter criticism in the face of the state media's increasing deterioration. The programme tackled controversial issues without breaching strict taboos.[26] The private broadcast sector has also developed a niche for primetime talk shows that gained large popularity, contributing to the diversification of the media content and widening the representation of tolerated civil society and political groups. For instance, Dream2's nighttime (10 p.m.) talk show *Al-Ashera Masa'an* with host Mona El-Shazly led the move towards a more critical, nuanced, yet still acceptable—by government standards—media content. The talk show distinguished itself by hosting Wael Ghonim, the Google executive who was behind the launch of the Facebook page, "We are all Khaled Saed", which played a major role in driving youth to the streets during the uprising. Ghonim, who was just released after being secretly detained by the Egyptian security, burst into tears during the interview.[27]

III. Watchdog or Activist: Blurred Identity

While the demonstrations were unfolding calling for the fall of the Mubarak regime, the majority of Egyptian television stars engaged in campaigns of slander against demonstrators. They claimed the demonstrators were foreign-trained protesters, spies for foreign regimes, or simply promoters of morally illicit activities.[28] After Mubarak's departure, talk show hosts followed the national state-run newspapers, whose headlines suddenly glorified the uprising, and became the defenders of the revolutionaries. After the military takeover, they simply reverted to defending the regime, displaying a populist, propagandist bent that went to the extreme of calling for the killing of political opponents.[29]

In the aftermath of the January 2011 uprising, a liberated mood within the media community encouraged journalists to push boundaries by tackling topics that used to be strictly taboo. Talk show hosts gained more courage, becoming bolder in challenging politicians directly on air. A prominent example is the talk show episode (*Baladna Bil Masri*) in which Ahmed Shafik, appointed Prime Minister by Mubarak during the uprising, was severely challenged by talk show hosts Reem Maged and Yosri Fouda on the private satellite television network ONT. ONT was owned by the Coptic businessman Naguib Sawiress, who is known for being close to the military through a large set of enterprises. The channel was sold to a new owner, the high-profile businessman Ahmed Abu Hashima, whose owns the company "Egyptians' Media" and was recently accumulating investments in domestic media. The following day, Shafik announced his resignation.[30] This was largely viewed as an indicator of national media's growing empowerment in relation to the political sphere. However, and as the case studies in this chapter demonstrate, this empowerment continues to serve the media owners' interests and reflects the nature of their relationship with the new ruler. As an example, the same TV channel, ONT, turned from being the voice of the revolution under the Brotherhood to the voice of the military-backed regime after the coup.

After the uprising, the deluge of talk shows and the fierce battle between presenters and channels over the hearts and minds of Egyptians confirmed the importance of these TV platforms as forums for debate, news providers, and main attractions for advertisers. The popularity of these TV slots can be explained by the extremely tense, fast-moving, and complex political transition: audiences desperately sought simple interpretations of these dramatic developments, in order to be able to understand them and take a position. This popularity was enhanced with new players introduced under the Brotherhood: religious preachers were granted the opportunity to discuss politics in their shows. Some of these shows became platforms for incitement, to the extent of defamation and public calls for killing. Khaled Abdullah, the previously prominent preacher of *al-Nas* Salafi TV station, believes his show significantly boosted the chances of Salafi candidates in the parliamentary elections of 2012 due to his statements openly calling upon his audience to vote for them.[31] His show was known as a strong platform for denigration of various parties, mainly the Coptic Christian community and secular leaders.

These talk show stars represent an exclusive club of media figures enjoying financial and professional privileges far above those of the large majority of Egyptian journalists, who endure fragile working conditions and low pay. Rather than exposing the wrongdoing of new regimes, these media personalities engaged in political activism and self-glorification: the main content of these talk shows were arguments between the guest(s) and/or the host(s). While the "watchdog" function has the aim of exposing wrongdoing in the name of the public interest,[32] the Egyptian-style talk show hosts are much more heavily engaged in creating a sustained culture of scandal on TV and boosting their personal popularity and status.

The format of these TV shows strengthened the trend towards self-glorification by making the personality of the presenter the centre of the show. Moderators use opening "monologues" in each episode to comment on the hottest news of the day, often using an emotional, redundant style. These monologues can be as long as the moderator wishes.[33] They can tackle personal, private matters in addition to the new political and social developments, thus confirming the centrality of the host's personality in the show. In debates, the moderator is an active contributor, expressing his or her views and frequently answering the questions addressed to the guest. It is customary to see hosts crying on screen, or slamming political opponents, or lecturing political leaders on how they should behave. For instance, the removal of deposed Mohamed Morsi at the hands of the army was announced on screens by an explosion of emotions: presenters crying, singing the national anthem, and waving the flag in their studios.[34]

For most of the talk show hosts I interviewed within the realm of this research, assuming neutrality could be understood as an act of treason; it is their "duty" to guide public opinion for the service of political agendas, interests, or ideals. Talk show host Reem Maged publicly supported the uprising from the beginning, and quickly became a media star/activist. Stationed in Tahrir square, Maged became a flagship figure, supporting demonstrators and giving direct reports to international media on the developments of the uprising. She acknowledges that her identity as a journalist blended with her political activism: "I have struggled between my professional and human identities. Talk shows are a powerful weapon. I will not renounce this weapon in the service of my cause while others are still using it for the service of their causes".

Other prominent figures in the television scene went equally silent after the military takeover, the most prominent among them is the satirist Bassem Youssef, who faced an arrest warrant issued under the Brotherhood government for allegedly insulting Islam and President Mohamed Morsi.[35] His satirical programme, "el Bernameg", frequently ridiculed the Brotherhood government, directly criticizing what he considered an antinational agenda, such as alleged plans by the administration to sell off national interests to regional connections like Qatar. After the military takeover, two private channels suspended his programme; the content was considered "disrespectful" of the new regime, especially the new head of state Abdel Fatah el-Sisi. The comedian finally decided to halt production of his show, which he was broadcasting through his YouTube channel. He explained his decision by stating "the present climate in Egypt is not suitable for a political satire program," adding in a press conference, "I'm tired of struggling and worrying about my safety and that of my family".[36] The satirist and his production company have been fined 13 million US dollars over a dispute with the one of the television channels which suspended his show, for the so-called "financial and literary losses" caused to the channel by the suspension of the programme.[37] A local arbitration body (the Cairo Regional Centre for International Commercial Arbitration) imposed the fine on Youssef and his company, Q-Soft, stating that his show was not "purposeful and constructive" but a platform for "smearing the country's political direction".[38]

IV. Case Studies from the Egyptian Talk Show Scene

After the military takeover, talk show hosts became one of the strongest instruments the military-backed regime used to assert its legitimacy. The alliance between the media and political elites was first framed, under the Brotherhood, as an expression of "patriotic duty"—the media stars supporting the political camp presented by them as best serving the interests of the country, but also serving their own interests as well. However, the so-called patriotic duty was mostly an occasion for them to assert their popularity and influence; their political positioning acted as a barometer to judge politician's performance. After the military takeover, the national "duty" dictated releasing blunt propaganda in support of the regime, to the extent that some hosts expressed their "pride" in being associated with the military and taking direct instruction from the regime.

The alliance between the Egyptian media elite and the political regime is fundamental for the survival of both parties. In a press article, Egyptian talk show host and investigative journalist Yosri Fouda describes a tradition established by late President Nasser in dealing with national media. Newly elected presidents launch their administrations by meeting leading journalists and writers in a bid to secure their support "for the sake of the country". Fouda describes the consolidation of this tradition by the informal designation of a prominent journalist who would be the voice of the president, which gradually lead to the erosion of professional standards, though the community of journalists, including few prominent critical writers, had actively resisted this wave.[39]

This alliance between the media elite and the regime is consolidated by the nature of the media's funding: most private broadcasters are owned by wealthy businessmen with strong economic and political connections to the regime. These businessmen helped in establishing a "parallel system" where newly launched private media present a more professional media product while remaining at all times under the control of security services, through the compliance of the media owner or the need to preserve his business interests.[40] The personal agency employed by the influential talk show host cannot extend to threatening the interests of the media owner and his relationship to political power.

Mostly trained in the print sector, these prominent television moderators are bound to the regime by a complex system of clientelism, making them one of its most steadfast proponents. For instance, some of them used to assume official functions within the apparatus of the former regime, such as the anchor Lamees el Hadidi (CBC private network), who used to serve as an advisor to former President Mubarak. They do not necessarily come from the upper class, socially or economically. Few of them had the experience of working in international media, without this experience necessarily impacting their perceptions of professional journalism. Their prominence is mostly linked to their loyalty to the regime and its entourage and to the media owner, as well as their ability to adapt to changes in the broadcast industry, quickly shifting their stance when this shift is needed to secure their survival and to sustain their popularity. The reciprocal need is acknowledged by new leaders, for whom securing the support of these "media stars" is important regardless of their fluid loyalties.

The complex interplay between the media and political elites transcends the political field, becoming an opaque exchange of political interests and business. The alleged deals are crucial for reinforcing the bonds of loyalty between the media stars and the regime's men, yet the deals can also be used, when needed, as a stick wielded to maintain control over the influential media figures and deter them from tackling touchy topics.

Asked about tools he uses to safeguard his independence, Sherif Amer, a talk show host who distinguishes himself by his sober style in contrast to the emotional model of his colleagues, talks about "avoiding mistakes" the regime can use to allegedly blackmail him. He contends that the Mubarak regime uses to blackmail prominent talk show hosts to push them not to tackle some topics—in return for turning a blind eye to some suspicious business projects/deals. "This is a dirty business, I don't play this game," he stresses.[41] While the alleged deals were not openly acknowledged under the Mubarak regime, it became customary after the military takeover to hear some of these media stars talking openly about "deals" made with politicians or military officers to suppress information or to disseminate derogatory rumours about opponents. For instance, a few prominent talk show stars, such as Wael el Ibrashi, Tamer Amin, and Mahmood Saad, were named in a leaked phone conversation between the chief of staff of the then powerful Minister of Defense, General Sisi, and an officer, in which the first instructs the second to intervene with them, to embellish the image of Sisi ahead of the 2014 presidential elections that he ultimately won. Wael al Ibrashi stated he is "proud" of serving the General,[42] while Tamer Amin declared in an interview that he frequently delivers some of his guests to the security services after inviting them to his show.[43]

In the following, I will present examples of the intricate interplay between some of these talk show hosts and the political powers that be. These case studies are based on media monitoring and interviews I conducted under the remit of my research project.

a. Ahmed Moussa: "Law Is the Bullets"

Unknown before the 2011 uprising, Ahmed Mousa is an excellent example of the dubious relations between media and political figures in Egypt. Openly acknowledging his connections to the security apparatus, he is nicknamed by colleagues as "the journalist detective". Recognized for his sharp voice, his programme ("Under My Responsibility", aired on *Sada al-Balad* private TV) is a prominent platform for slamming the regime's opponents, to the extent of calling directly for killing, shunning, and violations of privacy. Moving from one private TV channel to another, Mousa sees himself as the spokesperson of the security forces. He frequently presents "exclusive information" glorifying what he presents as future actions by security forces against certain target groups, especially supporters of the Brotherhood. In one episode, he announces, "the free army officers decided that anyone suspected of killing a security member will be killed by them directly in the street. There is no need for courts anymore".[44] While reporting from the scene of explosion in the city of Mansoura in December 2013—a car bomb targeted a building of the Interior Ministry, killing 13 people, according to official records—he wept and urged the government to declare the Brotherhood a terrorist organization. Lately he has campaigned against revolutionary figures and human rights activists, labelling them "traitors" and tools of "foreign hands".

The anchor became one of the fiercest defenders of the military-backed government post-coup, praising even the most repressive actions of the security apparatus. When 12 people were killed in Matariya, a neighborhood of Cairo, in demonstrations marking the fourth anniversary of the uprising, Moussa urged the Interior Ministry to strike the area and eradicate all protesters, stating that "law is the bullets"[45] and that he wished "the police would have killed 400 terrorists". The violent crackdown on protests that followed caused the deaths of 23 people; most of them were shot by security forces in various demonstrations throughout the country. Commenting on the death of activist Shaimaa el Sabbagh, shot while taking part in a peaceful demonstration on January 24, 2015, Moussa played the role of the detective, pretending to have special information on the activist's killer.[46] He showed a photo of the alleged perpetrator, one of the victim's fellow activists and a prominent human rights lawyer. At the same time he accused Brotherhood supporters of involvement in the shooting.[47] The government blamed the death on the activist herself, stating she died as a result of the shotgun wounds because she was "too thin".[48] The spokesman for the Medical Forensics Authority Hisham Abdel Hamid said in a television interview that "Shaimaa el-Sabbagh, according to science, should not have died," adding, "her body was like skin over bone, as they say. She was very thin. She did not have any percentage of fat. So the small pellets penetrated very easily".[49]

Moussa had an exclusive interview with former President Mubarak in November 2014, after a Cairo court dropped murder charges against Mubarak brought on behalf of the hundreds of protesters killed during the uprising. The ruling sparked uproar from human rights activists throughout the country. In his interview with the former president from the latter's hospital bed, the anchor asked Mubarak if he thought there was an American interference behind the uprising that led to his removal.[50] Mubarak evaded the question but talked about "phone calls" he received in the last ten years of his rule.[51] Moussa has recently sparked a new controversy by hailing what he considers to be the "success" of Russian attacks in Syria, and claiming to have special footage that proved their superiority over the allied forces' operations in the region. This footage was from a video game.[52] A court prison sentence issued against Moussa in a defamation lawsuit was finally annulled in a decision by an appeals court.[53] The original verdict had not stopped Moussa from accompanying President Sisi on his visit to Germany with a large media delegation in May 2015, before the sentence was abrogated.[54]

b. Lamees El Hadidi: Students Are "Thugs"

Lamees el Hadidi is a former adviser of the Mubarak regime and the prominent anchor of the talk show "Huna el Assima" ("From the Capital"), aired on the influential private network CBC. In a press interview, she notes she is proud of being named among the 50 most influential women in Africa by the francophone magazine "Jeune Afrique", a matter she relates to her "battle against the Muslim Brotherhood and the religious trends is general" in Egypt.

Acting as a political mentor and an expert on economics, the anchor, who is frequently commended by the new regime for her role in supporting the military takeover, does not limit her role to commenting on the news of the day but rather often "coaches" the government on how to deal with pressing economic, political, and security issues. Commenting on a possible rapprochement between Egypt and Qatar, Hadidi advises the Egyptian government to impose "conditions" for such rapprochement, stating, "the emir of Qatar should first seek pardon from the Egyptian people", and adding that any reconciliation should require the extradition of the Muslim brotherhood leaders who fled to Doha after the coup.[55] Commenting on the growing number of street protests against the regime, she slams the Brotherhood, stating, "The blood of one of the army or police martyrs is equivalent to thousands of the Muslim Brotherhood 'dogs'" and claiming that "foreign funds" are supporting these demonstrations.[56]

Along with other media presenters from the pro-military regime camp, Hadidi actively defends the actions of the security forces, even when they are clearly abusive. Her programme is one of the main TV platforms praising the security forces, proudly stressing the message that the security forces will use "excessive force" and respond "toughly and violently" to any potential attack.[57] For instance, commenting on a wave of student protests on campuses in Cairo that led to a violent crackdown by security forces, including the use of a private security agency, Hadidi labelled the students "thugs" who wanted to "test the power of the State and its security apparatus". She showed a series of reports in which she claimed students were attacking the police, calling for a tougher response to students' activism.[58] Universities are one of few pockets of visible opposition to the military-backed government, bringing together Islamist and left-leaning youth groups, who were instrumental in the 2011 uprising against Mubarak regime. According to sources within the organization of students, at least 14 students were killed in clashes with police and thousands were arrested in response to this wave of protests in October 2014.[59]

Hadidi, who led Mubarak's electoral campaign in 2005, is considered an elite figure in the pro-military government camp: Her previous work for pan–Arab and international media is a distinctive feature of her profile. However, this international experience did not make the style and content of her programme different from that of colleagues who did not enjoy such exposure. While the uprising was unfolding, her previous programme that used to air on the state-owned television actively defended Mubarak's regime. Like other televised media figures, she shifted immediately to the opposite camp post-uprising, launching fierce campaigns against the Brotherhood government in the name of defending the gains of the revolution.

c. Mahmoud Saad: The Ambivalent "Witness"

Considered among the highest-paid talk show host in Egypt today, Mahmoud Saad is well known for his humble personal style that speaks directly to the hearts of ordinary Egyptian citizens. A prominent talk show hosts on Egyptian screens before the uprising, Saad distinguished himself by lauding the success of the Tunisian uprising, siding with the revolutionaries when the street demonstrations in Cairo became an undeniable fact. He decided to stop presenting his show, saying he would not follow directives from the network to describe the demonstrators as "thugs".

Saad is known for his frequently changing stances and views, praising a party or a politician one day and criticizing them another day. He openly supported Mohamed Morsi, the Muslim Brotherhood's candidate in the first presidential elections following the uprising in 2012. He later became one of the fiercest critics of the Brotherhood's governmental policies. He considers himself a "columnist who happens to work for television". For him, his talk show is a televised translation of his ideas: "I'm a journalist and I've been used to expressing my opinions from an early age," he says.[60]

While resistant to directives, Saad can be conciliatory when it comes to topics he believes involve national security. Under the rule of the Supreme Council of the Armed Forces (SCAF),[61] the military generals deployed a PR campaign to seduce media by organizing regular briefs for senior journalists in an attempt to preempt any possible critical reporting on them. Saad was one of the main figures invited to these meetings. He describes how influential these meetings were in shaping his views and attitudes towards the military institution. He recounts, "They (the generals) met every one of us alone, they briefed us on on-going events. The aim was to provide us with accurate information so when we address our audiences we don't mess up and we avoid rumours on the military. I could understand the real role of secret services, the nature of their work and to what extent they are involved in everything".[62] Asked if he follows the instructions of the generals in positively reporting on the military, his answer is simple: "I cannot criticize the army as the army. It is a national institution. It is not possible".[63] For him, investigating topics in relation to security forces is not possible for lack of information. "It is a closed box. We don't know what is going on inside it. This is why I cannot talk about it".[64]

Saad frequently stresses his independence from political or governmental pressure. However, he was one of the talk show hosts cited in the leaked phone conversation in which President Sisi's Chief of Staff talks about collaborating with media figures to support Sisi's election. In the leaked conversation, the Chief of Staff describes a phone call he allegedly received from Saad, in which the presenter made sure that Sisi's camp sees him in a positive light.[65] However, Saad continues to represent a distinctive feature of the talk show scene under the military-backed regime, sporadically offering criticism of the regime. For instance, he was suspended from his programme, aired on the *An-Nahar* private television channel, after an episode in which he commented on a photo showing Sisi with a group of young activists. Saad said, "General Sisi is now president and he deserves it. Where are these kids (young people) today?" alluding to the fact that a great number of the activists in the photo were in prison at that time, mostly for criticizing regime. He added, "I wonder what General

Sisi thinks about this photo: Does he think they are traitors and deserve what they are facing now"?

Saad's ambivalent positions, criticizing the government and defending the case of imprisoned activists while in the same time glorifying the fight against terrorism, allow him to maintain the image of an independent commentator. However, he is a good example of the limits of this media elite's ability to use their personal agency and popularity in defending causes when it comes to challenging red lines. Commenting on suspending Saad's programme, the head of *An-Nahar* declared that he will not tolerate "any infringements since the unusual circumstances—of the country—require unusual measures" on media platforms.[66] Saad is absent from media platforms recently after his talk show contract ended. He explained his absence by his unwillingness to appear on any talk show platform.

d. Ibrahim Issa: From Outspoken Critic to Regime Mouthpiece

Ibrahim Issa is one of the most controversial media figures to shift from fiercely opposing the Mubarak regime—and later the Brotherhood government—to defending the military-backed regime. Issa was the co-founder of the popular weekly *al Dostour*, which criticized Mubarak using colloquial language and cartoons, in a departure from the official tone of state-owned newspapers. The weekly was able to tackle touchy topics, such as the relationship between the political regimes and businessmen, and wealth disparities among Egyptians.

The controversial paper cemented Issa's fame and influence within the media community. The journalist's populist and provocative style made him a special feature of the media landscape; the so-called "enfant terrible" of the Egyptian press, Issa presents himself as an observer of political life as well as an acute critic. He perceives himself as a reformer of the national media industry, gathering around him enthusiastic young journalists following in his footsteps as disciples. In his rocky career, he has embarked several times on new media projects that did not survive, having been either suspended by the authorities or sold under controversial and opaque circumstances.[67]

Issa's sudden U-turn from supporting the uprising to praising the military was a great source of disappointment for his fans. A flagrant example is Issa's decision to change his testimony given in 2011 in which he accused police forces of shooting protesters. When the case was sent to re-trial after the military coup, Issa gave totally different testimony, stating that he did not witness any shooting and stressing that Mubarak couldn't have ordered such violence because he was a "patriotic president".[68] The previously outspoken critic of the Mubarak regime, who had been supportive of a political role for the Brotherhood, began denouncing the Islamist group to the extent of calling Islam itself a source of violence. He frequently voices opinions considered scandalous, such as claiming that sexual harassment was a daily practice in the Prophet's time[69] or that ISIS crimes are committed based on Islamic sources[70] in his show ("With Ibrahim Issa", aired at Cairo and People TV channel [*al-Kahera wel Nas*]). He described Egyptian people as "illiterate and non-educated" while at the same time ordering them not to join revolutionary activists, condescending to them as "kids" and "material for exportation" to the West.

Along with his fellow anchors, Issa is spreading the idea of a Western conspiracy being fomented against Egypt. He claimed that Egyptian people and politicians are subjects of "a European and American espionage", justifying frequent leaked phone conversations that are becoming a powerful tool to disclose the shortcomings of Sisi's government. Stressing the existence of a "conspiracy" targeting Egypt, the prominent journalist is confident that "the US is monitoring and taping any phone conversation in Egypt". Issa also linked the Russian plane crash in Sinai (November 2015) to the alleged involvement of Western secret services seeking to "teach Russia a lesson" and "reward terrorists by punishing Egypt through pulling the tourists from the country".[71] Egyptian media widely spread the notion of a conspiracy behind the plane crash, accusing the British government of preempting the investigation on the crash by quickly declaring that the plane was likely to have been brought down by a bomb.[72]

Conclusion

Egyptian talk shows are instrumental in disseminating information to ordinary citizens, who rely on the hosts' interpretations of the news to understand the world around them. The wide influence of these shows makes them a precious platform for political mobilization, able to fuel people's dissatisfaction or absorb it, depending on the needs of the political agendas they serve. The changing allegiances of the media stars who host these shows—from fiercely opposing un-democratic practices by the Brotherhood government to aggressively supporting abusive measures by the military-backed government after the military takeover—are reflective of the excessive political manipulation of these programmes.

The polarized political landscape under the Brotherhood allowed these media stars to wield influence over both their audience and politicians, thus shifting the balance of power. Were these media elite truly political players in shaping public opinion during this particularly tumultuous phase, or was this media activism simply an expression of solidarity with the traditional political elite, without the latter directly instructing them on how to address their audiences? Asked in an academic conference to reflect on the shift in anchors' attitudes from critiquing the Brotherhood to abiding by the new regime's discourse and directives post-takeover, anchor Reem Maged simply replied, "The State was happy when we were criticizing them. Some anchors were criticizing dictatorship, others were slamming the Brotherhood and they are continuing today to do the same".[73]

The promotion of a populist style of journalism in support of the military-backed regime raises questions about the ability of talk show stars to use their personal agency in order to make change happens. The current glorification of the military indicates the limits of the influence exercised by these moderators in shaping the news agenda, and the political awareness of their audiences. The organic alliance between the media and political elites makes the tendency of leading media figures to conform to the views of the political ruling class a natural and smooth process. Today any critical media figures are silenced.

The examples provided in this chapter indicate that the dynamism injected into the public realm by these talk shows during the Brotherhood rule was simply a characteristic of the diversity of the new political landscape whereby different voices were allowed to coexist and express themselves. Their popularity and ability to attract huge audiences and plentiful advertisers gave them control over the content they delivered under the Brotherhood, including that which challenged the authority of media owners. Asked about managerial control of influential talk shows aired by the *an-Nahar* TV station, the chairman, Walid Moustafa, responded, "The talk show host is responsible for what he is saying in his programme. It is very difficult to control him. On air, it is difficult for us to intervene. After the programme, we can discuss[74]." Hassan Rateb, the owner of *al-Mehwar* network, found a simple way to control the content of talk show hosts by appointing "loyal" presenters: "I carefully choose my people, those who really care about our interests and that of the TV station. I have principles such as avoiding causing sectarian strife, or attacking the security forces…."[75]

The dynamism of these media platforms could not survive the descent of the previously diverse political landscape into tough autocracy. The current media elites have definitely not succeeded in challenging the entrenched taboo of the so-called "protection of national security". They are largely not willing to do so, rather using their personal agency to exacerbate fears of change and call for tougher responses from the regime to any questioning of its authority. The examples provided in this chapter confirm their active role in supporting and fuelling repression, rather than consolidating trends toward democratization. With the relapse of the transition into autocracy, the tenuous balance of power between these media stars and the political powers that be again shifted in favour of the latter. Critical voices, even when mild, are no longer tolerated on televised screens. The reaction is swift, and ranges from temporarily suspending the programme to forbidding the talk show host from presenting it or stopping its production entirely. The suspension of Bassem Youssef's satirical programme is reflective of this situation. Although that programme attracted formidable advertisement revenues, the host TV channel, CBC, known for its staunch support for the military-backed regime, decided to suspend it after the satirical presenter mildly criticized General Sisi. The surprisingly blunt criticism of President Sisi from Azza el-Henawy, a TV presenter on state television, led to her prompt suspension for "unprofessional conduct". She criticized Sisi for failing to hold officials accountable during a flooding crisis in areas north of Cairo in which dozens died.[76] Commenting on her suspension, el Henawy stressed that senior staff at the state broadcaster applied a policy of "The king died, long live the king", shifting their allegiances from one regime to another. She added that guests on her show lie frequently out of fear for their security and express opinions off the air contrary to what they state when they are on the air.

However, the above cases are not indicative of a trend; within the privileged club of television anchors, few engage in any meaningful resistance against the political dictates or the restrictions imposed by the media owners. On the contrary, they compete to prove their loyalty to the new regime by attacking its opponents, labelling them terrorists, dangerous cells, gangs, mafia, anti-Islam, anti-Egypt, etc. While some critical reactions from these media stars seem contradictory to their general stance, these sporadic expressions of dissatisfaction are perceived as an opportunity to absorb some of the widespread anger regarding the deterioration of political, security, and economic conditions post-coup. These critical expressions are also viewed as the reflection of a power struggle within the political regime between competing currents manipulating these televised platforms for the sake of serving internal dissentions.

The duality often observed in democratization processes between collaborative journalism (towards ideological friends) and oppositional journalism (towards ideological enemies)[77] was best expressed under the Brotherhood rule and faded after the military coup, leaving a chorus of voices all competing for the favour of the new political masters by actively fostering legitimacy for an autocratic regime. The majority of these media stars perceive their role as serving the "people" and responding to the street's mood. As argued by Sherif Amer, another prominent talk show host who lately opted for non-political content for his programme, "the pressure on media moved from being exercised by the regime to being enforced by the society. Every time I host a representative of an Islamic current in my programme, I receive extreme reactions from the audiences, some of them saying they don't want to see bears on television screens anymore".[78] These statements were made by this anchor in an interview immediately after the military coup. It is now nearly impossible to imagine a representation of radical dissent on Egyptian televised media platforms that would not be silenced.

While the media elites' role in fostering an environment permissive of abuses and fuelling its most radical manifestations is not to be denied, the media orchestration is in tune with an environment of hyper-nationalism, spanning all areas of everyday life. As only one example among many, a public service television advertisement urges Egyptians to be extremely cautious about any "stranger" inquiring about their internal affairs, as he or she is probably a spy. The government pulled the advertisement due to acute criticism of its content from human rights groups and on social media feeds.[79] Several incidents of reporting foreigners' to the police have been recorded, including the detention of prominent French journalist Alain Gresh by the police for chatting with two Egyptian journalists in a café in Cairo.[80]

The wave of populism swamping Egyptian televised shows and other media outlets is such that some extraordinary rumours that stretch logic and reason are being presented as solid facts. Examples abound: The daily partisan *al-Wafd* newspaper published a front-page headline claiming that US President Barak Obama was a secret Muslim Brotherhood member. An advertisement by a mobile phone operator featuring the popular puppet Abla Fahita was accused of containing subversive messages calling for terrorism. The debate on the alleged terrorist actions of the puppet suffused the talk shows, finally forcing the mobile phone company to issue a press release denying the allegations.[81] In this hysterical environment of fear and intimidation, it is unrealistic to think the media elite are truly lending any support towards democratic change.

Notes

1. Serge Halimi, Les nouveaux chiens de garde [the new watchdogs] (France: Liber-Raisons D'Agir, 1997), 76.
2. Remy Rieffel, L'elite des journalists [The Elites of Journalists] (France: Presses Universitaires de France, 1984).
3. Marc Martin, Media et Journalists de la Republique [Media and Journalists of the Republic] (Paris: Editions Odile Jacob, 1997), 428.
4. Owen Jones, The Establishment: And How They Get Away With It (London: Allen Lane, 2014), 5.
5. Dan Sabbagh, "How Proprietors are Taking Over the Biggest Media Companies in the UK," *The Guardian*, June 20, 2011, accessed November 20, 2015, https://www.theguardian.com/media/2011/jun/20/media-ownership-proprietors-families.
6. *Democratic Audit UK*, "The Political Affiliations of the UK's National Newspapers have Shifted, but There is Again a Heavy Tory Predominance," December 18, 2013, accessed November 20, 2015, http://www.democraticaudit.com/?p=1948.
7. Robert Lichter, Stanley Rothman, and Linda Lichter, The Media Elite (Chevy Chase, MD: Adler & Adler, 1986).
8. Des Freedman, "Media Moguls and Elite Power," Political Economy Research Centre, Papers Series: Elite, Power & Inequality, Goldsmith university, 2015.
9. Gaye Tuchman, Making News; A Study in the Construction of Reality (New York: Free Press, 1978).
10. Daniel C. Hallin and Paolo Mancini, Comparing Media Systems: Three Models of Media and Politics (Cambridge, UK: Cambridge University Press, 2004).
11. Silvio Waisbord, "In Journalism We Trust? Credibility and Fragmented Journalism in Latin America," in Mass Media and Political Communication in New Democracies, ed. Katrin Voltmer (Abingdon: Routledge, 2006).
12. Chantal Mouffe and Ernesto Laclau, Hegemony and Socialist Strategy: Towards a Radical Democratic Politics (London: Verso, 1985), 127.
13. Bessma Momani, "In Egypt, 'Deep State' vs. 'Brotherhoodization'," *Brookings*, August 21, 2013, accessed September 20, 2015, http://www.brookings.edu/research/opinions/2013/08/21-egypt-brotherhood-momani#.
14. Khaled Dawoud, "The Motives behind Salah Diab's Arrest and Release," *Atlantic Council*, November 17, 2015, accessed December 1, 2015, http://www.atlanticcouncil.org/blogs/menasource/the-motives-behind-salah-diab-s-arrest-and-release.
15. They are mainly anti-Islamic agendas and mostly linked to the former regime.

16. Nathan Field and Ahmed Hamam, "Salafi satellite TV in Egypt," Arab Media & Society, Spring 2009.
17. Marwan M. Kraidy, "Media Industries in Revolutionary Times," Media industries, 1 no. 2 (2014).
18. Mai Shams El–Din, "As Egypt-Qatar Relations Thaw, Al Jazeera Pulls Mubasher Misr Off Air," *Mada Masr*, December 22, 2014, accessed September 25, 2015, http://www.madamasr.com/sections/politics/egypt-qatar-relations-thaw-al-jazeera-pulls-mubasher-misr-air.
19. 25.9 % of Egypt's population above 10 years of age is illiterate, according to a report conducted by the Central Agency for Public Mobilisation and Statistics (CAPMAS) for the year 2013.
20. According to the European Commission' study (The EU Barometer poll 2012–2014 yet to be officially released), the level of TV consumption in Egypt is between 80 to 90 per cent of the interviewees in the poll.
21. Marwan M. Kraidy, "Media Industries in Revolutionary Times".
22. Mahmoud R. Al-Sadi, "Al Jazeera Television: Rhetoric of Deflection," Arab Media & Society 15 (2012).
23. Mohamed Zayani (ed.), The Al Jazeera Phenomenon: Critical Perspectives on New Arab Media (London: Pluto Press, 2005).
24. Muhammad Ayish, "Political Communication on Arab World Television: Evolving Patterns," Political Communication 19, no. 2 (2002): 137.
25. See an episode of the programme where guests exchanged swearing and indecent comments, https://www.youtube.com/watch?v=w109jPRtar0.
26. Fatima El Issawi, "In Post-Revolution Egypt, Talk Shows Redefine the Political Landscape," *Foreign Policy*, October 10, 2012, accessed September 25, 2015, http://foreignpolicy.com/2012/10/10/in-post-revolution-egypt-talk-shows-redefine-the-political-landscape/.
27. Amy Davidson, "Don't Cry Wael," *The New Yorker*, accessed November 25, 2015, http://www.newyorker.com/news/amy-davidson/dont-cry-wael.
28. *Al-Jazeera* Arabic created a documentary called "Manufacturing Lies" (*Sena'aet El-Kathib*) looking at state media during the 18 days of Egyptian protests https://www.youtube.com/watch?v=JfRHrK7uORQ.
29. Fatima El Issawi, "In Post-Revolution Egypt, Talk Shows Redefine the Political Landscape".
30. See the following clip on YouTube from the talk show: http://www.youtube.com/watch?v=jo61wpG_9i4.
31. See Ahram Online, "Religious Preacher Slapped with Fine for Insulting Egyptian Actress," May 29, 2013, accessed October 10, 2014, http://english.ahram.org.eg/News Content/1/64/72643/Egypt/Politics-/Religious-preacher-slapped-with-fine-for-insulting.aspx.

32. Silvio Waisbord, "Scandals, Media and Citizenship in Contemporary Argentina," *American Behavioral Scientist* 47, no. 8 (2004).
33. See Heba Afifi, "Lessons in Morality from Egyptian Media," *Mada Masr*, May 16, 2015, accessed October 10, 2015.
34. See *The Huffington Post*, "Egypt's President Morsi Ousted in Military Coup, Sparking Wild Celebrations," July 3, 2013, accessed September 10, 2014, http://www.huffingtonpost.co.uk/2013/07/03/egypt-president-morsi-ousted_n_3542451.html.
35. *BBC*, "Egypt Satirist Bassem Youssef Faces Arrest Warrant," March 30, 2013, accessed September 25, 2015, http://www.bbc.co.uk/news/world-middle-east-21980343.
36. Patrick Kingsly, "Egyptian Satirist Bassem Youssef Winds Up TV Show Due to Safety Fears," *The Guardian*, June 2, 2014, accessed September 25, 2015, https://www.theguardian.com/media/2014/jun/02/bassem-youssef-closes-egyptian-satire-tv-show-over-safety-fears.
37. *The Guardian*, "Egyptian Satirist Bassem Youssef Fined Millions in Dispute with TV Channel," December 23, 2014, accessed September 30, 2015, https://www.theguardian.com/world/2014/dec/23/egyptian-satirist-bassem-youssef-fined-tv-channel-al-bernameg-military.
38. Ibid.
39. See the opinion article by Yosri Fouda published by *Ashourouk* Egyptian newspaper, http://www.shorouknews.com/columns/view.aspx?cdate=29112015&id=7fbe315d-cae4-483e-919c-6f718c2be497.
40. Ibid.
41. Fatima El Issawi, "Egyptian Media Under Transition: In the Name of the Regime…in the Name of the People?", 78.
42. See Patrick Kingsley, "Will #SisiLeaks be Egypt's Watergate for Abdel Fatah al-Sisi?," *The Guardian*, 5 March 2015, accessed October 05, 2015, https://www.theguardian.com/world/2015/mar/05/sisileaks-egypt-watergate-abdel-fatah-al-sisi.
43. Mohamed Safaa el Din, "Media as a Trap for the Opposition," *Al Badil*, March 28, 2015, accessed September 25, 2015, (Arabic) http://elbadil.com/2015/03/28/%D8%A7%D9%84%D8%A5%D8%B9%D9%84%D8%A7%D9%85-%D9%85%D8%B5%D9%8A%D8%AF%D8%A9-%D8%A7%D9%84%D9%85%D8%B9%D8%A7%D8%B1%D8%B6%D9%8A%D9%86-%D9%85%D9%86-%D8%AA%D9%88%D8%B6%D9%8A%D8%AD-%D8%A7%D9%84%D8%AD/.
44. See Nour Youssef, "How Egyptian Media has Become the Mouthpiece for the Military State," *The Guardian*, 25 June 2015, accessed July 10, 2016, https://www.theguardian.com/world/2015/jun/25/egyptian-media-journalism-sisi-mubarak.

45. *Egypt Independent*, "TV Host Urges Interior Ministry to Strike Matariya district," January 27, 2015, accessed September 25, 2015, http://eg.b2.mk/news/?newsid=Fj.
46. See Leslie T. Chang, "Egypt Media: Endorsing Repression," *The New York Review of Books*, September 15, 2015, accessed October 01, 2015, http://www.nybooks.com/daily/2015/09/15/egypt-media-endorsing-repression/.
47. Ahmed Azab, "Ahmed Moussa and Shaimaa Killing: Lies, Lies and Lies," *al-Araby al-Jadeed*, January 26, 2015, accessed September 25, 2015, http://www.alaraby.co.uk/medianews/b7e245f3-20bd-4c5b-9ef9-6ec705b44dea.
48. David Kirkpatrick, "Egyptian Official Says Protester, Shaimaa el-Sabbagh Died in Shooting Because She was Too Thin," *The New York Times*, March 22, 2015, accessed September 20, 2015, http://www.nytimes.com/2015/03/23/world/middleeast/egyptian-medical-examiners-spokesman-blames-shaimaa-el-sabbaghs-death-on-her-thinness.html?_r=0.
49. Ibid.
50. See *Ahram Online*, "Egyptians Should Stand behind Their President, Says Hosni Mubarak," April 26, 2015, http://english.ahram.org.eg/NewsContent/1/64/128728/Egypt/Politics-/Egyptians-should-stand-behind-their-president,-say.aspx.
51. Ibid.
52. Abby Philipp, "Egyptian TV Anchor Mistakes Video Game Footage for Russian Airstrikes in Syria," *Washington Post*, October 12, 2015, accessed November 20, 2015, https://www.washingtonpost.com/news/worldviews/wp/2015/10/12/egyptian-tv-anchor-mistakes-video-game-footage-for-russian-airstrikes-in-syria/.
53. *Mada Masr*, "Court Overturns Talk Show Host Ahmed Moussa's 2-Year Prison Sentence," June 23, 2015, accessed November 20, 2015, http://www.madamasr.com/news/court-overturns-talk-show-host-ahmed-moussas-2-year-prison-sentence.
54. Ibid.
55. *Al Masreyoon*, "Lamees el Hadidi: These are My Conditions for the Reconciliation with Qatar," November 22, 2014, accessed September 30, 2015, http://almesryoon.com/%D8%AF%D9%81%D8%AA%D8%B1-%D8%A3%D8%AD%D9%88%D8%A7%D9%84-%D8%A7%D9%84%D9%88%D8%B7%D9%86/601837-%D8%A8%D8%A7%D9%84%D9%81%D9%8A%D8%AF%D9%8A%D9%88-%D9%84%D9%85%D9%8A%D8%B3-%D8%A7%D9%84%D8%AD%D8%AF%D9%8A%D8%AF%D9%8A-%D9%87%D8%B0%D9%87-%D8%B4%D8%B1%D9%88%D8%B7%D9%8A-%D9%84%D9%85%D8%B5%D8%A7%D9%84%D8%AD%D8%A9-%D9%82%D8%B7%D8%B1.
56. *Al-Masreyoon*, "Lamees el Hadidi: The Blood of a Martyr from the Army is Equivalent to Thousands of the Muslim Brotherhood' 'dogs'," October 25,

2014, accessed September 25, 2014, http://almesryoon.com/%D8%AF%D9%81%D8%AA%D8%B1-%D8%A3%D8%AD%D9%88%D8%A7%D9%84-%D8%A7%D9%84%D9%88%D8%B7%D9%86/582565-%D9%84%D9%85%D9%8A%D8%B3-%D8%A7%D9%84%D8%AD%D8%AF%D9%8A%D8%AF%D9%8A-%D8%AF%D9%85-%D8%B4%D9%87%D9%8A%D8%AF-%D8%A7%D9%84%D8%AC%D9%8A%D8%B4-%D8%A8%D8%A3%D9%84%D9%81-%D9%85%D9%86-%C2%AB%D9%83%D9%84%D8%A7%D8%A8-%D8%A7%D9%84%D8%A5%D8%AE%D9%88%D8%A7%D9%86%C2%BB.

57. See Mohamed Abdel Salam, "Egyptian Universities between the Brotherhood and the Military," *Sada, Carnegie Endowment for International Peace*, 20 December 2013, accessed October 10, 2014, http://carnegieendowment.org/sada/?fa=53998.
58. See an article reproducing some statements by Hadidi in which she labels students as "thugs", http://elsaba7.com/NewsDtl.aspx?Id=127847.
59. David D. Kirkpatrick, "Crackdown on Student Protesters in Egypt," *The New York Times*, October 13, 2014, accessed September 25, 2015, http://www.nytimes.com/2014/10/14/world/middleeast/egypt-cracks-down-on-new-student-protests-arresting-scores.html.
60. Fatima El Issawi, "In Post-Revolution Egypt, Talk Shows Redefine the Political Landscape".
61. SCAF was a council of higher military officials that ruled Egypt after the departure of Mubarak on 11 February 2011 and stayed in force until 30 June 2012 when Mohamed Morsi started his term as president.
62. Fatima El Issawi, "Egyptian Media Under Transition: In the Name of the Regime…in the Name of the People?", 38.
63. Interview with author, Cairo, June 2012.
64. Ibid.
65. *Mada Masr*, "New Leaks Expose Military Hold over Media," January 20, 2015, accessed September 25, 2015, http://www.madamasr.com/news/new-leaks-expose-military-hold-over-media.
66. *Al Watan News*, "The Head of *An-Nahar*: Saad Back on Wednesday…and We will Exclude no One," October 27, 2014, accessed September 25, 2015, http://www.elwatannews.com/news/details/584879. (Arabic)
67. Heba Afify, "Ibrahim Eissa is "The Boss," But at What Cost?," *Mada Masr*, April 28, 2014, accessed October 2, 2015, http://www.madamasr.com/sections/politics/ibrahim-eissa-%E2%80%9C-boss%E2%80%9D-what-cost.
68. See an article by prominent Egyptian activist and commentator Belal Fadel in which he slams the changing positions of Ibrahim Issa after the military takeover, http://www.shorouknews.com/columns/view.aspx?cdate=30122013&id=cf4e218c-4414-4a9b-ae8c-cbebadaa57b7.

69. See *Mada Masr*, "Azhar and Endowment Ministry Slam Ibrahim Eissa Remarks," July 31, 2014, http://www.madamasr.com/news/azhar-and-endowment-ministry-slam-ibrahim-eissa-remarks.
70. Ibid.
71. See an article published by *Araby 21* news website relating statements by Issa on a conspiracy against Egypt, http://arabi21.com/story/871901/%D8%A5%D8%A8%D8%B1%D8%A7%D9%87%D9%8A%D9%85-%D8%B9%D9%8A%D8%B3%D9%89-%D9%84%D8%A7-%D9%8A%D8%B3%D8%AA%D8%A8%D8%B9%D8%AF-%D8%AA%D9%88%D8%B1%D8%B7-%D9%85%D8%AE%D8%A7%D8%A8%D8%B1%D8%A7%D8%AA-%D8%A7%D9%84%D8%BA%D8%B1%D8%A8-%D8%A8%D8%AA%D9%81%D8%AC%D9%8A%D8%B1-%D8%A7%D9%84%D8%B7%D8%A7%D8%A6%D8%B1%D8%A9-%D9%81%D9%8A%D8%AF%D9%8A%D9%88.
72. Ahmed Aboulenein, "Egyptians See Conspiracy behind British Flight Suspension," *Reuters*, November 12, 2015, accessed November 20, 2015, http://www.reuters.com/article/us-egypt-crash-conspiracy-idUSKCN0T11ZB20151112.
73. Conference on "Egyptian Media & Journalism between Change and Continuity," Free University, Berlin, November 12–14, 2015.
74. Fatima El Issawi, "Egyptian Media Under Transition: in the Name of the Regime…in the Name of the People?", 79.
75. Ibid., 79.
76. Hamza Hendawi, "Egyptian TV Presenter Suspended after Criticizing El-Sissi," *The Huffington Post*, November 13, 2015, accessed November 20, 2015, http://www.huffingtonpost.com/entry/egyptian-tv-presenter-suspended-after-criticizing-elsissi_56463ef4e4b045bf3def0209.
77. Katrin Voltmer, "The Media, Government Accountability, and Citizen Engagement," in Public Sentinel: News Media & Governance Reform, ed. Pippa Norris (Washington, DC: The World Bank, 2010).
78. Fatima El Issawi, "Egyptian Media Under Transition: in the Name of the Regime…in the Name of the People?", 80.
79. *Associated Press*, "Egyptian TV Yanks Ads Warning against Talking to Foreigners," June 10, 2012, accessed September 25, 2015, http://www.foxnews.com/world/2012/06/10/egyptian-tv-yanks-ads-warning-against-talking-to-foreigners.html.
80. Alain Gresh, "I Was Arrested for Chatting in a Cairo Café," *al-Jazeera*, November 15, 2014, accessed September 30, 2015, http://www.aljazeera.com/indepth/opinion/2014/11/i-was-arrested-chatting-cairo-20141114175012955778.html.
81. *The Economist*, "Hounding the Muppet Brotherhood," January 1, 2014, accessed November 30, 2014, http://www.economist.com/blogs/pomegranate/2014/01/silly-season-egypt.

State Media: A Public Service?

The lack of a genuine will to liberate state media in the so called Arab Spring countries from the grip of political power was, and is still, a major handicap. In the immediate aftermath of the uprisings, state media journalists managed to challenge the reverential, uniform style and content they'd had to adopt for decades, but only very briefly. They quickly reverted to old practices in the face of raging political battles and attempts by current regimes to again use state media as a means to justify and legitimize their policies.

The reform of state media in Tunisia is without a doubt more advanced than that achieved so far in Egypt and Libya—the relative success of state broadcasts in gaining popular legitimacy and becoming the main provider of national news is in itself tremendous progress. However, state broadcasts are still largely perceived by audiences as failing to reach professional standards and compete on an equal footing with private television channels. The return to an autocratic regime in Egypt and the hegemony of militias in Libya obstructed state media reform plans. While the structural reform of state media has proved difficult, the process of identity change among state media journalists (who perceive themselves as the regime's guards) is an even greater challenge. The reshaping of this sector, from regime mouthpiece to provider of quality public media, faces a set of complex and long-lasting obstacles: lack of political support and vision, poor professional skills, financial and structural burdens, self-censorship habits, and the journalists' own entrenched conceptions of their profession.

I. From the State to the Public

A. *Theoretical Discussion*

The rationale of a public service provider lays in a set of principles and values that are meant to distinguish it from market-oriented, profit-based media organizations. Public service media is expected to provide society with information and cultural products that serve the public interest (beyond narrow and immediate individual preferences) and have intrinsic merit. This can take the form of educating the public, diffusing the nation's culture, or propagating high-quality cultural content.[1] The provision of impartial and independent information by public service media seeks to support an informed citizenship and promote democratic values through the encouragement of public debate that respects human rights and the fair representation of diverse groups in society. By so doing, public service media promotes social cohesion, a crucial requirement for a healthy and stable democratic system.[2] The production quality of public service media is mostly defined by its independence (from political and commercial pressures) and distinctiveness from commercial broadcasting services.[3]

However, the public service media has faced rapidly changing technological and market dynamics, placing a further strain on its capacity to deliver its objectives. To remain relevant, public service media must evolve and adapt to a new, highly digitalised information environment.[4] In addition to shifts caused by the advent of new media, the switch from analogue to digital TV broadcasting and the erosion of public service media's audience base by private competitors are strategic challenges that they must confront.[5] Furthermore, the unique values of a public media service are being questioned for several reasons: It is arguable that publicly funded or operated media are wasteful at a time when governments are being asked to reduce spending.[6] Digital media's ability to quickly create small, cheap, accessible productions makes it easier for their purveyors to cater directly to specific minority communities, vitiating a significant part of public service media's *raison d'etre*. By receiving public funding and operating unconstrained by traditional market forces, the public service media is arguably an anticompetitive and distorting entity in the wider media market.[7] Another major challenge is the practical implementation and preservation of the main value of public service media—the impartial representation of diverse views and experiences in a society. Public service media needs to keep firm demarcation lines between itself and politics to safeguard its credibility and independence.[8] As Lowe and Martin stress, "it would arguably be the 'kiss of death' for PSM to be tainted as a politically partisan institution".[9]

International experiences of transforming state-funded media into public service media demonstrate that the window of success is narrow. For instance, in both Poland and Hungary, ambiguity in the public service media mandate and frequent political interference have weakened the potential of these institutions. Factors such as societal politicization, weak political and civil cultures, and lack of necessary technical and administrative expertise have constrained success. Despite concerted attempts to establish such media organizations during the 1990s, nearly two decades later they had not yet developed into true public service media providers.[10] Likewise, the creation of public service media organizations in Bulgaria, Croatia, Russia, and Ukraine faced tremendous obstacles because, as Rozanova[11] contends, "the political elites expected journalists to assist the government as the leader of the process rather than exercising an impartial and critical watchdog role". In Eastern European countries, the absence of "cultural prerequisites" meant that public service media had to be established in unfavourable societal environments.[12] In addition, the nascent public service media organizations had to compete with private media players which raised market competition beyond levels these fragile institutions could reasonably withstand. Other factors which hindered the attempt to replicate the Western public service media model included political hostility, political ambivalence, and the lack of a market receptive to the democratic and economic values of such media institutions.[13]

After a brief theoretical discussion and some examples of transitional experiences in building public service media, I will describe the process of transforming the state-owned media in the so called Arab Spring countries into providers of public service media as it has happened so far. Before analysing the dynamics that are shaping such processes, I will first describe the major actors within the state media of Tunisia, Egypt, and Libya.

B. *State Media Landscape: Different Trajectories*

Tunisia
The former state media landscape in Tunisia comprised two main press publication houses: the "New Company for the Print, Press and Publication" (*al-shareka al jadeeda lel tebaa wal sahafa wal nasher*), publisher of the

dailies *La Presse* (in French) and *al-Sahafa* (in Arabic); and *Al-Sabah* publishing house, producer of two daily publications, *al-Sabah* (in Arabic) and *le Temps* (in French), and a weekly in Arabic (*al-Sabah al Usbuee*, al-Sabah weekly). The shares of what was initially a private publishing house were largely (70%) sold to the son-in-law of Ben Ali, Sakhr al Materi, in 2009. After the uprising, the publishing house was confiscated by the Tunisian state and put under the administration of a "judicial administrator".

Tunis Africa news agency (TAP)[14] had a monopoly on official political news under Ben Ali and was the main propaganda tool. After the uprising it is still considered the major provider of news, given its large staff and resources. The news agency had to face competition after it lost its monopoly, but it was not restructured.

The state-owned broadcast sector comprises two main TV channels (*Wataniya 1* and *Wataniya 2*), whose role under the former regime was to report on the activities of the president, his family, and the broader "clan" in the last decade of the regime's rule. Since 2011, channel 1 has been defined as a national generalist channel, while channel 2 has focused on children and regional news.[15] The Tunisian state radio broadcast corporation has nine FM radio stations, four of which are national. Two stations which were owned by Ben Ali's circle were confiscated by the ministry of justice after the uprising: the religious *Radio Zeitouna* (formerly owned by Sakhr al Matari, the son-in-law of Ben Ali) and *Radio Shems FM*, (formerly owned—largely—by Sirine Ben Ali, daughter of the former president).

The struggle between opposing currents, reform versus control of state media, became one of the major battlefields of the political transition. The reform of the state media sector, initiated by a consultative body of journalists and legal experts (*Instance Nationale pour la Reforme de l'Information et de la Comunication, INRIC*[16]), focused on removing the nomination of high ranking managers from the control of executive power and creating a more competitive and professional hiring process; thus they began a power struggle with interim governments who were reluctant to give up what they perceived as their "prerogatives". The independent body, the Authority for Audiovisual Communication (*Haute Autorite Independante de la Communication Audiovisuelle, HAICA*[17]), was tasked with regulating the broadcast industry, including approving license applications, monitoring media output, and nominating heads of state broadcasters. In addition to the delays in the formation of HAICA[18] and the reluctance of successive governments to endorse it, the body faces the challenge of safeguarding its prerogatives and implementing them efficiently (see

Chapter 2). The 2007 law organizing the state broadcast sector put the institution under the total control of executive power but without a clear definition of its mission. There is today an urgent need for new regulations to guarantee state broadcasters' editorial and managerial autonomy.[19]

Egypt
The large state-owned media apparatus in Egypt was established with clear goals to enhance the regime's image, assert its leadership in the Arab world, and spread a nationalistic message. President Gamal Abdel Nasser's decision to nationalize the press (May 24, 1956) introduced the concept of a "national press" (*assahafa al qawmiyya*), transforming the media into a tool of the regime, controlled by various legal and administrative instruments. The state media developed as one of main political instruments of the regime (under the umbrella of the Ministry of Information[20]); its key task was to draw a positive profile of the regime and showcase its "achievements". The state media encompasses six publishing houses[21] producing 55 daily, weekly, and monthly print publications.[22] Its mission is defined by the Press Law as providing "a free national platform for all political voices and trends and key actors". The reality is totally different, as these publications are not allowed to represent dissenting views or narratives counter to the regime's messages. The state print media sector is governed by a heavy bureaucracy. Every publication is managed by a board of directors who appoint an editorial board with five members, chaired by the editor-in-chief. The chairs of the two boards used to be appointed by the Shura Council, the upper chamber of the Egyptian Parliament.[23] The Supreme Press Council (headed by the speaker of the Shura Council) oversees the management of these publications. After the military takeover, the interim President Adly Mansour formed a new Supreme Press Council tasked with assuming the functions of the dismantled Shura Council.[24]

The state broadcast sector is managed by an equally strict and complex hierarchy. The Egyptian Radio and Television Union (ERTU), established in 1970, was conceived as the control and regulatory body of all terrestrial channels. According to the Arabic Network of Human Rights Information (a local NGO), the ERTU operates 30 TV stations and nine radio networks.[25] Six departments manage the ERTU, with the news department operating a central newsroom and acting as sole producer of political programming. The ERTU is governed by the 1979 Law 13, which defines its mandate as fulfilling the "mission statement of the audio-visual media and broadcasting services [...] in compliance with overall public policy and widely acknowledged professional standards and criteria".[26] A strong bureaucracy dominates the ERTU: the general assembly, the board of trustees, and the board of managing directors are all under the umbrella of the Minister of Information, who appoints the senior managers. With the recent abolishment of the Ministry of Information, the head of the ERTU exercises de facto ministerial powers in managing state broadcasts.

All administrations post-uprising successfully resisted restructuring this sector. One of the main challenges of reform is to find a resolution for the redundant staff, many of them appointed through nepotism without professional scrutiny. There are an estimated 70,000 staff in state media outlets, most of them technical and administrative: the ERTU employs around 43,000 staff; *Al-Ahram* publishing house alone employs over 14,000.[27] The government has recently approved a presidential decree that allows the ERTU to dispose of assets in order to settle its debts.[28] The ERTU's debt is worth 22 billion Egyptian pounds (2.8 billion USD) according to the government, and its assets include an estimated 32 pieces of land in Egyptian provinces.[29]

Libya
The Libyan state media was managed by a bureaucracy of institutions directly linked to the regime, making the margin for manoeuvre limited if not nonexistent. These controlling institutions were, however, continually reshaped according to the leadership's changing vision of the media as a platform to serve policy. In the 1970s, the broadcasting sector was developed under the umbrella of the *Libyan Jamahiriya Broadcasting (LJB)*. In 2001, a new body, the *Jamahiriyya General Information Corporation*, was established to cluster all media outlets. Under its remit was the *Jamahiriyya General Broadcasting Corporation* (for audio-visual media) and the *General Press Corporation* (for print publications), as well as related industries (printing, distributing, documentation, music, publishing, etc.).[30] The state media, considered as a tool for *tawjih* (regime orientation), had no respect or credibility among Libyan audiences, who were able to access alternative media content via pan-Arab media in the last decade of the regime. The role of this state media in defending the regime was amplified during the uprising, when state TV channels became a platform for libel and slander against the rebels.

The Libyan state media had approximately 5,000 employees, mostly technicians and administrative staff, less than half of the latter being journalists.

The *Jamahiriyya National News Agency* (*JANA*) holds a monopoly over political news which enabled the regime to continuously control the state media, who were reduced to the function of publishing the content provided by *JANA*. The four main state press publications[31] published the same headlines, editorials, and political news, all provided by the national news agency. The format of the "news" was extremely redundant, mostly lengthy prose in praise of the regime interspersed with insults to its opponents.

The post-uprising era witnessed a conflicting strategy: opting for maintaining existing state broadcasters but closing the former state print outlets, considered to be strongly linked to Gaddafi's ideology. The Committee for Supporting and Encouraging the Press—formed after the regime's fall with the task of reforming the state print media—decided to publish new state-funded newspapers in order to maintain employment of existing staff (around 1200, mostly technical and administrative).[32] Several print publications were launched post-uprising with financial support from the state in Tripoli and in regional areas: the daily *February*, its name alluding to the February 17th revolution, is considered to be the official print publication. However, the new state-sponsored papers were launched without a clear mandate or sufficient resources. Their content is still far from professional, and they are frequently accused of replicating the practices of the old state media, such as flattering political powers and militia leaders.

Immediately after the uprising, state broadcasters became the centre of a power struggle between various groups claiming ownership rights over the state media apparatus in the name of "the revolution's legitimacy". The *al-Libiyya TV* channel (the flagship TV station under Gaddafi) was renamed *Libya station* and given the role of official state TV station. It was recently rebranded again as *Libya al-Rasmiya* (*Libya the Official*) and tasked with reporting on parliamentary activities. The former *al-Jamahiriyya* TV station (the first TV station under Gaddafi) was also the subject of fierce battles over control of its management and logo. The station was rebranded as *al-Wataniya* and is now considered as a main state TV station alongside *al-Rasmiya*. The stations had finally fallen under the control of Islamic militias in Tripoli, leading to a decision by the elected parliament (based in Tobruk, to the East) to take two state TV stations off-air after they followed an anti-government editorial line.[33] However, both *Al-Wataniya* and *Al-Rasmiya* resumed broadcasting.[34]

II. A Shock But Not a "Revolution"

In the immediate aftermath of the uprisings, the reform of the redundant state media was central in the debate on media's role in shaping emerging political systems. However, this debate resulted mainly in chaotic movement in newsrooms, focused on removing the editors who were linked to former regimes and considered guardians of the media's obedience. Another important focus for this movement was improving journalists' working conditions and salaries. The movement led to the removal of a few powerful editors. But most of the former managers remained by simply shifting their loyalties after the regime's fall. A comment by Tunisian journalist, Hanen Zbeis, best represents the lack of a radical change in newsrooms: "We were trying to make new out of old", she said.[35]

In the first phase post-uprisings, journalists themselves began informally implementing change in leadership—a process that turned into a competition for who could win the staff's approval. This led to little more than promises of salary increases. Some journalists vied for newsroom leadership by requesting to be "compensated" for their previous exclusion by former management. In all cases, these internal movements rarely led to the nomination of new managers on the basis of professional competence. For instance, immediately after the uprising, journalists with the Tunisian *Assabah* newspaper attempted to exclude managers who were close to the former regime. This led to severe instability whereby managers were continuously changed while journalists were not sure about the future of the newspaper and their jobs. Rafic Ben Abdullah, the parliamentary reporter for *Assabah*, reflects on the chaos inside newsrooms as a result of the leadership competition: "After the revolution, we organized an action against the editor-in-chief, who was nominated by the former owner. We told him, "degage!" ["leave"]. We chose an editorial body but some journalists were opposed to it, so this body was changed many times".[36]

The idea of electing editorial boards was popular among journalists in several Tunisian state media newsrooms but was later abandoned after the campaigns turned into power struggles with little regard for the competence of the candidates. The quest for new leadership yielded similar results in Egypt. Journalists of the state-owned *al-Ahram* newspaper forced their editor-in-chief, Osama Saraya, to leave his office under police protection; the state-owned newspaper turned suddenly from disgracing to glorifying the demonstrators.[37] However, as Khaled Sarjani,[38] a journalist from the newspaper *al-Ahram*, describes, this shift in leadership did not bring real change in newsrooms: "New editors replicated the old managerial style. They did not take any measures for liberalising the internal structures, such as enforcing editorial independence and setting clear editorial policy and standards".[39] This view is echoed by Issam Zakariya, a journalist from the Egyptian state publication *Roz el-Youssef*, who argued that state media newsrooms witnessed an internal shock that did not amount to a "revolution" in editorial practices, given the focus on the pay raises and the lack of connection between state media journalists and the ideals of the revolution.[40] New management often used salary increases to win the support of their staff and consolidate leadership, but these aggressive increases often aggravated the acute financial crisis within state media.

In the Libyan context, new state print publications couldn't attract former media staff, who were reluctant to join for lack of interest or fear of retaliation. Also, although oppressive, former state media offered a secure work environment for journalists, as opposed to the chaotic transitional media institutions. However, these former state journalists have continued to collect wages from the state—a matter tolerated by the then head of the Committee for Encouraging Journalists, Idris al-Mismari, who argued that, "In Libya, a salary is considered a right to the person and their family especially in this sensitive period. We don't want to create animosities".[41] The head of a new committee appointed by Tripoli's government (and backed by Islamic militias) Mahmood Abu Shaima warned journalists that they must resume work or their salaries would be halted. The old committee headed by el-Mismari resumed its functions from the city of Benghazi; the internationally recognized government has lately appointed the writer Nouriddine al Makni the new head of the committee. Alike al-Mismari, al Makni is a former political detainee under the Gaddafi regime with few links to the journalistic profession.[42] Already suffering from a shortage of mid- to high-level managers, the exodus of former media staff has aggravated the dearth of experienced leadership in new state press and broadcasters. Yet, former state media journalists who remained in the country were marginalised in this new structure despite their professional training: prominent or well-known media figures under the Gaddafi regime are never allowed to appear on screen.

The "war" between old and new—those who used to work inside Libya and those who fled and later returned to the country—prominently fractured the new media community post-Gaddafi. Labelled as a supporter of the former regime (popularly called *Tahaleb*, "algae") former state media journalists were further excluded through the controversial Political

Isolation Law, a bill passed in May 2013 banning anyone who used to be involved in Gaddafi's regime from assuming functions in governmental bodies and institutions. The law was passed under duress when the MPs were besieged by armed groups in Tripoli; it was finally revoked by the internationally recognized parliament in Tobruk in February 2015.[43] The fall of both state media and private outlets into the hands of militias imposed further reshuffling on the journalistic body, with many journalists leaving their jobs and others leaving the country under security threats. Some unconfirmed reports suggest militiamen are directly involved in producing programmes for state TV channels.

III. PUBLIC SERVICE MEDIA IN TRANSITION

In the aftermath of the uprisings, the ideal of transforming the outdated state media sector into a provider of quality public information was mainly understood by journalists as the establishment of a media that "represents the people", but with no clear vision of how this ideal could be translated into daily practices. The need to liberate the media from the grip of political power was largely endorsed by journalists. However, the nets of resistance against political control which had developed within state media newsrooms were not empowered enough to trigger an open debate on the mission of this media, especially regarding how to guarantee content independence and what guidelines should govern relations with the political sphere in editorial decision-making processes.

A New Identity for State Media?

Editorial decision-making was usually limited to following directives from editors loyal to the regime. Post-uprising(s), the deep "loyalty" state media journalists had developed towards political powers still went mostly unquestioned, as many journalists still perceived their role to be protecting the regime rather than scrutinizing it. It was not even possible to imagine state media monitoring the government' policies, as Osama Saraya, former editor-in-chief of the Egyptian *al-Ahram* state newspaper, contends: "The main function of state media was to embellish the face of the regime. It was impossible to imagine a different role for it".[44]

In the Libyan case, reformulating the identity of a state media sector that used to be a major propaganda tool was unachievable with significant growth in interest and investment for private media and the expanded role of these private outlets in political campaigning. The vague positioning of state media outlets and their transformation into a main battleground between armed groups reinforced the futility of hopes the state media's would be part of the new media landscape. Uncertainty about the identity of the state media post-Gaddafi was exacerbated by a lack of vision regarding restructuring this redundant sector and its role in the transition to democracy. The hopes of transforming the old state media into a provider of public service rapidly faded, given the poor conditions of the former state media and the growing hegemony of militias. As Mohamed Baio, former head of the General Press Corporation (the state press body under Gaddafi) contends, "The staff and capacities are so poor. We need years and years of training and support to be able to deliver professional journalism".[45]

The notion of a new state media that would represent "the people" meant that journalists had to regain their audience's trust. In Tunisia, after the uprising, state media journalists had to overcome the stigma that made them accomplices of the regime in the eyes of their audience—whether they were actively engaged in deception or merely passively applied directives. Their rehabilitation necessitated a shift in practices and a process of self-criticism. The change in practices was noticeable through field reporting and an unprecedented diversity in media content. However, self-criticism was not something that journalists (state and private alike) were ready for; most of those interviewed for this research stressed they had no choice but to serve the regime. The state media's sudden U-turn (a few hours after Ben Ali's departure) from praising the regime to glorifying "the people" who overthrew it, confirmed their proclivity for hailing the victorious. Tibr Nouaimi, who used to work for the former ruling party magazine, *Hurriya* (Freedom), reflected on this mindset. She is now a reporter for Youth radio (*Shabab*), part of the state broadcasting apparatus. Tibr says she was and is still proud of her long years of work at the paper of the former ruling party, closed on the day of Ben Ali's departure (January 14, 2011):

> We were honest. We used to report events as they unfolded. But we were only reporting events that supported the policy of the party. This was the policy of the paper. As one of its journalists, I had to respect it. I was doing a professional job. The opposition media was also biased.[46]

The trust-building process was also hindered by divisions among journalists, with debates raging about excluding those who actively contributed to deception under the former regimes. While part of the media community vehemently called for accountability by applying a "naming and shaming" process, others warned that this would open the door to vendettas among journalists. Sofian Ben Hamida, head of news at the Tunisian private *Nessma TV*, is one of those labelled a former supporter of Ben Ali regime. For him, talking about blacklists for journalists is a dangerous approach when so many journalists were to some degree complicit:

> *Even if some journalists were not responsible for the editorial decision-making, they were applying these policies. No one forced them to do this work. Those who said that we did not have the choice but to serve the regime are using the logic of prostitution, not journalism. We were all implicated, even by our silence.*[47]

These divisions were exacerbated by an initiative from former Tunisian President Moncef Marzouki's office to list complicit journalists in a book titled, *The Propaganda Apparatus Under Ben Ali: The Black Book*. The release of the book, which neither followed a legal process nor involved the media community, sparked controversy and raised accusations of political manipulation and selective justice.[48] The initiative did not lead to any further action or debate.

In Egypt, the relaxation of restrictions over state media in the aftermath of the uprising gave state media the ability to publish news bearing content critical of new rulers, provided they did not breach strong taboos such as openly criticizing the military institution. However, this change was not strong enough to overcome the habit of working upon directives. Ahmad Hamdy, a junior reporter with the Egyptian state Nile TV, talks about the heavy bureaucracy of editorial decision-making in the coverage of issues considered sensitive, although field reporting became—for a brief phase post-uprising—more reflective of the realities in the street and less dependent on official press releases. An example is Nile TV's coverage of the violent clashes between demonstrators and security forces in the so-called Mohamad Mahmoud street events (November 2011)[49] in a departure from the TV station's traditions:

> *Our correspondent was not relying on the news provided by the official news agency as we used to do. He was in the street when the police issued a communiqué saying that they did not use gunfire, our correspondent was reporting live showing us the empty cartridges in the streets. We were telling what we were seeing and not what we were told to say.*[50]

However, this change did not evolve to become a sustained trend, as Hamdy explains: "The quality of reporting is very much linked to the personality of the editor of the day. There is no clear editorial policy".[51]

Gamal Fahmy, the former first secretary of the Egyptian journalists' syndicate, describes the ongoing need of state media journalists to censor themselves for fear of retaliation: "The idea of prohibited information no longer exists but journalists are used to it. They continued to define new red lines even if no one asked them to do so. They had to be reassured by the publication of the information by private media to consider the news as non-prohibited."[52]

The rampant confusion in state newsrooms was also observed in Tunisia and Libya. Amira Arfawi, from Tunisian state TV, describes the work environment in the newsroom, with journalists unable to deal with the overwhelming news of the departure of Ben Ali. According to her, the fear of breaching taboos set by the regime was rapidly replaced by a fear of contradicting what journalists perceived as the new power: the "people" who overthrew the regime and thus became the new censor. Amira brilliantly describes the situation within the newsroom at that time:

> *We used to be the trumpet of the regime. We did not have the choice. Now, we find ourselves the trumpet of the people, and we also don't have a choice. Before, we feared the regime. Now, we fear the people. How can we dare say something that is against the people?*[53]

In Libya, *Febrayer*, the new state daily newspaper, struggled to define its identity and its relation to the new political players. According to one of its editors, Ahmed al Ghomari, the newspaper is not clear on its new identity, given that it was established with the main goal of countering Gaddafi's propaganda while the revolution unfolded.[54] When reporter Zeinab al-Habbas took the initiative to do an investigative report on the demolition of religious Sufi shrines by militias (in which she managed to interview a militia leader) her editor simply refused to publish the report.[55] According to her, editors avoided any possible confrontation with politicians or militias' leaders, especially as the latter continued to deal with journalists according to the old practices. Both journalists and their sources were unable to move away from the practices of the former regime even though they were technically no longer dominated by a dictatorial culture.

Tunisian State Media Reform: Tentative Success

In Tunisia, the media reform launched by the INRIC focused on the liberalization of state media. In contrast to partisan private media, the liberalization of state media was meant to provide citizens with unbiased and balanced reporting, as stressed by the head of the consultative body, journalist and activist Kamel Laabid.[56] Multiple governments resisted the liberalization process by refusing to give up the privilege of nominating close editors as the head of state broadcasters. This struggle was relatively won by imposing a competitive and professional nomination process; however, this process is still very fragile and not immune to the governments' interference. The recent dismissal of the chairman of the state broadcasting service Mustapha Ben Letaief by the Prime Minister sparked an uproar from the journalists' syndicate, who argued both nomination and dismissal of senior executives in state broadcasting positions is no longer the government's prerogative.[57] The decision came after criticism of state TV's coverage of an extremist group's decapitation of a 16-year-old shepherd boy; channel 1 *al Wataniya* had shown a picture of the teenager's severed head in a news bulletin.[58] The local reporter and the Editor-in-Chief Hamady Ghidawi (who was also fired) are facing trial and possibly imprisonment for up to five years for "the glorification of a terror crime" pursuant to article 31 of the new anti-terror law.[59] The International Federation of Journalists and the Tunisian Syndicate of Journalists denounced the use of anti-terror stipulations against the two journalists as "a great danger threatening freedom of expression" in the country.[60] "Tunisian journalists are frequently interrogated by the police and security forces on issues related to their professional practices, under the anti-terror stipulations".

In addition to the battle for a professional nomination process for state broadcasting executives, other major challenges are also yet to be met, especially improving the professional skills of journalists (many of them appointed through nepotism) and providing necessary resources and a vision for state media. According to the former chairman of the state broadcasting service Mustapha Ben Letaief, "The main problem with redundant staff is not its large number but the fact that their rehabilitation would be very difficult given their appointment did not follow professional criteria".[61]

Media reform did achieve some major feats: for example, the new plurality in the content of state media and the diversification of sources in the storytelling. The head of the official news agency (TAP), journalist and academic Hamida el Bour, summarises the main changes in news production dynamics: "Field reporting is now the basis of the production; the press release comes in second place. Before, journalists would wait to receive a government press release to be able to treat the information and to follow the story."[62] She stresses the need for more professional training of staff and talks about a new relationship to official sources of information: "They asked us to black out information in some cases and we refused".[63] As an example, she brought up the reporting of the news agency in the south where the Tunisian army is conducting an anti-terror campaign; the local correspondents' reports frequently contradict the army's press releases. Nevertheless, el Bour notes that the challenges remain numerous, especially the diversification of the agency's content and operations to match the new competition from private news agencies, and the need to implement a fairer representation of various currents and groups going beyond the simply coverage of their daily activities.

Tunisian television has gained some legitimacy, with news bulletins by *al-Wataniya* 1 scoring very high with audiences and becoming the main source of information on national affairs for Tunisians. According to a first survey conducted in 2013 by BBC Media Action, 91.9% of respondents said they had watched the state television programmes within the last week, of whom 75.8% said they specifically watched the news bulletins. A second survey commissioned by the same media development agency in 2015 confirmed the leading role of the state broadcasting service, as the majority of respondents rated the Wataniya 1 and Wataniya 2 channels as the most trusted for information on local and national issues.[64] Although the state broadcasting service has opened up televised debates to all voices and currents, it is still not reflective of the diversity of the Tunisian society in its staffing (most presenters being from Tunis' bourgeoisie), and it does not yet report efficiently on rural regions.[65] The accusation that it is driven by anti-Islamic lobbies is rejected by the former news editor-in-chief at al-Wataniya 1 Hamady Ghidawi. He talks about "personal mistakes but not policies" in reporting on the former Ennahda-led government: "When the government took power, we put the information second in the news agenda. We committed a mistake and we recognized it".[66]

State television met the challenge of providing fair representation for contenders in the latest legislative elections: parties and candidates were given equal timing in news bulletins during election campaigns.[67] However, the reform of the Tunisian state broadcasting sector is a long process. The former chairman of the corporation Mustapha Ben Letaief cited one of the major handicaps to its liberalization as the lack of political support: "It is not clear for us if there is a genuine political will to support this process. I don't think the political powers are concerned with the need to develop this media sector".[68]

IV. State Media: The Battlefield of Politics

The move towards a relative diversity of content in state media and a reasonably fair representation of antagonists was a major evolution for this sector. However, the excessive polarization of the political landscape rapidly transformed state media into a major battleground in the struggle between political opponents, leading to the sabotage of important gains. As political polarization took hostage all national media platforms, state and private, the control of state-owned media was particularly important for new and old political actors, given the symbolic importance of this medium as representing the voice of new regimes. The transformation process of this sector was stalled by new regimes' attempts to manipulate state media, as well as journalists' loyalties to political powers and their natural tendency to submit to directives.

Tunisia: The Media of Shame

After the victory of the Islamic *Ennahda* party in elections of the Tunisian Constituent Assembly, and the formation of a tripartite government in 2011, state media was viewed as the spearhead in the battle to preserve a secular state amidst the grassroots Islamization of the country. *Ennahda* supporters relentlessly accused the media of replicating old practices of disseminating negative content in covering the Islamic-led government's policies, and in their portrayal of Islamic groups who rose to prominence post-uprising. The political change ushered in by the victory of an Islamic party was not reflected in the news agenda of the state media, especially the state television, which *Ennahda* accused of being the new mouthpiece of the secular opposition.

The former *Ennahda*-led government's supporters perceived state TV's reports on the challenges of the transition as an attempt to delegitimize the new regime by exaggerating its deficiencies and thus bringing the ruling tripartite coalition to its knees. The battle for control of state media exacerbated the divide between secularists and Islamists in the new Tunisian society. At the other end of the spectrum, the troika government and its supporters were actively engaged in delegitimizing state media because they saw it as a prominent platform for their opponents; they regularly called for its purge and accused it of being "rotten with elements from the former regime".[69] The government resorted to tools used by the former regime, mainly the nomination of heads for state media outlets across all platforms. These nominations sparked the fury of journalists who objected that new managers were appointed without consultation with the journalistic community, and especially that new managers tried to re-impose censorship—for example, by requiring that all content for state radio stations be checked by them 24 hours before its dissemination.[70]

The slogan "The Media of Shame" became a prominent headline of the political struggle between the government and its opponents, aggravating the fragmentation of the media community and its divide into two opposing ideological camps. The slogan was rejected by the Tunisian Syndicate of Journalists and by civil society groups, who claimed it was a tool to silence dissent by intimidation. However, others in the community decried this syndicate as failing to represent all voices and interests within the media. The tension was aggravated by major setbacks and challenges during the transition, chiefly very low economic performance, political assassinations, and the rise of Islamic extremism. The testimony of journalist Amira Arfawi on the working conditions in the state TV newsroom (after the election of the *Ennahda*-led government) is reflective of this power struggle. Interviewed immediately after the uprising, Amira described an environment of confusion where journalists and their editors were unable to make editorial decisions. Interviewed again after the formation of the *Ennahda* led government and the fight over control of state media, Amira had a different account of the situation. She stressed that professional standards had improved but that pressure had become more subtle. According to her, the editors (newly appointed by the government) put pressure on staff to give positive coverage of government policies. But the pressure now appeared in forms such as commissioning new journalists considered more receptive to directives than the old staff to cover government-related activities. However, this is not a new version of the former Ben Ali state media propaganda, according to Amira:

> *We are no longer disseminating blunt propaganda for the service of the new regime, because we now work under the eyes of the public and political parties, and the government now fears the scandals that can result from imposing direct pressures on journalists.*[71]

"Akhnawat al iilam": Egyptian State Media Under the Brotherhood

In Egypt, the fight for control of state media by new regimes took its sharpest form under the Muslim Brotherhood's short-lived rule. As in Tunisia, the new regime struggled to control the news agenda due to a lack of loyalty from journalists, leading them to reshuffle senior positions. The government also exerted control over the content of opinion columns by restricting them to views that were positive or friendly towards the regime. The so-called *akhwanat el iilam* or "Brotherhoodisation" of media became a prominent symbol of the power struggle between a bloated civil servant apparatus (the "deep state", with strong loyalty to the former regime) and the new regime, in the latter's quest to assert popular legitimacy. This struggle occurred in the context of great animosity between the anti-Brotherhood private media and the new Brotherhood government. The animosity was reflected in an unprecedented wave of legal cases against journalists (mostly by civil parties from Islamic currents) based on provisions that criminalised insulting the president or the religion.

The quest to liberate media content from the regime's grip did not translate into a redefining of professional practices for journalists, but rather a chaotic expression of opinions rejecting the regime's control. Examples of this rejection are numerous. The television news anchor and former presidential candidate Buthaina Kamel called a news bulletin *Annashra al Ekhbariyya*, the Brotherhood bulletin, (*Annashra el Ekhwaniyya*), while presenting the news, using her personal agency as anchor to criticize the government live on air. She explained her move was a reaction to the high number of news items that related to government activities.[72] Another anchor, Hala Fahmy, was subjected to punitive measures for presenting an episode of her show on state TV in which she carried a shroud as a symbolic gesture of what she saw as the "death" of the Egyptian state.[73] The excessive personalisation of internal opposition by a few media stars hindered the institutionalization of a debate on editorial standards that might dissect problems and look for a way forward. The government's response was to resort to disciplinary measures. A report by the Arabic Network for Human Rights Information counted 28 forms of retaliation against journalists and staff in state broadcasting[74] during this phase, including referral to Public Prosecution, administrative investigations, arbitrary salary deductions, suspension, prohibition of workplace access, and cessation of a programme or change of its identity.[75] Asked about these punitive measures, the Minister of Information from the deposed Brotherhood government said, "In any media system journalists and staff can be subject to investigation when they commit professional mistakes. A presenter, for example, praised a guest while he was expressing insults. This is not professional. Would this be accepted in Western media?"[76]

Journalists interviewed talked about a trend to lower the tone of criticism in state media by limiting the representation of radical voices critical of the government, although this was strongly denied by management. The former head of the state TV news department Ibrahim Sayyad did not hide his preference for "moderate voices which aim to build the nation and not to destroy it".[77] The practical translation by journalists of these directives was to avoid inviting guests who could be considered "troublemakers" for fear of retaliation, according to state TV journalist Somaya al-Shinnawy.[78]

Libyan State Media: The Voice of the Strong

In Libya, the media's newfound freedom opened the door for a professional journalism that included political reporting, which was unprecedented. The new state media benefitted from governmental financial support without being under the editorial control of media reform bodies or the reinstated Ministry of Information. However, various elements hindered journalists' quest for independence from political and military powers. The inability of the new rulers to understand media's role beyond their dictate, and the internal resistance of journalists to professional discipline and their links to militias hampered the process of consolidating new trends of independent reporting. The power struggle to control TV and radio stations immediately after the uprising reflects the symbolic importance of these media outlets in shaping the new regime. The battle for ownership rights of the state media apparatus is best illustrated by the conflicting decisions made by transitional bodies regarding the fate of these outlets. The struggle to control the flagship *al-Libiyya TV* (currently *al-Rasmiya*), known for its high-tech facilities, is an excellent example. The station went off the air after the fall of the regime, but a team from the privately held

(Benghazi-based) *Libya al-Hurra* TV station, close to Islamic currents, took control of *al-Libiyya*, broadcasting from the station's headquarters using its own logo. This "occupation" of a state TV channel ended with the "occupiers'" withdrawal after staff refused to deal with the newcomers. The former director of *Libya al-Hurra*, Saleh Majdoub, claimed the decision to broadcast from state TV headquarters was a symbolic gesture to mark the end of Gaddafi's era:

> *In that time, there were no institutions. Under the legitimacy of the revolution, all can change. We wanted to seize the occasion. We wanted to be the new official voice of the state.*[79]

After the fall of Gaddafi's regime, the rise of militias pushed journalists to develop dynamics of "coexistence" with the strongmen (who were regularly capturing media buildings and using them as headquarters under the guise of "protecting" them). These dynamics included developing chains of "friendships" with them, avoiding expressions and labels that could anger them (such as calling them "militias"), and accepting their authority. The cases of state TV stations and the official news agency are very relevant here. The old news agency (*JANA*) was rebranded the Libyan News Agency (*LANA*) post-uprising, but the reform of this outdated body into a professional news provider faced many handicaps, especially the link between militiamen and journalists, making the authority of new management obsolete. The reluctance of staff to obey basic management directives plunged the agency into turmoil, to the extent of obstructing news production. Bashir Zoghbiya, nominated as head of the news agency's steering committee,[80] was pushed out by an internal protest accusing him of links to the former regime. He explained the difficulties of the news agency reform:

> *Most journalists have the mentality of employees. They understand freedom as being able to do whatever they want. One of the staff was absent from work and when he returned he brought me a letter from a rebel faction stating he was on a special revolutionary mission!*[81]

The reactions of the new state media editors and journalists to all this pressure ranged from coping with it to simply leaving the office. The head of news at *al-Wataniya* TV station Mohamed Salem described the process of coexisting with the station's guards, who gradually became involved in staff management:

> They are not controlling the TV stations. Sometimes they express some opinions and it could be the right thing to do. I call this a revolutionary caution. We are in transition. Things will return to normal after a while.[82]

The interferences of former rebels who took control of state media facilities through "revolutionary legitimacy" pushed Mariam Hajjaji, newly appointed director of *al-Libiyya Radio*, to resign her job. She explained, "The real bosses became our guards. The interference was to the extent that some of them went into the studio and asked the presenter to leave. In other cases, they shut down the broadcast".[83]

Recently state media has come under the control of factions ruling Tripoli, leading to reshuffling in top positions until the editors declare allegiance to the new rulers. Another journalist, Raafat Belkhair, who worked for the state broadcasting service, resigned due to political pressure. "I was told to amend my coverage in favour of the 'right' political side. Either you are with us or not, so I left," he said.[84]

V. Old Practices Die Hard: The Journalist Guard Dog

In state media newsrooms, self-censorship has slowly replaced formal censorship over media content, evolving from overt to indirect control. For instance, the censorship in Egyptian state newsrooms has moved from the presence of a censor in newsrooms to the appointment of a security official in printing houses (who could halt production of controversial content), to the nomination of editors-in-chief who are close allies of the regime and can exercise "professional control" over what is to be published. The regimes' allies, the "professional controllers", use a "stick and carrot" approach, offering promotions to reverential journalists and punishing the rebellious with punitive measures or exclusion. Journalists understand these limits and generally abide by them without the need for enforcement.

Reverential reporting in defence of regimes did not vanish post-uprisings but was mitigated by a relative plurality in views for a limited period before restrictions were re-imposed, forcefully by managers or willingly by obedient journalists. Recently, the exclusion of dissent on Egyptian state media platforms has not been limited to political opponents but extends to criticism of the military or the regime expressed by third parties. State TV journalist Somaya el-Shinnawy talks about daily directives from management on what is not allowed to be aired in programmes and news bulletins[85]: "We had heated debates after editors decided not to air news of a communiqué by al-Qaeda slamming the Egyptian army. We told them it is not possible to ignore such news". The return to a populist propaganda is embraced by a large majority of staff as an expression of their support of the regime against "terrorists". Consider the testimony of a journalist from state TV who asked to remain anonymous: "After the announcement of the removal of Morsi, we celebrated the news, dancing on desks. We were happy to get rid of the Brotherhood. The pressure became stronger on what is allowed to say but we live with it and understand the need of applying such measures as the state is facing terrorism".[86]

These so-called patriotic trends are also impacting the Tunisian state media; however, they have not adopted a propagandist tone or a uniform content in support of the security forces. The anti-terror operations sparked fears of a return to the authoritarian days of the Ben Ali regime, especially with the arrest of journalists and others and the killing of people described as "terrorism suspects" in military or security operations.[87] Asked about the coverage of these operations, the former head of news for the *Wataniya* 1 TV channel explains:

> *We are not neutral when it comes to terrorism. The protection of the security institution is important but we are not a trumpet of the army. We cover all news related to the operations, including bombing by the army, but we don't give a platform for people voicing their frustration about the impact of these operations, as national security comes first.*[88]

The natural alignment of state TV journalists is mainly driven by their perceived identity as being employees of a state institution and by their lack of experience. According to former journalist and activist, Bechir Oaurda "We are no longer in the era of propaganda; the news bulletins provide information from all sources, but there is a clear prioritization of communiqués from the Ministry of the Interior and governmental positions"[89] in reporting on these military operations.

In Libya, the short-lived reform of state media did not allow real change in practice. As stressed by Idriss el Mismari, former head of the Committee for Supporting and Encouraging the Press, "Our newspapers are still the same. The same news is published by all publications without any change; journalists are used to copy and paste statements from sources," as they did under

Gaddafi's regime.[90] This view is supported by Bechir Zoghbiya, former head of the official news agency, whose reform strategy was resisted by staff:

> In the first anniversary of the revolution, journalists wrote stories using the same glorification style that used to be applied in covering the regime's "revolution" anniversary. They just replace the phrase "September Al Fateh revolution" [Gaddafi's coup] with "the February revolution".[91]

The process of building professional skills cannot realistically take place when raging violence targets media staff and institutions and media professionals disseminate propagandist content in the service of belligerent forces. The year 2014 witnessed the highest number of attacks against journalists and media staff in Libya.[92] The Committee to protect Journalists has rated Libya among the deadliest countries for journalists in 2016, third after Syria and Yemen.

Discussion/Conclusion

The experience of state media reform in the so-called Arab Spring countries mirrors obstacles and challenges endured by media reform bodies in similar transitional contexts. These handicaps include the lack of a clear mandate for public service media, fierce political struggles over control of content, and weak political and civil cultures that could monitor and support reform. Outdated structures are also a common problem, encompassing lack of modern technical resources and administrative expertise as well as journalists' entrenched habits of working under instructions and press releases. Most importantly, the political hostility towards the liberalization of state media and the lack of a receptive attitude from new political powers, societal groups, and audiences weakened the popular legitimacy of such processes.

This reform was perceived by journalists as a thorny, if not unrealistic, project. The notion of social utility was recognized by state media journalists post-uprising as the main quality of a public service media. Independence from political control was considered by journalists crucial to enable the sector to regain credibility and to represent diverse societal groups. Although the "public value" of state media was recognized by journalists, it was hard to say how this could be measured or defined—especially with extreme political polarization deepening existing divides among groups and using state media as its favoured battlefield.

The role of state media in enhancing civic participation in public affairs was largely acknowledged and (relatively) implemented by journalists as the need to represent various political currents, groups, and sides of the story. This relative diversification of views and sources represents in itself tremendous progress after decades of uniform official content. The ability of state media to provide a platform for political opponents was crucial in the process of legitimizing political adversaries as partners in democratization processes as well as legitimizing disagreement as an important element of these processes. It was also crucial for this media sector to build trust with audiences and gain credibility after decades of manipulation.

However, the values of public service media did not enjoy a solid structure or genuine support from political actors or journalists themselves. Given the increasingly polarized political scene post-uprising(s), plurality of content regressed as ideological and political opponents were again portrayed as the ultimate enemy. In the case of Egypt, the return to a reverential role for state media is even more evident, with private media joining the race to obey the new political and military masters. While state media journalists acknowledged the importance of independence from political power, they rapidly conceded this battle in the name of the "patriotic" duty. It is questionable whether journalists' short-lived resistance to the dictates of new regimes is an expression of "collaboration" with the old political and military elites and a rejection of the new political actors, rather than a genuine attempt to liberate practices from the grip of power. This is partly explained by the natural rejection among state media journalists of political opponents who became rulers, after years of being denied any legitimacy by both regimes and the state media that served them.

The upheavals of the political transitions were a major factor in hampering any meaningful change within state media newsrooms. The descent of the Egyptian transition into autocracy with a fierce crackdown on civil rights and liberties (including critical reporting) makes any attempt to liberalize state media unrealistic under current conditions. The relative success of Tunisian state media reform could be explained by the progress in the political and media reform process in general and the creation of entities with the mandate to protect this process. But it is also solidly linked to the eagerness of the media community to safeguard these gains and the dynamism of a civil society continuously lobbying in their defence. However, the lack of a comprehensive restructuring of this sector makes these gains the fragile prey of political swings, especially within the heightened environment of anti-terrorism policies and the alarming indications of the new government using these policies to quell critical reporting.

Furthermore, the lack of resources to modernize outdated apparatuses makes state media a weak player, unable compete with wealthy private media.

Notes

1. Karol Jakubowicz, "PSB 3.0: Reinventing European PSB," in Reinventing Public Service Communication: European Broadcasters and Beyond, ed. Petros Iosifidis (Basingstoke: Palgrave Macmillan, 2010); Chris Hanretty, Public Broadcasting and Political Interference (Abingdon, Oxon: Routledge, 2011).
2. Heap Hargreaves and others, "Television in a Digital Age: What Role for Public Service Broadcasting?," Economic Policy 20, no. 41 (2005): 116.
3. Monroe E. Price and Marc Raboy (ed.), Public Service Broadcasting in Transition: A Documentary Reader (Oxford: Programme in Comparative Media Law and Policy for the European Institute for the Media, 2001).
4. Karol Jakubowicz, "PSB 3.0: Reinventing European PSB"; Fiona Martin and Gregory Ferrell Lowe, "The Value and Values of Public Service Media," in The Value of Public Service Media, ed. Gregory Ferrell Lowe and Fiona Martin (Göteborg: Nordicom, 2014).
5. Jean K. Chalaby, "Public Broadcasters and Transnational Television: Coming to Terms with the New Media Order," in Reinventing Public Service Communication: European Broadcasters and Beyond, ed. Petros Iosifidis (Basingstoke: Palgrave Macmillan, 2010).
6. Martin and Lowe, "The Value and Values of Public Service Media".
7. Katharine Sarikakis, "For Culture and Democracy: Political Claims for Cosmopolitan Public Service Media," in Reinventing Public Service Communication: European Broadcasters and Beyond, ed. Petros Iosifidis (Basingstoke: Palgrave Macmillan, 2010).
8. Ibid.
9. Martin and Lowe, "The Value and Values of Public Service Media", 27.
10. Pawel Stępka, "Public Service Broadcasting in Poland: Between Politics and Market," in Reinventing Public Service Communication: European Broadcasters and Beyond, ed. Petros Iosifidis (Basingstoke: Palgrave Macmillan, 2010); Mark Lengyel, "From 'State Broadcasting' to 'Public Service Media' in Hungary," in Reinventing Public Service Communication: European Broadcasters and Beyond, ed. Petros Iosifidis (Basingstoke: Palgrave Macmillan, 2010); Julia Rozanova, "Public Television in the Context of Established and Emerging Democracies: Quo Vadis?," International Communication Gazette 69, no. 2 (2007).
11. Julia Rozanova, "Public Television in the Context of Established and Emerging Democracies", 134.

12. Karol Jakubowicz, "Ideas in Our Heads: Introduction of PSB as Part of Media System Change in Central and Eastern Europe," European Journal of Communication 19, no. 1 (2004).
13. Ibid.
14. See the website of TAP news agency http://www.tap.info.tn/en/index.php.
15. UNESCO, "Un état des lieux de la télévision publique Tunisienne," February 14, 2013.
16. See the website of the *Instance Nationale pour la Reforme de l'Information et de la Comunication, INRIC* http://www.inric.tn/fr/.
17. See the website of the regulator http://haica.tn/.
18. It was finally formed in May 2013 after several calls from NGOS and media watchdogs. See a communique by Reporters Without Borders on the government's move to finally form the regulatory body https://rsf.org/en/news/government-finally-appoints-independent-broadcasting-authority.
19. UNESCO, "Un etat des lieux de la television publique Tunisienne".
20. Fatima El Issawi, "Egyptian Media Under Transition: In the Name of the Regime…in the Name of the People?," *POLIS*, London School of Economics and Political Science, 2014.
21. These are *al-Ahram, al-Hilal, Roz el-Youssef, al-Akhbar, al-Tahrir, al-Qawmiyya lil tawziee*, (The National [company] for Distribution).
22. Fatima El Issawi, "Egyptian Media Under Transition: In the Name of the Regime…in the Name of the People?",15.
23. The Shura Council was dissolved after the military coup. The then interim President Adly Mansour, ordered the dissolution of the Shura Council in a constitutional declaration in July 2013.
24. *Ahram Online*, "Egypt's Interim President Forms Supreme Press Council," August 28, 2013, accessed September 2, 2015, http://english.ahram.org.eg/NewsContent/1/0/80205/Egypt/0/Egypts-interim-president-forms-Supreme-Press-Counc.aspx.
25. *The Arabic Network of Human Rights Information*, "Maspero in the Reign of the First Elected President," April 8, 2013.
26. ERTU Law, Law No 13 of Year 1979 on the Egyptian Radio and Television Union, 1979.
27. *The Arabic Network for Human Rights Information*, "The Liberalization of State Media," October 9, 2012 (Arabic).
28. Mostapha Hassan, "Maspero Assets Up for Sale," *Sada Elbalad*, May 14, 2015, accessed September 2, 2015, http://www.el-balad.com/1532979.
29. Safiaa Mounir, "Egypt's State-owned Media Ripe for Restructuring," *AlMonitor*, August 11, 2015, accessed September 2, 2015, http://www.al-monitor.com/pulse/originals/2015/08/egypt-government-channel-financial-crisis-restructuring-plan.html.

30. Fatima El Issawi, "Libya Media Transition: Heading to the Unknown," *POLIS*, London School of Economics and Political Science, 2013.
31. These publications were: *al Jamahiriyya, El shams, el Zahf al Akhdar and el Fajr el Jadid*.
32. Fatima El Issawi, "Libya Media Transition: Heading to the Unknown".
33. *Committee to Protect Journalists*, "Two Journalists Abducted and Two TV Channels Forced Off the Air in Libya," August 21, 2014, accessed September 2, 2015, https://cpj.org/2014/08/two-journalists-abducted-and-two-tv-channels-force.php.
34. *Reporters Without Borders*, "News Media Targeted Amid Libyan Chaos," August 28, 2014, accessed September 3, 2015, http://en.rsf.org/libya-news-media-targeted-amid-libyan-28-08-2014,46858.html.
35. Interview with author, Tunis, December 2011.
36. Ibid.
37. See this article by *Al Arabiya* news website describing changes in the state press immediately after the fall of the Mubarak regime http://www.alarabiya.net/articles/2011/02/09/136952.html.
38. The journalist died of a heart attack in September 2014.
39. Fatima El Issawi, "Egyptian Media Under Transition: In the Name of the Regime...in the Name of the People?", 35.
40. Ibid.
41. Fatima El Issawi, "Libya Media Transition: Heading to the Unknown", 25.
42. See an article on the nomination of the new head of the journalistic body published by Afrigatenews.net http://www.afrigatenews.net/content/%D8%AA%D8%B9%D9%8A%D9%8A%D9%86-%D8%B1%D8%A6%D9%8A%D8%B3-%D8%AC%D8%AF%D9%8A%D8%AF-%D9%84%D9%87%D9%8A%D8%A6%D8%A9-%D8%AF%D8%B9%D9%85-%D9%88%D8%AA%D8%B4%D8%AC%D9%8A%D8%B9-%D8%A7%D9%84%D8%B5%D8%AD%D8%A7%D9%81%D8%A9-%D8%A7%D9%84%D9%84%D9%8A%D8%A8%D9%8A%D8%A9.
43. *BBC*, "Libya Revokes Bill Which Banned Gaddafi-era Officials from Office," February 2, 2015, accessed September 3, 2015, http://www.bbc.co.uk/news/world-latin-america-31104099.
44. Fatima El Issawi, "Egyptian Media Under Transition: In the Name of the Regime...in the Name of the People?", 30.
45. Fatima El Issawi, "Libya Media Transition: Heading to the Unknown", 24.
46. Interview with author, Tunis, December 2011.
47. Ibid.

48. *Al Arabiya*, "Blacklist' of Former Pro-Tunisian Regime Journalists Sparks Controversy," December 2, 2013, accessed September 3, 2015, http://english.alarabiya.net/en/News/middle-east/2013/12/02/-Blacklist-of-former-pro-Tunisian-regime-journalists-sparks-controversy-.html.
49. Security forces attacked a sit-in organised to demand that Egypt's then-ruling Supreme Council of Armed Forces (SCAF) relinquish power to a civilian authority. The clashes left 47 killed and hundreds injured. See http://english.ahram.org.eg/NewsContent/1/64/58444/Egypt/Politics-/Mohamed-Mahmoud-clashes,--year-on-A-battle-for-dig.aspx.
50. Fatima El Issawi, "Egyptian Media Under Transition: In the Name of the Regime...in the Name of the People?", 36.
51. Ibid.
52. Fatima El Issawi, "Egyptian Media Under Transition: In the Name of the Regime...in the Name of the People?", 36.
53. Interview with author, Tunis, December 2011.
54. Fatima El Issawi, "Libya Media Transition: Heading to the Unknown", 26.
55. Ibid.
56. Interview with author, Tunis, December 2011.
57. Mohamed Moameri, "65 journalists fired from Tunisian media organizations" *al Araby al Jadeed*, September 11, 2016, accessed September 14, 2016, (Arabic) https://www.alaraby.co.uk/medianews/2016/9/11/65-%D8%AD%D8%A7%D9%84%D8%A9-%D8%B7%D8%B1%D8%AF-%D9%84%D8%B5%D8%AD%D8%A7%D9%81%D9%8A%D9%8A%D9%86-%D9%85%D9%86-%D9%88%D8%B3%D8%A7%D8%A6%D9%84-%D8%A5%D8%B9%D9%84%D8%A7%D9%85-%D8%AA%D9%88%D9%86%D8%B3%D9%8A%D8%A9.
58. *AFP*, "Head of Tunisia TV Suspended for Decapitated Head Picture," November 16, 2015, accessed November 25, 2015, http://english.alarabiya.net/en/media/television-and-radio/2015/11/16/Tunisia-sacks-state-TV-chief-after-grisly-broadcast-.html.
59. Mohamed Moameri, "Tunisian Journalists Threatened by Trial Pursuant to Anti-terror Law," *Al Araby Al Jadeed*, November 19, 2015, accessed November 25, 2015, http://www.alaraby.co.uk/medianews/2015/11/19/%D8%A5%D8%B9%D9%84%D8%A7%D9%85%D9%8A%D9%88%D9%86-%D8%AA%D9%88%D9%86%D8%B3%D9%8A%D9%88%D9%86-%D9%85%D9%87%D8%AF%D8%AF%D9%88%D9%86-%D8%A8%D8%A7%D9%84%D9%85%D8%AD%D8%A7%D9%83%D9%85%D8%A9-%D8%A8%D9%82%D8%A7%D9%86%D9%88%D9%86-%D8%A7%D9%84%D8%A5%D8%B1%D9%87%D8%A7%D8%A8.
60. See the communique by the media rights watchdogs http://www.ifj-arabic.org/page-ifj-546.html#.Vk8KgGqyAEY.twitter.

61. Interview with author, Tunis, June 2015.
62. Ibid.
63. Ibid.
64. Alexandra Buccianti and Sara el-Richani, "After the Arab Uprisings: The Prospects for a Media that Serves the Public," *BBC Media Action*, September 26, 2015.
65. UNESCO, "Un etat des lieux de la television publique Tunisienne".
66. Interview with author, Tunis, June 2015.
67. An agreement was signed between HAICA and a body formed to oversee the elections, *Instance Superieure Independante pour les Elections*, in order to insure fair representation in private and state broadcasters during the elections. The media performance was monitored by several civil society groups as well as the journalists' syndicate and the HAICA.
68. Interview with author, Tunis, June 2015.
69. See a statement by a leader of *Ennahda in* response to criticism of the government's decision to nominate heads of state broadcasters: http://eqrar.blogspot.co.uk/2012/09/blog-post_3.html.
70. See this article published by *al Modon* online magazine on the return of old tools to muzzle media http://www.almodon.com/media/86a9f8ad-278d-4edd-b243-1ef2c0a6edcc.
71. Interview with author conducted by phone from London, November 2013.
72. See the video YouTube of the related news bulletin https://www.youtube.com/watch?v=g-Ba5OSXh30.
73. Fatima El Issawi, "Egyptian Media Under Transition: In the Name of the Regime…in the Name of the People?", 46.
74. The state broadcaster building is popularly called Maspero in allusion to the name of the street where the building stands in centre Cairo.
75. *The Arabic Network for Human Rights Information*, "Maspero in the Reign of the First Elected President".
76. Fatima El Issawi, "Egyptian Media Under Transition: In the Name of the Regime…in the Name of the People?", 46.
77. Ibid., 45.
78. Ibid.
79. Fatima El Issawi, "Libya Media Transition: Heading to the Unknown", 50.
80. In the aftermath of the uprising, the news agency was put under the direction of a steering committee of five members who used to be senior journalists and/or managers in the agency but without formal ties to the former regime.
81. Fatima El Issawi, "Libya Media Transition: Heading to the Unknown", 52.

82. Ibid., 51.
83. Ibid.
84. Alexandra Buccianti and Sara el-Richani, "After the Arab Uprisings the Prospects for a Media that Serves the Public", 17.
85. Interview with author conducted by phone from London, November 2015.
86. Interview with author conducted by phone, November 2013.
87. Conor Sheils, "Tunisia: A Return to a Police State?," *Al Araby Al Jadeed*, April 2, 2015, accessed October 10, 2014, http://www.alaraby.co.uk/english/comment/2015/4/2/tunisia-a-return-to-a-police-state.
88. Interview with author, June 2015.
89. Interview with author conducted by phone from London, September 2015.
90. Fatima El Issawi, "Libya Media Transition: Heading to the Unknown", 26.
91. Ibid., 39.
92. See Freedom House report on press freedom in Libya for 2014, https://freedomhouse.org/report/freedom-press/2014/libya.

Journalists Versus Activists? Traditional Journalists and Cyber-Activism

In August of 2013, I met Zeinab Zaiddi, a Libyan talk show presenter, in a coffee shop in Tripoli. With the rebellion that would lead to the overthrow of Gaddafi regime raging, Zeinab, who used to moderate televised debates on family topics, found herself playing the role of a political activist, using her platform on an opposition TV station to incite her audience to break through the wall of fear the regime had built. When I asked her how she was reconciling the contradictory roles of neutral moderator and engaged activist, she strongly defended her dual role, arguing that her opinions are always based on facts when they are expressed in her programme. But after few seconds, she added, "I feel confused. Am I right or wrong?"

The model of the journalist as a champion of change is not unusual or new; indeed, the ideal of unveiling the truth is one of the most attractive features of the profession for aspiring journalists. Historically, few prominent Arab journalists contributed to opening up the media and political landscape by advocating against the autocratic practices of existing regimes. A few are currently critiquing and advocating against autocratic practices, and enduring harsh retribution for doing so. But in the overall context of the Arab uprisings, traditional journalists played a minimal role in supporting democratic change, or even reporting on it, because the large majority of the journalistic community, especially those holding top-ranking positions, were politically aligned with the current regimes. Zeinab, in refusing the role of the regime guard while an uprising was unfolding, was an exception to the general trend, among few others of her peers.

Celebrated as an engine of political change in the context of Arab uprisings, bloggers and social media activists presented a role model for traditional journalists, while also inciting their jealousy and rejection. As will be demonstrated in this chapter, the interplay in roles and identities between the two groups is complex and multifaceted. In the shaky political landscape post-uprisings, official forms of communication—such as the governmental communiqués that were regularly accepted as factual without appropriate investigative follow-up—broke down. This led to the flourishing of social media tools as the main provider of information for traditional newsrooms, creating an unprecedented shock in news production mechanisms.

I. Social Media: A Voice for the Voiceless

In the context of Arab uprisings, cyber-activism is largely recognized as a catalyst of change,[1] having served as the mechanism for mobilizing support, coordinating mass protests, and providing up-to-date information. Social media platforms provided these movements with fluid networks, allowing them to cross national boundaries and spread throughout the region.[2] In bypassing the official storytelling fiercely propagated by state-controlled traditional media, new media platforms "undermined the theatre of the state … with the theatre of the 'street'".[3] However, these platforms were active in challenging the regimes' narratives long before the outbreak of mass protests.[4] These flexible platforms allowed users to channel and communicate forms of collective action beyond traditional forms of political activism. The politicization of Facebook transformed it into a prominent tool to advocate for radical political change. For instance, the "We are all Khaled Said" Facebook page became an important source of information, mobilization, and advice for Egyptian protesters.[5] Blogger Wael Ghonim, who launched the page to denounce police brutality, rose to global prominence through his ability to use his large cyber networks to promote the protest, leading to his secret detention for 11 days in police custody.[6] Facebook activism was a chief player in empowering political change in Tunisia. According to Khaled Koubaa, president of the Internet Society in Tunisia, only a few thousand people communicated via Twitter, while around two million used Facebook as a platform to exchange ideas and information. The activism of the first group informed that of the latter, according to the activist.[7] Furthermore, the dynamic social networks enabled by the new media tools focused on specific demands, instead of simply revolving around a charismatic central figure. This allowed these movements a flexibility that helped them resist regimes' attempts to break them.[8]

However, scholars celebrating these movements as evidence of new media's ability to trigger change—to the extent of labelling these movements as Facebook and Twitter Revolutions[9]—ignore the other factors that empowered the outbreak of these protests. The success of social media as a vehicle for empowerment is intractably linked to the willingness of activists to physically bring their demands to the public, through marches and other concrete forms of protest, rather than limiting themselves to the virtual exchange of ideas, as scholars Mohamed Nawawy and Sahar Khamis contend.[10]

We must also acknowledge the historical trajectories of these movements and their roots in the dynamics of civil society, as these predate the existence of modern social media. In Tunisia and Egypt, protest movements had been actively engaged in challenging regimes' policies way before the advent of cyber-activism. Mass protests did not erupt from nowhere, but rather were informed by preceding grievances and ambitions for change.[11] For instance, the street demonstrations that led to the departure of Ben Ali echoed social movements of large magnitude, notably the revolts in the Gafsa mining basin in 2008 in which the mobilization of the workers and their families for several long months was violently repressed by the regime.[12] We must also acknowledge the important role played by international television networks such as al-Jazeera and CNN, which were equally instrumental in widely disseminating content provided by social media activists. These networks granted activists regional and international visibility and, as scholar Simon Cottle has said, "a human face," so they appeared "less distanced, less humanly remote".[13] While admitting the central role of social media, Cottle is right to insist on a "more holistic appreciation of the interpenetrating ways in which media systems and communication networks have complexly conditioned and facilitated" the revolutionary movements and moments of Arab democratization.[14]

Before the advent of the internet in the Arab world, the Arab media landscape was already witnessing a growing dynamism caused by the proliferation of satellite television channels and the growing investment in private media. The increased private ownership of media has played a role in, as scholar Naila Hamdy says, "bringing pluralistic and diverse perspectives to the public",[15] leading to dramatic shifts that have also afforded media a "key role in the debate about Arab democratization".[16] The rise of pan-Arab satellite media was a major step forward. The so-called Al-Jazeera effect, translated as the network's impact on shifting regional public attitudes towards supporting a democratic agenda, has been widely emphasised by many scholars.[17] Some scholars have denied the ability of these media platforms to push for meaningful reforms, arguing that the window of expression they provide acts as a nothing more than a safety valve to vent the population's frustration. As stressed by scholar Muhammad Ayish, the changes in the Arab media scene are not "conducive to political pluralism and diversity in Arab societies dominated by authoritarian political systems. No matter how professional and independent television is, it cannot replace true political transformations that would ensure participatory governance".[18]

The advent of the internet was a major turning point in widening the diversity of views and information expressed in the public sphere. Internet and mobile phone usage has undergone formidable growth since the 1990s, reaching their strongest expansion in developing countries.[19] Between 2009 and 2010, Twitter usage in the Arab region was estimated to include around 5.5 million users, an impressive 136.5% annual growth rate.[20] Empirical research confirms a steady growth of social media users in the Arab world, especially among the youth. For instance, in 2013, a total of 64% of all Arab youth admitted to having a Facebook account, and nearly half said they respond to tweets from others.[21] According to the 6th Arab Social Media Report conducted in 2014, more than 22% of Arabs were actively using social media platforms, with around 82 million Facebook users and 5.8 million active Twitter users, thus confirming the primacy of Facebook as the main social media platform.[22] Mobile penetration has increased rapidly in the past 12 years, from just 3% in 2000 to 105% in 2012, representing an average annual growth rate of over 32%, according to figures by Arab States Mobile Observatory for 2013.[23]

The recent relapse into autocracy within the context of raging counter-revolutions in the Arab world, as well as the strong comeback of self-censorship habits in newsrooms, is contributing to re-imposing social media platforms as the main—if not the sole—provider of an alternative discourse to the official storytelling again being fiercely propagated by traditional media.

II. Journalists Versus Activists: Who Leads?

In the immediate aftermath of the uprisings, bloggers and social media activists became important references for traditional media in a complex relationship of attraction and rejection. Largely considered by traditional journalists as "amateurs", citizen journalists still managed to impact newsroom dynamics by first integrating themselves in these newsrooms, and later embedding their advocate style in various features of media production. In interviews conducted immediately after the uprising that led to the fall of the Ben Ali regime, Tunisian journalists expressed scepticism about the conception of bloggers as professional competitors in telling the story of the uprising and its aftermath. The journalists suggested that the comparison was inequitable, as the bloggers' pre-uprising anonymity had made them freer than traditional journalists, who, working for larger media organizations, were restricted in their ability to challenge taboos. Khaled Haddad from the *Ashourouq* daily newspaper admits that "social media played our role" in reporting the uprising. "We were not able to take risky initiatives. We work for established organizations. People know us. The regime knows us," he said.[24] In the same vein, Rafic Ben Abdullah, a parliamentary reporter for the *Assabah* daily newspaper, stresses, "Bloggers can hide behind fake identities, we journalists are public figures. It is very difficult for the regime to know who published a blog, while the journalist is well known and his production bears his signature".[25]

This popular perception among traditional journalists denies the leading role bloggers played in the struggle for civil liberties under the Ben Ali regime and minimizes the tough retaliations some of them had to endure. These bloggers were crucial in unveiling violations committed by the former regime before the 2011 uprising, supporting campaigns like the one launched in 2010 to counter internet surveillance by urging people to post grievances against it.[26] This activism continued post-uprising, as most of these bloggers remain strong voices in challenging new regimes and advocating for political action. In 2011, bloggers organized a campaign urging voters to participate to the first free elections in the country.[27] More recently, bloggers denounced alleged corruption in the management of the country's resources in a controversial campaign that used the question, "Where is our oil?" as its slogan.[28] Activists were accused of undermining the newly formed, largely secular government and acting as pawns manipulated by politically minded religious groups.

Furthermore, many Tunisian bloggers became personally engaged in politics post-uprising. Riad Guerfali, Tarek Kahlaoui, Slim Amamou, Amira Yahyaoui, and Mehdi Lamloum all ran on independent lists for the constitutional assembly in the 2011 elections.[29] Some took office in interim governments: Selim Amamou was appointed Minister of Youth and Sport in the first Tunisian interim government, and later resigned in protest of the government's move to shut down some online websites.[30] Many continue to challenge the recent upsurge of autocratic practices and face retaliation. In one example among many, blogger Yassin Ayari was tried before a military court and jailed for three months, pursuant to the Tunisian military justice code, for "defaming the military" in a series of Facebook posts in which Ayari criticized leadership appointments within the military.[31]

The new-born liberty should put traditional journalists on equal footing with these bloggers. However, many bloggers and cyber-activists continue to dispute the leadership of traditional journalists in the role of watchdogs of the new regimes. According to Hani Shukrallah, former Editor-in-Chief of Egyptian state news website *Ahram Online*, published in English, social media is still leading in breaking news when it comes to uncovering serious violations by regimes. He explains—

> *The story is not here in print, it is not on television screens either, it is in social media. They still lead in disclosing controversial information such as reporting on the military when firing bullets on demonstrators.* [*It's*] *only after they break out the news that the printed press and TV channels take it.*[32]

The lack of professional training for journalists, and the reluctance of media management to invest in building a tradition of investigative reporting, has led to citizen journalist's and cyber-activist's continuing to inform the public on controversial topics, thus preserving the leading role they played before the uprisings in questioning regimes' practices. However, there are rare instances when traditional media has managed to dispute this leadership. A photo taken by the private Egyptian newspaper *al-Masry al-Yom* of a woman being stripped of her clothing by security officers during a demonstration in Cairo was widely shared in social media feeds and national and international media (December 2012).[33] Footage of a civilian dragged naked through the streets of Cairo by police was captured by cameras of the *al-Hayat* private Egyptian TV network[34] (February 2013).

III. The Battle for Professional Legitimacy

A phenomenon of interdependency and reciprocal influence could be observed between bloggers and traditional journalists post-uprisings. While bloggers were attempting to win professional legitimacy by creating or adopting institutional news production structures, traditional journalists were tempted to adopt the advocate style of activists in rallying political agendas and ideological camps, using social media tools extensively to disseminate their productions but also to follow up on news. This reciprocation can be seen in the transformation of *Nawaat*[35]—a Tunisian collective blog which had played an eminent role in challenging the Ben Ali regime since 2004— into a provider of news services with an institutional structure post-uprising. Riad Fargali, one of the founders of the blog, explains that their aim in launching a news service was "to support civil liberties such as investigating corruption as well as giving jobs to young journalists who may have no place in traditional news institutions".[36]

The complex interplay between bloggers and traditional journalists took its most dynamic yet controversial form in the Libyan media. Traditional Libyan journalists interviewed about the current situation frequently described their newly re-launched newsrooms as "invaded by newcomers". Labelled as pro-regime or "Tahaleb" ("algae") due to the stigma surrounding their previous work within Gaddafi media, staff of the former media are largely excluded from the new media landscape unless they occupied a very low rank in these older media outlets. The newcomers, citizen journalists who captured the revolution's momentum, have the upper hand in new traditional newsrooms—but several editors and managers have argued this came at the expense of professionalism. Mariyam al-Hajjaji, another of the few former staff who integrated into the post-Gaddafi media, stated—

> *The revolution brought us a new wave of journalists who have no link to the profession. We found ourselves invaded by thousands who pretend having worked in media during the revolution—although we never heard of them. The real journalists are at home. The newcomers took over, benefitting from their connections to the revolutionaries…*[37]

Yet many also praised these citizen journalists for bringing new blood and energy to the industry, as most Gaddafi media journalists considered themselves simple employees and lacked enthusiasm for their work. As stressed by Hussam Zaagar, head of the Free Media Centre, one of main providers of professional training in Libya, citizen journalists, commonly called the "frontline media community", "are quite ready to transform into successful professionals. They have unusual energy and capacities. They are not professional but they have trained on the ground with extremely limited resources. They are very enthusiastic in comparison to most of those who worked in the regime's medi".[38] Take the example of the *Febrayer* newspaper, the new state-funded Libyan newspaper launched after the uprising. New staff were appointed not for their professional experience, but rather their lack of connection to the former regime; the paper's editors acknowledged the arduous challenge of reaching professional standards, but consider the situation necessary as part of escaping the former regime's legacy. The inclusion of former media staff is also met with questions over their ability to provide a different model than what they applied for decades under the former regime. Mahmoud el Misrati, the owner and Editor-in-Chief of *Libya al-Jadida* newspaper, reflects on the problems of hiring former staff:

> *We tried to engage journalists from the former media. They could not work at our rhythm; they are still working under the mentality of the state media where they consider themselves to be employees. I told them they have to work, to deliver, or they will be fired.*[39]

The private print media sector flourished post-uprising and quickly posed a serious threat to state-sponsored print publications. An acute competition over attracting professional journalists led to the fragmentation of the media landscape, given the limited number of these journalists and the exclusion of a large number of them for their perceived link to the former regime. A Benghazi journalist who used to work for state media under Gaddafi chose to launch her own weekly magazine, which was poorly sponsored by governmental advertisements. Asked why she opted for such a venture after having enjoyed the job security of a state-funded media outlet, she said, "I am tired of working under directions. We want finally to be free, to express our opinions".[40] The journalist, one of the few from the old guard who found a place for herself in the post-Gaddafi media, had to face the competition of citizen journalists heavily engaged in launching personal media projects. She recounts, "After the revolution, everyone wanted to become a journalist, from medical doctors to street workers. I told colleagues we should accept this situation. Most of these new projects will ultimately vanish. Things will go back to normal after a while".[41] Yet this division between the "frontline media" and the former media staff remains a prominent feature of the new media landscape.

It cannot be said, however, that the old guard is excluded simply due to perceived bias in favour of the regime; many leading figures who could pursue careers in this new environment opt out, as a result of legal prosecution (mainly conducted in obscure conditions), intimidation, or simply reluctance to resume work in an unwelcoming environment and amid shaky security conditions. The statement of Abdel Hakim Maatook, the former editor-in-chief of *Al-Shams* newspaper, one of the four dailies published under the former regime, is reflective of the struggle of leading journalists from the old guard to find a place in the new media landscape:

> *After the fall of the regime, I gathered my former team to discuss publishing a new newspaper with a new discourse. In the middle of the meeting, three armed persons stormed the room and took me away. They interrogated me and insulted me. I finally managed to talk to their leader, who appeared to be wiser. They let me go after they took my passport. After a week, I managed to contact their leader, who finally agreed to give me back my passport.*[42]

IV. THE JOURNALIST ADVOCATE WITH A CAUSE

Although denying any professional legitimacy for bloggers, traditional journalists swiftly adopted the fervent tone applied by these bloggers in lobbying for their preferred causes. The shift in journalists' perception of their roles, from informing audiences to preaching to them, paved the way for a flourishing of the journalist advocate for the revolutionary cause.

In Tunisia and Libya, where national media used to be extremely closed, newfound liberty translated into an explosion of personal opinions and emotions on screen. The model of journalist advocate was not a new feature in media industries such as the Egyptian national media, where dissent was narrowly expressed. After the uprisings, this model expanded to various layers of the media community to become a main feature of media production, especially under the Brotherhood. The euphoric expression of personal views and emotions on various media platforms took several forms. Some journalists and television personalities waved the national flag and chanted the national anthem in studios in response to national events like the announcement of the removal of the Brotherhood president. Others would cry or scream in studios or while reporting from the field of tragic events. In a monologue addressed to the audiences of her televised show that aired on the "al Assima" private channel, presenter Riham Noaman tearfully urged viewers to rally with her in support of the Egyptian President, General Sisi, who, she alleged, was facing a powerful conspiracy:

> We couldn't believe that we finally had a patriotic president who saved us from this cancer called the Muslim Brotherhood. I feel saddened to see this dream becoming finally reality while elements from inside the regime are conspiring against him—Sisi—and against Egypt...

On the one hand, this adoption of a more personal and heated style increased journalists' courage to approach long-standing taboos, reporting on topics that used to be unapproachable, and thus expand the scope of information disseminated to audiences. On the other hand, it hindered the development of a critical and inquisitive reporting based on facts, exacerbating the use of media for political distortion and manipulation, especially in the context of highly divisive events. The extremely polemical tone many journalists adopted, praising their ideological friends and slamming the opposing ideological camp, extended to the dissemination of all kinds of rumours and misinformation, aggravating confusion within a public struggling to understand the extraordinary events of the political transition. The political activism of these journalists was somehow the reflection of the cohabitation of the two models of the reverential journalist—with ideological friends—and the radical/oppositional journalist—with ideological enemies—together in the practices of the same professional group.

The model of the journalist advocate was especially celebrated during the uprisings, when challenging an autocratic regime from a media platform was an extremely risky venture that could just as easily lead the journalist to prison as to fame. Reem Maged, the former anchor of the pro-secular Egyptian television station ONTV, was one of few journalists who took this risk. Reem rapidly became a strong voice against the military rule under the Supreme Council of the Armed Forces (SCAF) and later the Brotherhood government. In May 2011, a military prosecutor summoned her and her guest, the prominent activist/blogger Hossam el-Hamalaway, after they openly criticized the military for attacking protestors.[43] For Maged, it is difficult to differentiate between the roles of activist and journalist, although she is aware of the risks of such blurred identity: "Some can be detached because they were not part of the revolution. They were not on the ground. Some told me that, because of my bias to the revolution, I am causing harm to the revolution. I am not able to attract the anti-revolution audiences. They are right, but I cannot change," she said.[44] Reem Maged was absent from screens since the military coup.

The Libyan presenter discussed earlier in the chapter, Zeinab Zaidi, is another prominent example of the journalist activist in support of the revolution. When the rebellion against Gaddafi erupted, she found herself presenting a political talk show on an opposition TV station based in Cairo, urging Libyan people to rebel against Gaddafi's regime: "I told my audiences stories of crimes committed by the regime. I wanted them to get angry, to cry. I was crying myself while recalling these atrocities," she remembers.[45] After the uprising, Zeinab became one of the prominent talk show hosts debating politics along with social problems brought on by the revolution, such as the degradation of women's conditions in post-Gaddafi Libya. She engaged in political activism by running for the first parliamentary elections after the regime's fall. In her televised talk show, she continued to challenge authorities as well as militias, interviewing leaders of extremist Islamic groups and producing reports on touchy topics such as torture of prisoners by former rebels. At the same time, she acts as a public figure, voicing her personal opinions in the media. Asked how she can reconcile the two roles of journalist and political activist, Zeinab defends her dual identity: "It is for you to label me as activist or as journalist. I found my soul in the experience of a journalist working to convey a message. I was always an activist acting for the service of the oppressed. I want to be the voice of people, those tired people".[46] She was elected member of the special commission tasked with drafting the new Libyan constitution.

The journalist advocates of the revolutionary cause, although widely celebrated, were not able to defy the interests of media owners, however. Prominent talk show hosts frequently disappeared from screens during particularly important events, such as elections, if their political leaning could compromise the political stance and interests of the media owner. On the Egyptian ONTV private TV channel, two prominent hosts, Reem Maged and Yosri Fouda, decided to halt their program during the presidential campaign of 2012 after they refused to tolerate alleged interference by management in the content of their programs. The former director of the TV station, Albert Shafiq, states—

> *During the presidential elections, presenters told us, 'we want to express our views'. We told them to leave this to the viewer, that we could no longer lead the streets. We told them that Egyptians are divided and that we don't want to aggravate the situation.*[47]

With the decline of revolutionary enthusiasm and the re-emergence of autocratic practices and control over media, the model of the journalist advocate for the revolution was itself replaced with a new one:

the journalist advocate for the patriotic cause, a more flattering interpretation of the role of regime's guard. The popularity of this "patriotic" activism is consolidated by the resurgence of self-censorship practices that fell out of favour but did not entirely disappear in the aftermath of the uprisings. For instance, the ongoing "patriotic" support of the military-backed regime is not new for Egyptian journalists, for whom defaming the regime's opponents is generally perceived as "a duty". Some state newspapers were dedicated to this role, regularly publishing reports defaming opposition figures, including opposing journalists. After having displayed unprecedented courage in challenging prominent taboos in the aftermath of the uprising, such as critiquing the president, Egyptian journalists quickly reverted to their traditional collaborative role, abiding by the patriotic "duty" of denigrating political opponents presented as the ultimate "enemy", as "the terrorists". This defence by traditional journalists of autocratic practices is allowing them to safeguard their role as "preachers" of public opinion. The scope of the regimes' manipulation of these journalists confirms the limits of such activism beyond the traditional role of the regimes' guard (see Chap. 4).

V. FACEBOOK: THE UNFILTERED NEWSFEED

Social media tools are impacting the mechanisms of production in traditional newsrooms, not only in this region, but also around the world. A 2014 study on the international impact of social media reported that 68% of journalists surveyed believe that journalism can no longer operate without social media.[48] The opportunities provided by new media for traditional journalists are tremendous, allowing them to access first-hand material produced by ordinary citizens in places they may struggle to reach, and on topics they may not able to investigate. In countries where mainstream media is not free, the significance of ordinary citizens' being able to disclose abuses is massive. William Dutton of the Oxford Internet Institute describes the power of social networks as a Fifth Estate, surpassing the institutional boundaries of traditional media since "highly networked individuals (helped by new platforms like social networking and messaging) can move across, undermine and go beyond the boundaries of existing institutions".[49] However, this easy access can negatively impact core values of investigative journalism,[50] as the chaotic flow of newsworthy material from ordinary citizens acting without regard for professional rules can make fact-checking challenging. Most large news organizations, including the BBC, *al-Jazeera*, and CNN, have developed special departments tasked with processing the user-generated content.

In the so-called Arab Spring countries, with social media platforms like Facebook serving as major providers of information and lacking clear journalistic oversight, it was easy for the division between news and rumour to blur, creating confusion for both journalists and their audiences. This confusion was aggravated by the decline of the conventional sources—the government communiqué—and the lack of fact-checking traditions in these newsrooms. Not to mention the fact that blurring opinions and facts was not foreign to the practices of these journalists.

Traditional media's dependency on social media for information was empowered by various factors: new governments resorting to old manipulation tactics to evade transparency; lack of clear standards in professional journalism; changes in the media community with the inclusion of citizen journalists; and finally the inability—or unwillingness—of management to train journalists in professional reporting and investigative techniques. Leaders who benefitted from extreme political polarization recognized media as the most efficient tool to fuel these divisions and quickly began learning how to wield it. Abdallah Kamal,[51] the former editor in chief of *Roz el Youssef* (an Egyptian state newspaper), gives an example of what he perceives to be as the dual impact of social media tools on media and on politics: "I can publish a few lines in my Twitter account in the morning. These lines will be published by a low key online website and later discussed in talk shows. Important political institutions will be dragged to comment on it. The journalist who published my tweet did not take the effort to check the information first".[52] As Kamal illustrates, the ability of new media platforms to shape media and politics has led to a naïve relationship between media, the political actors, and the public opinion.

Journalists rely even more heavily on new media as a source of information when new governments, reacting to accusations and allegations, simply deny charges without further clarification. According to Mohamed Hawari, a managing editor for the Egyptian private newspaper *al-Masry al-Yom*, the lack of transparency of official sources is leading to a media scene controlled by rumours: "The reaction of official sources to rumours comes usually very late and is limited generally to denying it, thus contributing to its wider dissemination", he argues. This confusion is contributing to eroding the public's trust in the media as a provider of accurate information: "Anything one says will be widely shared. At the same time, people would say, 'this is all media talk'; they don't trust media anymore," said Hawari.⁵³ For Mahmood Mosallami, the former editor-in-chief of the Egyptian private newspaper *Al Masry Al Yom*, the excessive dependency of journalists on social media, especially Facebook, as a provider of original news, is linked to a culture of professional laziness among journalists, who are keen to access original information without effort. It is also directly related to the race among journalists and managers for sensational news, usually published without being verified by independent sources.⁵⁴

In Libya, the excessive use of social media tools in breaking news is exacerbated by the raging violence in the country. Journalists are kept from the streets—not only due to a lack of professional training (as they are used to disseminating pre-packaged stories,) but also the dangers of field reporting. Most of the managers I interviewed confirmed they could not send their reporters to certain areas, especially when the political leaning of the media organization is considered hostile to the armed groups in control on the ground. With the division of the country into two belligerent parties and the fall of Tripoli into the hands of Islamic militias, media organizations find themselves again reduced to mouthpieces of the forces in control or silenced altogether.

The excessive use of Facebook pages of political or tribal groups as a main source of information has contributed to fuelling the mistrust of audiences towards the national media. This suspicious attitude is heightened by the lack of transparency on media funding and a general perception labelling private media as the mouthpiece of political groups. Newly established private TV stations have been frequently accused of using Facebook as a source for serious and unverifiable allegations, which help to fuel political and tribal dissensions. A good example is the fight that erupted between militias from two cities, Misrata and Bani Walid, over the alleged torture and killing of a Misrati rebel, believed to be involved in the killing of Gaddafi, by militias in Bani Walid in October 2012. The situation escalated dramatically, with Libyan forces launching an operation against the town of Bani Walid; an eight-day battle resulted, which ended with at least 20 people dead.⁵⁵ In their coverage on this battle, most Libyan media failed to report both sides of the story for fear of retaliation, resorting to reporting news from politically charged Facebook pages representing the two groups involved in the struggle. The local TV stations of the two towns took the lead in the incitement campaign, a discourse largely propagated by national TV stations according to their political leaning and position on the struggle.

VI. Social Media as Platform for Political Dissent

With the recent upsurge of censorship and self-censorship practices among journalists, cyber-activism is again thriving as a unique platform to express political dissent. In the aftermath of the coup in Egypt, social media platforms regained their role as the provider of a diversity of views after traditional media, state and private, engaged in an orchestrated propaganda campaign in praise of the military-backed regime. Online websites and social networking pages again became the main venue to share information on human rights violations, spread the messages of those excluded from the political arena (many of whom had been labelled by the traditional media as "terrorists" or "traitors"), and provide supporters with a platform to express their grievances and communicate. According to Hazem Ghourab, the head of the Misr 25 TV station (one of main media outlets representing the Brotherhood, which was closed immediately after the coup), "the communication of our message is mainly now by direct contact with activists in demonstrations and via social media platforms which are becoming the main platform for us, not only to communicate but also to uncover the wrongdoings and scandals of the military government".[56] In addition to giving voice to those excluded from the political arena, new media is allowing the dissemination of counter-narratives to regimes' discourse, providing information on controversial topics that are willingly or forcibly ignored by mainstream media, such as torture in prisons, rape of female detainees, journalists under detention, and other issues. Facebook pages of activists or opposition groups are becoming a main venue for learning about the growing injustice and oppression in the region. Egyptian Facebook pages such as "al Huriyya lel Gedaan" ("Freedom for the Brave"), which reports mainly on political prisoners and the youth opposition movement of April 6th, are among the few sources of information available on abuses of rights and civil liberties inflicted by the new regime. This information is rarely reported by Egyptian traditional media. The news website *Mada Masr*, a major provider of alternative narratives to the dominant official discourse, is threatened by a lack of funds and reprisals by the regime.[57] Hossam Bahgat—one of main contributors to the independent news website and a prominent human rights activist—was arrested and charged with spreading false information in November 2015. His release occurred only after the ensuing international outrage spread to the highest levels, including statements condemning his arrest from the UN Secretary General Ban Ki Moon.[58]

Although instrumental in providing an alternative to the official storytelling propagated by traditional media, the counter-narratives provided by these social networks are not able to balance the dominant media discourse. According to a report by Article 19 on alternative media in Egypt, independent websites and those affiliated with the banned Muslim Brotherhood are challenging the pervasive homogenization of reporting and the dominance of a single voice in the media. However, the trend of a single-voiced media is extending to digital space, due to the spread of the self-censorship habits to the online sphere and anticipated new media laws and surveillance systems. Online journalists are in an extremely vulnerable situation, especially when it comes to reporting on military matters. According to the report, "the overwhelming majority of interviewees, especially these from independent and Muslim Brotherhood affiliated websites, believe that it will be increasingly difficult to continue as a journalist in Egypt in the coming year".[59]

Awakened to the impact of new media in challenging their policies, the Egyptian government is trying to develop a mass surveillance system that monitors all users' digital activity, including private conversations and messages sent through mobile applications like Viber and WhatsApp.[60] Unconfirmed reports circulate about plans to provide monitoring units within security services the right to block websites or cyber-networking pages if they consider them a threat to national security.[61] The new Egyptian Constitution gives a new body, yet to be formed, the responsibility of regulating state broadcasters, as well as power over all forms of broadcast via satellite and online, thus putting websites providing such production under the government's control.[62] A new law project aiming at reviewing the legislations and structures of print, broadcast, and electronic media has opted for a dated and restrictive formula for electronic media, including networking pages, according to media expert Naglaa el Emary. Restrictive measures include the need for prior authorization in order to launch any webpage which "deals with public affairs" at the risk of facing exorbitant fines of up to 500,000 Egyptian pounds, as well as the limitation of the dissemination of videos online to media organizations with large capitals.[63]

Other restrictions have been imposed in the name of preventing cyber-crimes and the use of the internet to spread terrorism. In December 2014, former Prime Minister Ibrahim Mahlab issued a decree forming the High Council for Cyber-Security aimed, according to the government, at combatting cyber-threats, but decried by online activists as a new tool to restrict freedoms. In February 2015, another decree was issued to form a committee tasked with considering legislative amendments to national security law, including giving courts the jurisdiction to remove any online content related to terrorism. The bill, currently under revision, aimed to fight cyber-crime via restrictive measures including criminal punishments for insulting citizens or the state on the internet or on social media.[64]

In the case of Egypt, counter-narratives extended recently from social media platforms to some of mainstream media outlets, sporadically publishing reports on torture, inhuman treatment, and wide abuses by security officials in prisons. This sudden U-turn in the tone of these prominent publications is widely attributed to the internal struggle between different regime's wings, but one of the managing editors of *al-Masry al Yom*, Mohamed Hawari, implicates the rise of social media as well, saying—

> *Traditional media are recently facing growing competition from social media networks that are providing consistent information on these abuses. National media first imposed a blackout on these stories in the name of national security, but they later found that we are left behind in reporting this story and that this situation should not continue.*[65]

Conclusion

The input of social media as provider of original information for traditional newsrooms is not specific to Arab media. This global trend coincides with a steady shift in news consumption from traditional to new media, although television is still the main news source in the MENA region. More than half of Tunisian audiences used Facebook as a key news source in 2013,[66] while a third of Qatari nationals said they use WhatsApp to find out the latest news in 2014, according to figures by the Qatari Ministry of Information and Communications Technology.[67] According to the Arab Digital Generation Study conducted in 2012, a total of 24% of respondents said they could not trust traditional media, as its content is controlled by the government. The study conducted among youth found that 83% of respondents use the Internet daily and 78% prefer the Internet to television.[68]

In the context of the "Arab Spring" countries, the identification of traditional journalists with the model of the blogger/cyber-activist increased their courage to tackle topics that were previously exclusively considered fields for political activism. However, the ability of traditional journalists to tackle such topics was chaotic and sporadic, and even now remains under the control of media owners who share interests and relations with the political elites. The resistance to political dictates in state media was also inspired by the emotionally charged activists' lobbying style and was repressed harshly by state media management. Journalists' advocate role proved to be a double-edged sword: it widened the scope of information provided by traditional media, but this activism also acted as a powerful tool in the struggle raging between political camps, leading to de-legitimizing political adversaries and widening the social and political divide. In Egypt, the engagement of journalists in so-called patriotic advocacy in praise of the military regime and its many violations indicated the resilience of the model of the reverential journalist whose main task is to defend the regime. This raises questions regarding these journalists' ability to advocate for a cause beyond the direct or indirect dictates of political elites.

The thriving social media landscape is enabling relative visibility for those excluded from mainstream media and politics, providing information and uncovering the regime's abuses that traditional media willingly keeps under wraps. The digital space is able to provide counter-narratives challenging the official discourse largely propagated by a deferential traditional media. Preserving the dynamism of the digital space is crucial today—in the heightened environment of a crackdown on media freedom and civil liberties—for informing the public on topics that traditional media is willingly obscuring or reporting in a biased and distorted manner.

However, the dependency of traditional journalists on social media platforms, especially in breaking news, creates confusion in the public space, transforming traditional media into platforms to disseminate rumours, thus fuelling dissension and widening social and political divisions. With the lack of professional training for new journalists, especially regarding mechanisms of fact-checking and accuracy, the dependency on new media in reporting on complex and fast-developing events is exacerbating the use of national media as a platform for political manipulation. In this environment, the fine line between rumours and news is often difficult to draw, leaving the public in disarray when it comes to making sense of the many perplexing challenges and difficulties of the transition.

Notes

1. Nezar AlSayyad and Muna Guvenc, "Virtual Uprisings: On the Interaction of New Social Media, Traditional Media Coverage and Urban Space during the 'Arab Spring'," Urban Studies 1, no. 17 (2013); Asef Bayat, Life as Politics: How Ordinary People Change the Middle East (US: Stanford University Press, 2013); Christos A. Frangonikolopoulos and Ioannis Chapsos, "Explaining the Role and the Impact of the Social Media in the Arab Spring," GMJ: Mediterranean Edition 8, no. 1 (2012).
2. Simon Cottle, "Media and the Arab Uprisings of 2011: Research Notes," Journalism 12, no. 5 (2011).
3. Dale F. Eickelman and Jon W. Anderson, New Media in the Muslim World: The Emerging Public Sphere (US: Indiana University Press, 2003). Preface.
4. See Philipp N. Howard, The Digital Origins of Dictatorship and Democracy: Information Technology and Political Islam (Oxford: Oxford University Press, 2011).
5. Sahar Khamis and Katherine Vaughn, "Cyberactivism in the Egyptian Revolution: How Civic Engagement and Citizen Journalism Tilted the Balance," Arab Media & Society 13 (2011).
6. Patrick Gingsley, "I'm No Traitor, Says Wael Ghonim as Egypt Regime Targets Secular Activists," *The Guardian*, January 9, 2014, accessed November 30, 2015, https://www.theguardian.com/world/2014/jan/09/wael-ghonim-egypt-regime-targets-secular-activists.
7. Peter Beaumont, "The Truth about Twitter, Facebook and the Uprisings in the Arab World," *The Guardian*, February 25, 2011, accessed November 30, 2015, https://www.theguardian.com/world/2011/feb/25/twitter-facebook-uprisings-arab-libya.
8. Charlie Beckett, "After Tunisia and Egypt: Towards a New Typology of Media and Networked Political Change," POLIS blog, LSE, February 11, 2011, accessed in September 10, 2014, http://blogs.lse.ac.uk/polis/2011/02/11/after-tunisia-and-egypt-towards-a-new-typology-of-media-and-networked-political-change/.
9. Stefano Passini, "The Facebook and Twitter Revolutions: Active Participation in the 21st Century," Human Affairs 22 (2012).
10. Mohammed El-Nawawy and Sahar Khamis, "Cyberactivists Paving the Way for the Arab Spring: Voices from Egypt, Tunisia and Libya," CyberOrient 2 (2012).
11. Simon Cottle, "Media and the Arab Uprisings of 2011".
12. Leyla Dakhli, "A Betrayed Revolution?: On the Tunisian Uprising and the Democratic Transition," *Jadaliyya*, March 5, 2013, accessed November 30, 2015, http://www.jadaliyya.com/pages/index/10463/a-betrayed-revolution_on-the-tunisian-uprisingand.

13. Simon Cottle, "Media and the Arab Uprisings of 2011", 648.
14. Ibid., 649.
15. Naila Hamdy, "Youth Perceptions of Media Credibility and Political Information in Post-Revolution Egypt," Global Media Journal 1, no. 2 (2012): 90.
16. Nael Jebril, Mattew Loveless and Vaclav Stetka, "Media and Democratisation: Challenges for an Emerging Sub-field," Medijske Studije 11 (2015): 26.
17. See Mohamed Zayani (ed.), The Al Jazeera Phenomenon: Critical Perspectives on New Arab Media (London: Pluto Press, 2005); Philip Seib, The Al Jazeera Effect (Washington, DC: Potomac Books, 2008).
18. Muhammad I. Ayish, "Political Communication on Arab World Television: Evolving Patterns," Political Communication 19 (2002): 151.
19. Philipp N. Howard, The Digital Origins of Dictatorship and Democracy, 19–20.
20. *Arab Crunch*, "Digital Marketing Trends in the Middle East: 5.5 Million Twitter Users in the Arab World," March 30, 2011, accessed October 15, 2015, http://arabcrunch.com/2011/03/infographics-digital-marketing-trends-in-the-middle-east-5-5-million-twitter-users-in-the-arab-world.html.
21. *Burson-Marsteller*, "ASDA'A Burson-Marsteller's 5th Annual Arab Youth Survey," 2013, accessed October 10, 2015, http://www.burson-marsteller.co.uk/newsarticles/5th-annual-asdaa-burson-marsteller-arab-youth-survey/.
22. *Dubai School of Government*, "The 6th Arab Social Media Report," 2014 accessed October 10, 2015, http://www.arabsocialmediareport.com/home/index.aspx?&PriMenuID=1&mnu=Pri\.
23. *Deloitte & GSMA*, "Arab States Mobile Observatory 2013," 2013, accessed October 15, 2015, http://www.gsma.com/publicpolicy/wp-content/uploads/2012/03/GSMA_MobileObservatory_ArabStates2013.pdf.
24. Interview with author, Tunis, December 2011.
25. Ibid.
26. See a letter to a parliamentary urging him to support the campaign to end internet surveillance, https://www.facebook.com/note.php?note_id=139717572707534.
27. Lina Ben Mhenni, "Tunisia: Time to Register for Elections," *Global Voices*, July 25, 2011, accessed October 10, 2012, https://globalvoices.org/2011/07/25/tunisia-time-to-register-for-elections/.
28. *Nawaat*, "Where's Our Oil?': The (Continued) Confusion of Politics and Resource Management in Tunisia," June 16, 2015, accessed October 10, 2015, http://nawaat.org/portail/2015/06/16/wheres-our-oil-the-continued-confusion-of-politics-and-resource-management-in-tunisia/.

29. Emma el Hammi, "Tunisie: les blogueurs à l'assaut de l'assemblée constituante," *Nawaat*, September 14, 2011, accessed October 20, 2015, https://nawaat.org/portail/2011/09/14/tunisie-les-blogueurs-a-l-assaut-de-l-assemblee-constituante/.
30. Angelique Chrisafis, "Tunisian Dissident Blogger Quits Ministerial Post," *The Guardian*, May 25, 2011, accessed October 10, 2015 https://www.theguardian.com/world/2011/may/25/tunisian-dissident-blogger-minister-quits.
31. Conor Sheils, "Freed Blogger Yassine Ayari: Tunisia's Revolution has Failed," *Al-Araby Al-Jadeed*, May 7, 2015, accessed October 10, 2015 https://www.alaraby.co.uk/english/features/2015/5/7/freed-blogger-yassine-ayari-tunisias-revolution-has-failed.
32. Interview with author, Cairo, June 2012.
33. Ahdaf Soueif, "Image of Unknown Woman Beaten by Egypt's Military Echoes Around World," *The Guardian*, December 18, 2011, accessed November 09, 2012, https://www.theguardian.com/commentisfree/2011/dec/18/egypt-military-beating-female-protester-tahrir-square.
34. *BBC*, "Cairo Police Beating: Victim Hamada Saber Blames Police," February 3, 2013, accessed October 10, 2015, http://www.bbc.co.uk/news/world-middle-east-21314782.
35. See the blog webpage http://nawaat.org/portail/.
36. Interview with author, Tunis, November 2013.
37. Fatima El Issawi, "Libya Media Transition: Heading to the Unknown," *POLIS*, London School of Economics and Political Science, 2013, 62.
38. Ibid., 46.
39. Ibid., 64.
40. Interview with author, Benghazi, October 2012.
41. Ibid.
42. Fatima El Issawi, "Libya Media Transition: Heading to the Unknown", 61.
43. See the video of Reem Maged and Hossam el-Hamalawy discussing the meeting with military prosecutor: http://www.youtube.com/watch?v=OEO11WLnaDc&feature.
44. Interview with author, Cairo, March 2012.
45. Interview with author, Tripoli, October 2012.
46. Ibid.
47. Interview with author, Cairo, March 2012.
48. *ING*, "2014 Study Impact of Social Media on News: More Crowdchecking, Less Fact Checking," 2014, accessed October 10, 2015, http://www.ing.com/Newsroom/Allnews/NW/2014-Study-impact-of-Social-Media-on-News-more-crowdchecking-lessfactchecking.htm.

49. Nic Newman, "The Rise of Social Media and Its Impact on Mainstream Journalism," *Reuters Institute for the Study of Journalism*, 2009, accessed October 10, 2015, https://reutersinstitute.politics.ox.ac.uk/sites/default/files/The%20rise%20of%20social%20media%20and%20its%20impact%20on%20mainstream%20journalism_0.pdf.
50. Jennifer Alejandro, "Journalism in the Age of Social Media," *Reuters Institute for the Study of Journalism*, 2010, accessed October 10, 2015, http://reutersinstitute.politics.ox.ac.uk/publication/journalism-age-social-media.
51. The journalist died from a heart attack in June 2014.
52. Fatima El Issawi, "Egyptian Media Under Transition: In the Name of the Regime…in the Name of the People?", 73.
53. Interview with author conducted by phone from London, May 2015.
54. Ibid.
55. Chris Stephen, "Gaddafi Stronghold Bani Walid Captured by Libya Government Troops," *The Guardian*, October 24, 2012, accessed October 10, 2015, https://www.theguardian.com/world/2012/oct/24/bani-walid-captured-by-libya-government.
56. Fatima El Issawi, "Egyptian Media Under Transition: In the Name of the Regime…in the Name of the People?, 67.
57. Miriam Berger, "With Morsi Out, Uphill Battle for Independent Media Intensifies," *Atlantic Council*, July 17, 2013, accessed October 12, 2015, http://www.atlanticcouncil.org/blogs/menasource/with-morsi-out-uphill-battle-for-independent-media-intensifies.
58. *The Guardian*, "Anger as Egypt Detains Campaigning Journalist," November 9, 2015, accessed November 30, 2015, https://www.theguardian.com/world/2015/nov/09/egyptian-journalist-hossam-bahgat-charged-military-prosecutor.
59. *Articles 19*, "Egypt: News Websites and Alternative Voices," 2014, accessed October 20, 2015, https://www.article19.org/data/files/medialibrary/37780/Egypt-Report-for-Web.pdf, 3.
60. Ahmed Ezzat, "You are being Watched!' Egypt's Mass Internet Surveillance," *Mada Masr*, September 29, 2014, accessed October 15, 2015, http://www.madamasr.com/opinion/politics/you-are-being-watched-egypts-mass-internet-surveillance.
61. *Al-Araby Al-Jadeed*, "First Egyptian Legislation that Allows to Block Websites," (Arabic), April 14, 2015, accessed October 15, 2015, https://www.alaraby.co.uk/medianews/2015/4/14/%D8%A3%D9%88%D9%84-%D8%AA%D8%B4%D8%B1%D9%8A%D8%B9-%D9%85%D8%B5%D8%B1%D9%8A-%D9%8A%D8%B3%D9%85%D8%AD-%D8%A8%D8%AD%D8%AC%D8%A8-%D8%A7%D9%84%D9%85%D9%88%D8%A7%D9%82%D8%B9-%D8%A7%D9%84%D8%A5%D9%84%D9%83%D8%AA%D8%B1%D9%88%D9%86%D9%8A%D8%A9.

62. *Egyptian Chronicles*, "Another Blow to Online Media in Egypt Coming on the way!!," April 27, 2015, accessed 08 October 2014, http://egyptianchronicles.blogspot.co.uk/2015/04/another-blow-to-online-media-in-egypt.html.
63. Naglaa el Emary, "To Draft a Media Law from the Last Century," *Al-Masry el Yom*, November 2, 2015, accessed November 27, 2015, http://www.almasryalyoum.com/news/details/837272.
64. Ragab Saad, "Egypt's Draft Cybercrime Law Undermines Freedom of Expression," *The Atlantic Council*, April 24, 2015, accessed November 30, 2015, http://www.atlanticcouncil.org/blogs/menasource/egypt-s-draft-cybercrime-law-undermines-freedom-of-expression.
65. Interview with author conducted by phone from London, May 2015.
66. Damian Radcliffe, "Social Media Catching Up with TV as Trusted News Source in Middle East," *BBC College of Journalism*, February 11, 2015, accessed October 10, 2015, http://www.bbc.co.uk/blogs/collegeofjournalism/entries/c3790641-d512-48d3-9616-228ea10abfea.
67. Damian Raclifffe, "WhatsApp Now Clear Social Media Leader in Qatar, Including for News," *BBC College of Journalism*, January 6, 2015, accessed October 10, 2015, http://www.bbc.co.uk/blogs/collegeofjournalism/entries/0d8a6f02-f9e6-35f5-98b7-a59bd8338b07.
68. *Strategy&*, "Understanding the Arab Digital Generation," October 9, 2012, accessed October 10, 2015, http://www.strategyand.pwc.com/reports/understanding-arab-digital-generation.

Ratings Are Votes: Media and Democratization

INTRODUCTION

During the first months after the overthrow of Gaddafi, Libyan journalists recently liberated from the regime's propaganda machine found themselves facing an uncertain future. Despite a great sense of relief, the journalists also feared a world where the censors they were so accustomed to became nothing more than, as one journalist described them, "ghosts". With no formal identity or address, obscure militiamen seized the chaotic situation as an opportunity to intimidate journalists and attack media offices and personnel with impunity. Libyan journalists faced a volatile security environment and an entrenched political culture of repression, where new political players often continued the old regime's tactics in dealing with media. For those journalists, limited to reverential reporting for decades, it was not clear what democratic governance would mean and what an independent and professional media industry would look like. For many of them, media reform was a kind of utopia: as idyllic as it was unrealistic.

Arab journalists operating in the traditional mold (as advocates for the current regime's political agendas and interests) coped with unsafe and unpredictable working conditions and a volatile political environment. Professional reform was less of a concern for them, and so attempts to move to a more "watchdog" role were not generally successful, especially for the elite. The heavy legacy of former media systems, along with a lack of clarity and planning regarding the goals of the media reform, reflect the complexities of the media democratization process. The media's impact on the process of building new democratic institutions proved equally problematic, with media often accused of fuelling antagonism by favouring a reporting style based on personal views, rumours, and libel.

In countries that have just emerged out of authoritarian rule, local political elites tend to reject a newly adversarial press, and new regimes are not ready to give up controlling the media content. Yet field investigation in Tunisia, Libya, and Egypt has confirmed the use of traditional national media to incite political animosity, which has in turn encouraged suppression of the rights and freedoms of the press, especially in Egypt. In this chapter, I will review some of the academic literature on the role of media as an agent to support democratic change. I will use data from the field to both reflect on and complement this analysis. In addition, I will investigate common trends and challenges in the pathways developed by the journalists covered by this study and their role in the democratization processes, applying a comparative analysis between these countries and international transitional experiences.

I. Democracy and Democratization

Modern democracy is defined by Philippe Schmitter and Terry Karl[1] as "a system of governance in which rulers are held accountable for their actions in the public realm by citizens, acting indirectly through the competition and cooperation of their elected representatives". In his definition of democracy, Dahl[2] goes further, identifying seven key criteria that citizens in a democratic system should enjoy: control over governmental decisions, fair and free elections, universal adult suffrage, the right to run for public office, freedom of expression, access to alternative sources of information free of manipulation from political powers, and freedom of association.

As opposed to a minimalist view, this definition of democracy emphasizes the importance of accountability by including the ability of citizens to hold their political leaders to account and mechanisms of accountability within the government itself,[3] as well as the ability of the civil society to play the role of watchdog in the political sphere with the support of an independent mass media.[4] Thus we must distinguish between the mere implementation of democratic processes, allowing for the electing competing elites,[5] and the notion of democracy as an inclusive and comprehensive culture reflected in a set of values that govern and guide citizen's everyday life.⁶

Democratization, then, is defined as a "lengthy process of social construction that is bound to be relatively open-ended" leading mainly to "a more rule-based, more consensual, and more participatory type of politics".⁷ Voltmer echoes this view, defining democratization as "a process leading towards more participation and a more open public sphere".⁸ Hence, democratization cannot be limited to a defined timeframe or measured by a set of elements that can be applied to all contexts; it cannot be rapid or linear. However, its success would be reflected in gradual change towards more open public spaces, and a political system that is more participatory, more inclusive, and more based on the rule of law and institutions. The Arab revolts confirm the diversity and complexity of these transitional processes; furthermore, they confirm that transitional processes don't necessarily have to follow the classical three-phased linear model: liberalization, democratization, and consolidation.⁹ The power struggle between old and new, conservative and revolutionary forces, renders the outcome unpredictable. It is not realistic to apply a model of democratization to all experiences, disregarding the particularities of the national context that inevitably define the emerging system.¹⁰

These particularities are not only applicable to Arab transitions: the European uprisings of 1848 were followed by counter-revolutions and renewed authoritarian rule. The 1989 collapse of the Soviet Union led to a diverse landscape where democratization was successful in some countries, and failed completely in others.¹¹ To successfully transition to democracy, the new ruling elite must be able to implement a fundamental restructuring of political institutions, including an efficient constitutional reform. When such restructuring processes do not occur or fail to realise their goals, newly elected regimes revert to old forms of repression.¹² The process of democratization is threatened by many factors, including authoritarian rule, the difficulty of building democratic institutions, and the challenge of convincing the elite of the regime to consent to the process.¹³ Even with the coercive state apparatus removed, revolutionaries often struggle in practice to imagine "what an alternative order would look like once such processes have taken place".¹⁴ As Voltmer points out, "democracy is not a one-way road and [...] a viable democracy requires more than the implementation of the key institutions of government".¹⁵

II. DEMOCRATIZATION AND THE ROLE OF MEDIA

Much of the academic debate regarding the role of the media in consolidating or hindering processes of democratization focused on specifically Western experiences.[16] In a democracy, the role of media is ideally to "impartially present factual information about candidates, programs, and policies that is adequate enough in volume and content to enable citizens to make informed voting choices and hold governments responsible for their actions".[17] But during a transition from an autocratic regime to democracy, when stakes are high and power struggles are fierce, media can rarely play such a role. The media's relationship to democratization processes depends on a number of contextual variables, including the level of cohesion or fragmentation of societal groups, the economic and regulatory situation, the literacy levels and the level of political knowledge among citizens, as well as their media consumption behaviour, and of course, the choices made by politicians and journalists as to how the media will approach the political transition.[18]

As of the Arab uprisings demonstrate, the success of the political transition in fostering a gradual implementation of a new system based on the rule of law is crucial for successfully democratizing media itself; reciprocally, the media democratization itself would be a strong asset to support the political transition to democracy and to consolidate the legitimacy of the new democratic rule. By facilitating citizens' participation, media helps in fostering social consensus and a friendly climate supportive of the implementation of the democratization process.[19] For instance, national media promoted democracy and good governance during Latin America's corruption deals of 1993 (Venezuela), 1997 (Ecuador), and 2000 (Ecuador), where investigative reporting put an end to corruption and increased press credibility. After the fall of the Franquist regime, the vast majority of Spanish press supported the reforms for a gradual and successful transition.[20] Similarly in Chile and East Germany, media facilitated the "erosion of the credibility and legitimacy of the nondemocratic regime; the development of pluralism in political attitudes, preferences, and partisan alternatives; and, eventually, re-socialization of both masses and elites to the new democratic rules of the game".[21]

However, the media response to challenges posed by a democratization process is not necessarily linked to a genuine will to help foster democracy. The media opposition to autocratic political practices before or during the transition to democracy can simply originate from rational self-interest. Furthermore, the degree of agency the media can exercise in supporting a move towards a democratic regime is questionable, as authoritarian regimes tend to initiate minor liberalization measures in order to vent public pressure for change.[22] Yet these reforms may lead to unintended consequences as newfound freedoms snowball further than the regime had anticipated—the media may find itself with more to say than it had bargained for, unexpectedly contributing to weakening autocratic regimes.[23] However, these gains are not solid unless they are institutionalized and strongly embedded in journalists' practices. The Egyptian private media's support of some of the most appalling abuses inflicted by the military-backed regime demonstrates that media, facing a shaky transition, may rather support a status quo that would ensure the survival of the complex interplay between the media and political elites.

Beyond the models presented by Hallin and Mancini[24] in their analysis of the relationship between media and the political sphere[25], the complexities of the interplay between media and politics in emerging democracies render the application of imported models unrealistic. In a democratization process, emerging media practices are quite often a blend of old and new, "a unique conjunction between the trajectory of the past and the immediate constraints of the transition itself".[26] If we examine the accounts the journalists I interviewed gave of their practices and how those practices evolved, we can observe how they adopt features of certain models and reject others depending on the imperatives of various phases of the political transition and the values that are strongly propagated in the political sphere to guide the process of shaping new regimes. After the regime change, the attempts to integrate new liberal values into entrenched old models often "cause considerable confusion and conflicts among journalists as to their role in the new democratic order".[27] The "fight" that erupted between old and newly introduced habits led to confusion in journalists' perception of their roles. While in some cases (mainly Tunisia) this confusion receded, allowing the new habits to take better shape in journalists' practices, in other cases (mainly Egypt) it allowed the forceful return of reverential practices, even exacerbating their scope in spreading regimes' populist propaganda. In Tunisia, while the struggle between the legacy of the past and the need for change raged, media reform remained central in the public debate. Civil society supported and monitored this process, encouraging noticeable change in newsroom practices. This change is reflected in a more balanced storytelling reliant on field reporting corroborated by multiple sources.

The democratization of the media sector itself, which under autocratic regimes is often governed by a repressive structural and legal framework, remains a major challenge in the context of political transitions. The democratization of the media requires independence from state and party control[28] but also a review of the practices and values that guided media production for decades and the willingness of professionals to question their own habits. In fragile and politically charged transitions, the weak civil society and grassroots mobilization can impair the media's ability to support the democratization process.[29] The media democratization process in these Arab countries proves how central civil society is to the success of such a transition. A dynamic civil society—such as we see in Tunisia—acts as a key support for media and political reforms, while the weak and fragmented civil societies of Egypt and Libya have not been able to protect the fragile democratic gains achieved post-uprising.[30]

In the following pages, I will identify some of the main challenges encountered by traditional journalists in their relationship to the democratization processes in Tunisia, Egypt, and Libya with a comparative focus. This analysis will tackle four major topics: the liberalization of media from the state control, the role of private media, media diversity, and media professionals' roles and identity shifts.

III. Towards Independent Media?

As previously discussed, Tunisian private broadcast media under the former regime had no political content, while Libya had no independent media to speak of. A regime can exercise control over state-owned media directly by appointing media executives, but it also wields influence over "independent" media through the issuing of licenses, selective law enforcement, allocation of funding (mainly subsidies and advertising), and exploiting the media's dependence on state-owned technology such as printing presses and broadcasting equipment. While state control covers all forms of media production, the broadcast sector, especially television, is most vulnerable and undergoes continuous state interference.[31] Given its high popularity among audiences, controlling narratives disseminated through these influential televised platforms is crucial for regimes to maintain the upper hand on their image and how it is framed and presented to large audiences. The popularity of broadcast media is confirmed by a recent study conducted by Northwestern University on media use in the Middle

East (2015). According to this study, the vast majority of respondents watch television programmes (97%) and two in three of them listen to the radio (65%).[32]

States in the Arab region have used all these tools against national media. In Egypt, where private "independent" media was legal, the Mubarak regime employed various tools—such as behind-the-scenes manipulation of advertising revenues—to limit the media's ability to provide counter-narratives to the official discourse propagated by state-owned media.[33] Since the governmental discourse often prioritized national security, the preservation of national identity, and cohesion for the sake of public welfare[34], media had no choice but to conform to these goals, especially for the broadcasting sector. Even when a state-owned broadcaster was granted autonomy and a public service mission on paper, it remained vulnerable to the interference of national leaders, and closed to dissenting voices.[35]

In the post-uprisings phase in these countries, the idea of media's representing "the people", as frequently mentioned by journalists interviewed in this research, did not translate into effective structures guaranteeing the independence of journalists' practices. Many factors contributed to this failure: first among them was the lack of support from new regimes for genuine efforts to restructure the state-owned media sector and end editorial and political dependency on the government. Practically speaking, all governments post-uprisings were eager to use state media as a mobilization tool to propagate a positive account of their policies. In Egypt, the Muslim Brotherhood allegedly reshuffled media management to promote executives sympathetic to their cause, instructing them to interfere with reporting both directly (through phone calls and overt directives) and indirectly (through the authority of an editor-in-chief or the head of News acting as a gatekeeper) to bring about the so-called "brotherhoodisation of media".[36] The return of state media to its former role as a platform for dissemination of the current regime's propaganda after the military takeover put an end to ambitious plans to transform this outdated sector into a provider of public information.

The inflated structure of the state-owned media was, and remains, a serious impediment to the reform of this sector. In Egypt where the state broadcast sector alone employs more than 40,000 people, most of whom have no official journalistic training, staff reductions were strictly avoided by all administrations. The poor professional skills of Libyan state media journalists were a major handicap, garnering them little trust from both the public and the new political elites. The managers I interviewed talked about internal resistance from their staff to implementing new practices and approaching their work in a different way, along with problems of discipline and difficult relationships with the new management.

Several managers told me about staff reluctance to show up for their work shifts on time and to provide the number of work hours required. The former head of the Libyan state-owned news agency (rebranded the *Libyan News Agency*, *LANA*), Bashir Zoghbiya, had to leave his position after being faced by an "uprising" from his staff, who refused to follow new practices like leaving their offices to report from the street or from governmental offices. Another important struggle was the rift within media leadership between new and former staff—those who were living inside the country under Gaddafi and those who fled and came back after the regime's fall to assume leadership positions. A prominent movement inside newsrooms urged rejection of the latter, under the guise that they were not knowledgeable in the Libyan internal context and that they did not pay the price of co-existing with Gaddafi's repression.

The many handicaps that have so far obstructed the process of transforming state media into an independent and quality provider of information echo similar failures experienced by other nations rebuilding after revolutions. Nations such as Bulgaria, Croatia, Russia, and the Ukraine have faced obstacles such as the political elites' expecting journalists "to assist the government as the leader of the process rather than exercising an impartial and critical watchdog role".[37] In both Poland and Hungary, lack of clarity in these media outlets' mandate and frequent political interference weakened the public service potential of these institutions. Factors like societal politicisation, weak political and civil cultures, and lack of necessary technical and administrative expertise constrained the success of such efforts.[38] The disappointment with the outcomes of the state media reform could be simply related to excessively high expectations from the start and underestimating the scope of the difficulties the process faced.[39]

IV. REGULATORY REFORM ON PAPER AND IN PRACTICE

If liberating state media in "Arab Spring" countries from the state's control proved troublesome, reforming the deeply coercive regulatory frameworks has been even more problematic. These regulatory frameworks limit both the scope of effective change in the national media and the media's ability to support the democratization process. Some major positive change has been introduced to the regulatory framework, such as abolishing the licensing system for print publications and opening private media ownership to individuals. Yet repressive legal provisions remain in force, including prison sentences for professional "offenses" and trials before military courts.[40]

Constitutional amendments guaranteeing freedom of expression, essential rights such as access to information, and the eradication of media censorship are frequently contradicted. The many exceptions included in these new constitutions provide opportunities to limit or to deny these rights, such as Egypt's provision allowing media censorship "in war time and general mobilization" without clearly defining the circumstances under which such measures can be applied. Criminalization of libel in legal cases related to offenses committed by journalists in the exercise of their profession remains the most alarming and widely used practice in muzzling critical reporting. Journalists still face prison sentences for the expression of "defamatory statements", which are in numerous cases an expression of political dissent. Many journalists and editors interviewed listed the threat of legal ramifications, resulting from reporting on critical views or investigating controversial cases, as having the most negative impact on their practices, leading in many cases to self-censorship.

Even when important milestones have been achieved, such as the ratification of a new Tunisian press code abolishing the restrictive features of the old one, this was not sufficient to protect independent reporting. Although operating freely in theory, Tunisian journalists face an extensive campaign of intimidation at the hands of the judiciary based on the provisions of the penal code, leading to double standards in the treatment of legal cases against journalists, with the judiciary applying the penal code in some cases and the press code in others. The frequency of these legal prosecutions threatens to revive the repressive media environment that used to prevail under the Ben Ali regime.[41] The extensive use of anti-terror laws to justify frequent arbitrary detentions and lengthy incarcerations of journalists and human rights activists, and their trial before military courts, shows the judiciary's ability to punish and thus deter dissent. New anti-terror bills impose serious restrictions on reporting, especially that concerning military operations, thus obstructing any independent reporting on the military and limiting the storytelling to official narratives. A flagrant example is the draft bill yet to be voted on by the Tunisian parliament that imposes heavy jail sentences for divulging state secrets or "denigrating" the army or police force. The vague wording of this bill, presented as part of the anti-terror measures, was decried by 13 local rights groups as potentially allowing the authorities to apply "wide discretion to make arrests on unjustified grounds", potentially paving the way for attacking "those who expose the government's wrongdoing".[42]

Constitutional reforms in the countries covered by the research have not really impact the daily practices of journalists positively and effectively. At the contrary, the experiences of journalists interviewed demonstrate an accentuation of restrictions and pressures exercised mainly in the name of protecting national security. The gap between constitutional texts and the practice is wide.

This situation is not different to challenges faced by journalists in similar transitional contexts. For instance, journalists in Latin America had to face an "antiquated and hostile legal climate" where libel was a punishable offence, with the existence of *descato* or "insult laws" which penalise "disrespect" towards public officials, effectively deterring critical speech. Journalists don't enjoy "legal standing to protect confidential sources", and "official data and reports that should be public are often quietly withheld or treated as state secrets".[43] Scholars Sallie Hughes and Chappell Lawson advocate for "abolishing existing criminal defamation and descato laws, and replacing them with well-defined civil procedures for addressing libel and slander and introducing access to information laws".[44]

The lack of political will to dismantle such a repressive legal arsenal is also not particular to the Arab case. For instance, Waisbord looks specifically at two cases in Latin America (Argentina and Uruguay) when civil society coalitions used advocacy to instigate change in media systems when the state and mainstream media themselves were not enthusiastic about such reform, leading to the passing of legislation favouring the diversification of media ownership and public access to official information; laws that discourage critical scrutiny of governments were also revoked.[45] According to Waisbord, "both cases show that civic mobilization was crucial in the processes that resulted in legal reforms. Civic groups jump-started public dialogue around the issues and drew attention to the need for chance among key political, business and civic actors".[46] This echoes the Tunisian experience, where civil society is acting as a strong platform for lobbying against repressive regulations and practices, with the new governments failing to provide necessary support for effective, long-term media reform.

V. Media Ownership: With Privatization Comes Independence?

The liberalization of the media is often understood as opening the door for commercialization of the industry by allowing private ownership in a sector that used to be exclusively owned by the state. However, a sudden and chaotic opening of the media market to private ownership often leads to the concentration of media ownership in the hands of a privileged elite with links to the political regime. Such swift and disorganized liberalization of the media is even more alarming in times of democratic transition, as it can lead to a very fragmented landscape, whereby political, religious, and sectarian forces control the media, reducing it again to its old role of ideological platform and hampering further development.[47] Liberal theory places high importance on the expression of diverse views in public spaces. The so-called "marketplace of ideas" is expected to naturally lead to the emergence of the truth, by the confrontation of arguments and counter-arguments on media platforms.[48] This is crucial to enable citizens to make informed choices in important matters in relation to their daily life. The ability of media to provide a diversity of views is therefore crucial to help citizens build a comprehensive understanding of major conflicts of the day, enabling them to make sound and independent political choices. By this logic, the multiplicity of information channels is essential to ensure that citizens can access a diversity of ideas and that these ideas can enjoy visibility.[49] However, critics of such logic contend that private media does not encourage media practices committed to defending the interests of citizens just because it is independent from state control. Rather, they allege it acts to protect the vested interests of the market forces.[50]

Under autocratic regimes in "Arab Spring" countries, the introduction of private media managed to diversify the media content without providing real plurality. The close link between media owners and traditional political elites led to a media inherently complicit with the regime's coercive practices[51], effectively engaging in de-politicising citizens and excluding dissenting views from the public sphere. This model can survive under a transition whereby media perpetuate undemocratic tendencies by providing biased information on the public life, thus exacerbating political and social divisions in a fragile transition process to democracy; Examples of this media contribution in fuelling dissension abound in Central and Eastern European states, where the link between post-communist politicians, entrepreneurs, and the media is hardly transparent.[52] Taking the example of media transformation in post-Soviet Poland, Russia, and China, Sparks[53] contends that "there is no evidence whatsoever of any correlation between marketisation and democratization, at least with regard to the mass media". Conversely, the trend is one of continuous control by the elite of the media sector. The Russian media landscape in the 1990s and early 2000s indicates that having numerous media outlets was no guarantee that they could provide unbiased reporting.[54] In Latin America, the political democratization did not lead to a media landscape that is bold to both market and state control. According to Waisbord[55] "democratic rule has not significantly altered the historical structural relations among media, state, and market". The media owners' collusive relations with political elites led to a situation where "family-run enterprises rarely allow a separation between ownership and political control, which tends to reduce diversity and assertiveness in coverage".[56]

As we have seen, the media transition in "Arab Spring" countries supports these conclusions. Privately owned media post-uprising largely replicated the old model of large private media owned by wealthy businessmen in connection with political elites new and old. Small media projects in their infancy could not sustain operations and gain momentum. Rumours of political funds being used to manipulate media and calls for media funding transparency were rife. In Libya, the explosion of private media post-revolution without legal and ethical frameworks transformed media into a tool for political and ethnic groups wielded to further fragment a sector already in deep crisis. The use of media to promote political agendas exacerbated tribal conflicts and internal cleavages, thus worsening the difficulties during the process of building new institutions. Egypt's private media sector's role in legitimizing non-democratic practices under the pretext of preserving national security shows how alliances between media owners and political elites can hinder democratic change.

In the three countries covered by this research, media was largely state owned. The outbreak of private media was controlled and used as a tool to embellish the regimes' face. In Egypt, the limitations on the private ownership of media led to the transformation of private media into a club for political and economic elites (see Chap. 2). The proliferation of private broadcast projects in Egypt post-uprising followed a similar trend of media empires with large resources and operations owned by business tycoons. Some of these businessmen were obscure before the uprising, and the source of their funding is often not clear to the public.[57] The opening of the political broadcasting sector to religious media outlets and business projects linked to political groups previously excluded from mainstream politics ended with the fall of the Brotherhood rule after the military takeover. This extension of the private media to new players contributed to further diversifying the media content while exacerbating its antagonism.

In Tunisia, private media flourished chaotically after the uprising, benefitting from the vacuum caused by the dismantling of the national media's former control system. This led to the outbreak of pirate broadcasters operating unlawfully, most of which having limited operations and audiences. The independent regulatory body for broadcast media (HAICA) had repeatedly warned these media outlets to follow the licensing process and present official applications to have their case studied, advising them that otherwise security services could forcibly close their premises.[58] The transparency of media funding and ownership was embedded in the new media regulations but with no process or structure on how to ensure this transparency. Some called for content regulation to ensure that these influential broadcast productions respected the fundamental rights of the public, regardless of the ownership of the media outlet and independently from media owners' political views and interests, moving sometimes from one extreme to another to safeguard their place in the political arena. The Chairman of *An-Nahar* TV network Walid Moustafa argues, "Regardless of the source of funding, which cannot possibly be truly transparent, the most important matter is to define and implement clear rules and criteria for the production itself. This is not possible yet".[59]

Ethical requirements for media content are contained in many codes of ethics, although they are rarely applied; some private broadcasters have adopted their own internal charters, such as the Egyptian An-Nahar TV networks, according to Amer al-Kahki, the head of the organization.[60] Despite the manager's claim, the network is responsible for airing some very controversial content, such as the programme anchored by Reham Saeed that was accused of frequently breaching persons' privacy and rights. For example, during a field visit to refugee camps in Lebanon, Saeed referred to Syrian refugees as "uncivilised", sparking heated criticism in traditional and social media and calls for her programme to be suspended.[61] Content regulation faces much scepticism, with many seeing it as a means of re-imposing censorship by portraying critical speech as a call for hatred and national discord.

The media owners' influence on media content extends to dictating content and a blunt change of identity and interests. Take the case of the widely viewed Tunisian TV channel *Nessma*. Although in violation of the charter stipulated by the new authority responsible for regulating broadcast media that bars media owners from political activity, the Tunisian media tycoon Nabil Karoui openly stated that he was one of driving forces behind the success of secularist *Nidaa Tunis* political party in the parliamentary and presidential elections of 2014. Having acted as the main platform for radical secularists calling for a halt of the alleged proliferation of Islamic trends in the new Tunisia, *Nessma's* identity was recently reshaped as the "TV station of the family", focusing more on light-entertainment shows and less on politically charged debates. The Tunisian media reported recently on several meetings between Karoui and leaders of *Ennahda* Islamic party. For a businessman eager to find a place for himself under all regimes, changing loyalties (as well as the identity of his prominent media outlet) is not a problem. The rapprochement between the media mogul and the Islamic party is explained as the expression of Karaoui's frustration at not having secured the gains he was seeking from supporting *Nidaa Tunis* political party during the latest elections.

The excessive use of powerful private television stations as platforms for political propaganda and the speculations about political manipulation of media through private investments confirm the limited contribution of private media in introducing diversity into the public space. The transformation of private Egyptian media into an orchestrated propaganda platform used to legitimize the military-backed regime demonstrates the weakness of editorial policies under the control of powerful media owners.[62]

VI. Media Diversity: The Loss of the Shared Narrative

Many see the ability of media to deliver a variety of viewpoints as crucial for a viable democracy: citizens' familiarization with a multiplicity of views presented as worthy of respect will eventually foster an environment of tolerance and peaceful coexistence between political opponents.[63] However, it is essential to distinguish between internal diversity, represented by the model of the public service media's providing a fair and balanced representation of different views, and external diversity, wherein a group of ideologically diverse media institutions can guarantee the broad representation of all views[64], following Manca's[65] concept of "pluralist objectivity". The danger of such a model is that, while encouraging political participation and civic engagement, it can lead to acute polarization, becoming increasingly adversarial to the extent of sabotaging the democratic experiment.[66] The media plurality enjoyed after the fall of autocratic regimes in so-called Arab Spring countries brought mainly external diversity, and even this diversification was fragile and short-lived. It vanished with the erosion of political diversity as a result of intense polarisation in the political sphere and the resurgence of autocratic governmental practices. A victim of political polarization, this external media diversification was, at the same time, a prominent tool to fuel this process, thus contributing to sabotaging the fragile democratic gains achieved by the uprisings.

In an environment where political and media dissent was limited or absent, the outbreak of a panoply of ideologically oriented media, echoing the new political plurality, was considered instrumental in encouraging political participation.[67] However, the extreme use of national media to support political campaigns and denigrate political enemies led to the fall of this new and fragile plurality. This media openness, which was one of main gains of the emerging democracies, was at once also one of main tools for sabotaging it, contributing to empowering adversarial trends as opposed to a climate of coexistence and tolerance. As Voltmer rightly points out, "the plurality of voices has to be counterbalanced by shared narratives and opportunities to communicate across the lines of difference".[68] Voltmer gives the example of the decision to launch three different broadcasters in Bosnia and Herzegovina, each targeting one of the ethnic groups of the country, as a mistake that would further divide and polarize the region. By contrast, the Switzerland model, where segmented public service broadcasters serve the different language communities of the country, contributes to consolidating a common sense of national unity among various communities.[69]

The extreme bias of ideologically driven media deepened the existing divisions between opposing political camps, each side understanding events in a different light. The extreme polarization that prevailed under the Muslim Brotherhood's rule in Egypt is a very relevant example. Divided into pro- and anti-Brotherhood, national media provided audiences with a narration of polemic events that aimed to reinforce the audiences' sense of belonging to their own political camp and their rejection of the opposing camp as a danger to the nation. This polarization, which is a normal feature of politics, became intolerable when the middle ground, the shared narratives, were denied in media narratives. The Egyptian media's continuous attempts to frame the tumultuous political transition as a battle between those who are "with the state" and those who are against it encouraged a culture that excluded and repressed political opponents. It was especially detrimental to social cohesion, as it made the crucial task of building such common narratives of the transition not realistically possible.

Furthermore, the external pluralism of Arab national media postuprisings did not lead to a radical change in practices and behaviours of journalists, media stakeholders, and their audiences. In Milton's view, the so-called "institutional traces"[70] inherited from the former regimes are entrenched not only in media regulations but also in media practices and behaviours. The application of pluralism has to take into consideration this heritage and propose solutions that can fit with its particularities. For instance, in Tunisia, where an independent body was tasked with regulating the broadcast sector, one of the major challenges of future strategies is normalising the situation of media outlets that used to operate before the uprising and those that mushroomed after the uprising (and operating unlawfully) while preserving the pluralism of the new media landscape and its representation of various social groups and interests. A debate erupted on the potential impact of widening this external plurality on Tunisian audiences and on the political transition. For Hicham Snnousi, a member of the new regulator HAICA, the licensing process for new private media had to deal with a complex reality on the ground. He explains—

> *We were faced by two choices: keeping the media landscape as it used to be with its ideological and political bias or creating competition in the market by granting new licenses to prominent media projects enabling certain balance and diversity. We opted for the second choice.*[71]

This is an opinion which is not shared by all. Kamel Laabidi, former head of the consultative body that worked on media reform after the uprising, argued—

> *Granting licenses for audio visual stations that are linked to political or religious parties or groups could represent a fatal blow to the country's march toward democracy, especially if we consider what is happening in countries like Libya and Iraq.*[72]

Despite the adversarial and negative impact of "polarized pluralism",[73] this model is nevertheless crucial for audiences to understand the new political landscape, which is often complex and fast moving, and to make sense of important developments impacting their lives.[74] During periods of transition, both partisan and objective reporting is crucial to help audiences to engage politically while acknowledging the existence of a diversity of views and accepting their existence peacefully.[75] However, the predominance of partisan reporting over objective reporting in the national media post-uprising led to a plural but highly adversarial media landscape that acted—in the case of Egypt especially—as a ticking time-bomb that sabotaged the fragile democratic experiment (see Chap. 4 on the media elite and the relationship to the political sphere).

VII. "We Are Not Neutral": Professional Identity Shifts

The liberal model of journalism focuses on the role of media as a provider of unbiased information and watchdog of the authorities' policies and performances. Among the values most strongly advocated by this model, objectivity is considered "a cornerstone of the professional ideology of journalists in liberal democracies",[76] and accuracy is cherished as "the most sacred belief held among journalists worldwide".[77] The emancipatory model,[78] in contrast, rejects this balanced approach and advocates expressing bias in support of such universal values as human rights, gender equality, democracy, and peace.[79]

The narratives provided by journalists of their experiences post-uprising(s) reveal a hybridity of journalistic practices: journalists' exposure to these new models led to their "domestication" and integration into new traditions of production.[80] The preconditions of the political transition and the nature of former systems and institutions often shape emerging systems. Thus, these new traditions are quite often "unique types of media systems", a blend of features adopted from various models.[81] The living experiences of journalists interviewed demonstrate that they tend to adopt different models depending on the political developments and roles they are expected to perform in various situations. They describe themselves as monitoring the policies of new authorities and providing platforms for diverse views, while they also adopt an advocate-based reporting style urging their audiences to side with certain political and ideological camps. According to journalists' narratives, this bias was not a choice but rather an obligation, as they saw themselves primarily as citizens and only secondly as professionals.

It is important here to recognize the choices made by journalists in adopting and rejecting various models. Journalists don't operate in a vacuum. They are not immune to ideologies that shape the political sphere in which they operate; nor are they indifferent to the raging struggle between these ideologies, especially in times of transition. Political transitions in the so-called Arab Spring countries were—and remain—particularity tumultuous, with power struggles often taking a violent shape. Thus the importance of distinguishing between the two levels of news value—the professional, formal one and the ideological one connected to the political debate in which reporting takes place.[82] For instance, the prevalence of a populist style in reporting the post-coup in Egypt is mostly not imposed on journalists but rather largely embraced by them as the expression of their loyalty and support for the new regime against others who are presented as the enemies of the state.[83] The testimony of Yamina Fouati, a journalist from the Tunisian public news agency, is particularly relevant. Asked how she adapted to the impartial model of reporting after years of reporting with a bias in favour of the regime, she explains—

> *We are impartial since we report accurately on all important political parties and forces, but we are not neutral. For example, I choose the headline I find the most attractive, I give more visibility for a statement over another.*[84]

The journalistic community's willingness to rapidly submit to new political masters, shifting loyalties from one camp to another, was and still a major handicap. The temptation to serve the powerful is embedded in a longstanding perception of national media—especially state media—as a platform controlled by the state in the interest of "stability". These practices continued after the regime change: We see this in the Egyptian state television's reporting of the so-called Maspero demonstrations. In October 2011, security tanks violently dispersed mostly Coptic demonstrators, leaving dozens dead and hundreds wounded. The peaceful demonstrations were protesting the burning and destruction of a church by Islamic extremists.[85] The state television did not report on the demonstrators' murders, but rather that the Coptic demonstrators had been armed and attacked the soldiers; a state TV presenter called directly on audiences to take to the streets in support of the army.[86] The story of the violent clash during the demonstrations was largely reported by international media, supported by social media feeds, but ignored by state media. The coverage of the violent repression of pro-Muslim Brotherhood sit-ins in Cairo which led to the killing of nearly 1,000 people on August 14, 2013 is another prominent example. The crackdown on the Brotherhood supporters' camps which was described by Human Rights Watch as the most serious incident of mass killing in the modern history of Egypt was totally ignored by Egyptian media, state and private alike, in favour of talking about an attack by the Brotherhood supporters on the state.

The attempt by national media to consistently report on the democratization as a negative process, a threat to people's interests and to the national security, contributed to the erosion of the public support for the process. The nostalgia towards former regimes currently rife in "Arab Spring" countries can be explained by the disappointing outcome of these uprisings in improving the living conditions of citizens. However, this nostalgia is strongly nurtured by national media through the revival and recitation of the so-called "glories of the past", compared to the difficult present and a doubtful future.[87] This is very true of the Tunisian media, where the reference to the achievements under late President Habib Bourguiba were continuously revisited by media supporting a secularist agenda, in their portrayal of the perceived failures of the former governing coalition led by the Islamic *Ennahda*, in the context of the latest elections that brought the secularist *Nidaa Tunis* to power.

In addition to the many setbacks to the political transition, the chaotic media environment could be considered a main engine fuelling the popular disenchantment with the democratization process, given the extreme use of media platforms as a tool for political polarization, incitement, and hatred. It is argued that the forces that helped bring about revolutionary change are not necessarily supportive or conducive to the implementation of democratic values. By contrast with their role in helping weakening the autocratic regime, these forces can hinder the establishment of stable democratic institutions, thus ultimately sabotaging the fragile democratic gains.[88]

The example of Egyptian talk show scene is reflective of the scope of political manipulation of media and the negative impact this can produce on a fragile democratic process. The frequent statements of leading Egyptian journalists claiming openly that they are collaborating with the security services to the extent of taking directives from them, prove the danger of the decline of factual reporting in favour of political activism, especially when democratic values are facing a fierce crackdown. As press editorial writer and scholar Arthur Charity rightly observes regarding the conflict between neutrality and engagement in journalists' practices, "journalism should advocate democracy without advocating particular solutions".[89]

Conclusion

Democratization processes are open-ended transformations that are often marred by fierce conflicts and power struggles, including the struggle over national media. The attempt to import the liberal model of media and implement it in a media landscape that used to be widely manipulated by regimes quite often proves highly problematic in a new and fragile democracy. The excessive collusion between journalists in the so-called

Arab Spring countries and politicians exacerbates antagonisms, leading to the portrayal of the political adversary as the enemy and thus limiting the potential for a tolerant climate where diversity and dissension can coexist peacefully. Journalists rejected the role of political monitor in favour of serving as a political activist, under the idea that their identity as citizens superseded their role as journalists. This showcases the realistic limits of importing models, and the need to learn from failures and successes of similar transitional experiences.

Journalists reporting on the Arab transitions are not working in a political and ideological vacuum. The expectation that they will report in a fair and calm manner amid raging political and ideological struggles over the identity and shape of new regimes is not realistic. The vulnerability of their relationship to the political elites and their continuous swing between patterns of deference and opposition reflect their confusion with regard to their role in the political transition. It also indicates their inability to figure out a media democratization process that is equally important to the power struggle in the political arena. This media democratization was not a priority for politicians or for journalists themselves having to cope with an unpredictable and chaotic environment amidst political and economic uncertainty.

Beyond the legacy of former media regimes and the challenges of political transition, the choices made by the media reform organizations and leaders are major elements in shaping emerging media systems. The excessive focus on privatization and lack of consultative frameworks with journalists, as well as a lack of expertise in dealing with complex issues, made the reform process unplanned and in some cases cosmetic, leading to the adoption of contradictory features and trends. The relative success of Tunisian media reform is closely related to professional deliberation and inclusion of international expertise, along with sustained support from the civil society, which acted as a monitor and a safety valve for the process. While consultation with international media reform bodies and experts was very limited in cases of Egyptian and Libyan media reform, the sustained deliberation between the national Tunisian body tasked with media reform and international experts helped to support the reform process with lessons learned from those with similar experiences on how to adopt and implement best international practices.

Inspired by democratization scholar Laurence Whitehead's constructivist approach to democratization, Voltmer applies the same logic to establishing independent media in emerging democracies, asserting that "understanding the democratization of media institutions and journalism as social construction, i.e., as a process of collective (re)interpretation and continuous practice has far-reaching consequences for the policy choices that are made and the evaluation of outcomes".[90] It is indeed this conjunction between the new models, the heritage of the past and the particularities of conditions shaping current political transitions, that would define the nature of emerging media practices and models. This process is nevertheless still largely a work in progress for the so called Arab Spring countries.

NOTES

1. Richard Gunther and Anthony Mughan, "The Political Impact of the Media: A Reassessment," in Democracy and the Media: A Comparative Perspective, ed. Richard Gunther and Anthony Mughan (Cambridge: Cambridge University Press, 2000), 421.
2. Robert A. Dahl, Polyarchy: Participation and Opposition (New Haven, CT: Yale University Press, 1973).
3. Guillermo O'Donnell, "Illusions about Consolidation," Journal of Democracy 7, no. 2 (1996).
4. Andreas Schedler, Larry Diamond and Mark F. Plattner, The Self-Restraining State: Power and Accountability in New Democracies (US: Lynne Rienner, 1999).
5. Joseph A. Schumpeter, Capitalism, Socialism, and Democracy (New York: Harper and Brothers, 1942).
6. Gabriel Almond and Sidney Verba, The Civic Culture Revisited (London: Sage, 1989).
7. Laurence Whitehead, Democratization: Theory and Practice (Oxford, UK: Oxford University Press, 2002), 27.
8. Katrin Voltmer, The Media in Transitional Democracies (Cambridge, UK: Polity, 2013), 10.
9. Terry Lynn Karl and Philippe C. Schmitter, "Modes of Transition in Latin America, Southern and Eastern Europe," International Social Science Journal 128 (1991).
10. Katrin Voltmer, "The Media, Government Accountability, and Citizen Engagement," in Public Sentinel: News Media & Governance Reform, ed. Pippa Norris (Washington, DC: The World Bank, 1991).
11. *Democracy Reporting International* & *The Portuguese Institute of International Relations of the New University of Lisbon*, "Paths to Democracy in Europe, 1974–1991: An Overview," April 2011, accessed October 10, 2015, http://www.ipri.pt/images/publicacoes/working_paper/pdf/Transitions%20Report%20DRI_IPRI%202011.pdf.

12. *The RAND Corporation*, "Democratization in the Arab World: Prospects and Lessons from Around the Globe", 2012.
13. Valerie Bunce, "Comparative Democratization: Big and Bounded Generalizations," Comparative Political Studies 33 (2000).
14. George Lawson, "The Arab Uprisings: Revolution or Protests?," in After the Arab Spring: Power Shift in the Middle East?, IDEAS series, LSE, May 2012.
15. Katrin Voltmer, "The Media, Government Accountability, and Citizen Engagement".
16. See Daniel C. Hallin and Paolo Mancini, Comparing Media Systems: Three Models of media and politics (UK: Cambridge University Press, 2004); James Frank Hollifield and Calvin C. Jillson (ed.), Pathways to Democracy: The Political Economy of Democratic Transitions (London: Routledge, 2000); Guillermo O'Donnell G and Philippe C. Schmitter, Transition from Authoritarian Rule: Tentative Conclusions about Uncertain Democracies, (Baltimore, MD: John Hopkins University Press, 1986); Vicky Randall, "The Media and Democratization in the Third World," Third World Quarterly 14, no. 3 (1993).
17. Richard Gunther and Anthony Mughan, "The Political Impact of the Media: A Reassessment", 15.
18. Ibid.
19. Sheila S. Coronel, "The Role of the Media in Deepening Democracy," European Journal of Communication 2002, accessed October 10, 2015, http://unpan1.un.org/intradoc/groups/public/documents/un/unpan010194.pdf.
20. Carlos Barrera and Ricardo Zugasti, "The Role of the Press in Times of Transition: The Building of the Spanish Democracy (1975–78)," in Mass Media and Political Communication in New Democracies, ed. Katrin Voltmer (London: Routledge, 2006).
21. Richard Gunther and Anthony Mughan, "The Political Impact of the Media: A Reassessment."
22. Nael Jebril, Václav Štětka and Matthew Loveless, "Media and Democratisation: What is Known about the Role of Mass Media in Transitions to Democracy," Reuters Institute for the Study of Journalism, September 2013.
23. Richard Gunther and Anthony Mughan, "The Political Impact of the Media: A Reassessment", 421.
24. Daniel C. Hallin and Paolo Mancini, Comparing Media Systems: Three Models of Media and Politics.
25. These are: The polarised pluralist model (the Mediterranean countries), the democratic corporatist model (northern and central Europe) and the liberal model (North Atlantic countries).

26. Katrin Voltmer, Building Media Systems in the Western Balkans: Lost between Models and Realities (Sarajevo: Analitika – Center for Social Research, 2013).
27. Katrin Voltmer, "Comparing Media Systems in New Democracies: East Meets South Meets West," Central European Journal of Communication 1 (2008): 27.
28. Robert A. Hackett and Yuezhi Zhao, Democratizing Global Media: One World, Many Struggles (Lanham, MD: Rowman & Littlefield, 2005).
29. Jason William Boose, "Democratization and Civil Society: Libya, Tunisia and the Arab Spring," International Journal of Social Science and Humanity 2, no. 4 (2012), accessed October 10, 2015, http://www.ijssh.org/papers/116-CH317.pdf.
30. Shelley Deane, "Transforming Tunisia, the Role of Civil Society in Tunisia's Transition," *International Alert*, February 2013, accessed October 13, 2015, http://www.international-alert.org/sites/default/files/publications/Tunisia2013EN.pdf.
31. Katrin Voltmer, "Comparing Media Systems in New Democracies: East Meets South Meets West," 26.
32. *Northwestern University in Qatar*, "Media Use in the Middle East 2015, A Six Nation Survey," 2015, accessed December 3, 2015, http://www.mideastmedia.org/2015/chapter/key-indicators.html.
33. Sahar Khamis, "The Transformative Egyptian Media Landscape: Changes, Challenges and Comparative Perspectives," International Journal of Communication 5 (2011).
34. Tourya Guaaybess, "Conclusion," in National Broadcasting and State Policy in Arab Countries, ed. Tourya Guaaybess (Basingstoke: Palgrave Macmillan, 2013), 212.
35. Belkacem Mostefaoui, "Algerian Public Authorities in the Face of Transnational Media Competition: Between Status Quo and Deregulation," in National Broadcasting and State Policy in Arab Countries, ed. Tourya Guaaybess (Basingstoke: Palgrave Macmillan, 2013).
36. Shahira Amin, "Egypt's Post-revolution Media Vibrant but Partisan," *Index on Censorship*, May 2, 2013, accessed October 11, 2015, https://www.indexoncensorship.org/2013/05/egypts-post-revolution-media-vibrant-but-partisan/.
37. Julia Rozanova, "Public Television in the Context of Established and Emerging Democracies: Quo Vadis?," International Communication Gazette 69 no. 2 (2007): 134.
38. Pavel Stępka, "Public Service Broadcasting in Poland: Between Politics and Market," in Reinventing Public Service Communication: European Broadcasters and Beyond, ed. Petros Iosifidis (Basingstoke: Palgrave Macmillan, 2010); Mark Lengyel, "From 'State Broadcasting' to 'Public

Service Media' in Hungary," in Reinventing Public Service Communication: European Broadcasters and Beyond, ed. Petros Iosifidis (Basingstoke: Palgrave Macmillan, 2010); Julia Rozanova, "Public Television in the Context of Established and Emerging Democracies: Quo Vadis?".
39. Monroe E. Price, "Media Transitions in the Rear-View Mirror: Some Reflections", 490.
40. *Doha Centre for Media Freedom*, "Egypt Military Court Gives Journalist Suspended Jail term," November 4, 2013, accessed October 22, 2015, http://www.dc4mf.org/en/content/egypt-military-court-gives-journalist-suspended-jail-term.
41. *Reporters Without Borders*, "Journalists' Work Hampered by Abusive Prosecutions and Arrests," September 17, 2013, accessed October 22, 2015, https://rsf.org/en/news/journalists-work-hampered-abusive-prosecutions-and-arrests.
42. Tarek Amara, "Draft Security Law Raises Concerns about Rights in New Tunisia," *Reuters*, April 20, 2015, accessed October 20, 2015, http://www.reuters.com/article/us-tunisia-security-rights-idUSKBN0NB 11O20150420.
43. Sallie Hughes and Chappell Lawson, "The Barriers to Media Opening in Latin America," Political Communication 22 (2015): 11–12.
44. Ibid., 17.
45. Silvio Waisbord "The Pragmatic Politics of Media Reform: Media Movements and Coalition Building in Latin America," Global Media and Communication, 2010.
46. Ibid., 139.
47. Katrin Voltmer, "Political Communication between Democratization and the Trajectories of the Past," in Mass Media and Political Communication in New Democracies, ed. Katrin Voltmer (London/New York: Routledge, 2006).
48. John Stuart Mill, On Liberty (London: Penguin, 1859/1972).
49. Philip M. Napoli, "The Marketplace of Ideas Metaphor in Communications Regulation," Journal of Communication 49, no. 4 (1999).
50. Edward S. Herman and Noam Chomsky, Manufacturing Consent (London: Pantheon Books, 1988).
51. Colin Sparks, "Media and Transition in Latin America," Westminster Papers in Communication and Culture 8, no. 2 (2011).
52. Vaclav Štětka, "Media Ownership and Commercial Pressures," University of Oxford and London School of Economics and Political Science, September 2013, Media and Democracy in Central and Eastern Europe (Research Project); Ainius Lašas, "Political Culture," University of Oxford and London School of Economics and Political Science, September 2013, Media and Democracy in Central Eastern Europe; Henrik Örnebring,

Journalistic Autonomy and Professionalisation, University of Oxford and London School of Economics and Political Science, September 2013, Media and Democracy in Central and Eastern Europe.
53. Colin Sparks, "Media Systems in Transition: Poland, Russia, China," *Chinese Journal of Communication* 1, no. 1 (2008).
54. Hedwig De Smaele, "'In the Name of Democracy': The Paradox of Democracy and Press Freedom in Post-communist Russia," in Mass Media and Political Communication in New Democracies, ed. Katrin Voltmer (London: Routledge, 2006); Colin Sparks, "Media Systems in Transition: Poland, Russia, China."
55. Silvio R. Waisbord, "Latin America".
56. Sallies Hughes and Chappell Lawson, "The Barriers to Media Opening in Latin America," 14.
57. Lina Attalah and N. Rizk, "Egypt's Evolving Media Landscape: Access, Public Interest and Control," in A New Frontier, An Old Landscape, ed. Dixie Hawtin and Andrew Puddaphatt, (New York: Ford Foundation, 2011); Miriam Berger, "What's Next for Egypt's Military and Media Moguls?," *Atlantic Council*, April 28, 2015, accessed October 12, 2015, http://www.atlanticcouncil.org/blogs/menasource/what-s-next-for-egypt-s-military-and-media-moguls.
58. See a communique by HAICA on the process of regularization of TV and radio stations operating without a license or with provisory ones. http://haica.tn/fr/2014/09/delivrance-de-15-nouvelles-licences-et-regularisation-de-la-situation-de-12-etablissements-audiovisuels/.
59. Fatima El Issawi, "Egyptian Media Under Transition: In the Name of the Regime…in the Name of the People?," *POLIS*, London School of Economics and Political Science, 2014.
60. Interview with author, Cairo suburb, March 2013.
61. *Al-Araby Al-Jadeed*, "Egyptian TV Host Attacked for 'Insensitive' Show on Refugees," September 25, 2015, accessed November 10, 2015, https://www.alaraby.co.uk/english/blog/2015/9/25/egyptian-tv-host-attacked-for-insensitive-show-on-refugees.
62. Shahira Amin, "In Post-Morsi, Egypt Journalists Toe the Military Line or Self-censor," *Index on Censorship*, December 3, 2013, accessed October 20, 2015, http://www.indexoncensorship.org/2013/12/post-morsi-egypt-journalists-toe-military-line/.
63. Katrin Voltmer and Mansur Lalljee, "Agree to Disagree: Respect for Political Opponents," in British Social Attitudes: The 23rd Report, ed. Alison Park, John Curtice, Katarina Thomson, Miranda Phillips, and Mark Johnson (London: Sage, 2006/2007).
64. Silvio R. Waisbord, "In Journalism We Trust? Credibility and Fragmented Journalism in Latin America," in Mass Media and Political Communication in New Democracies, ed. Katrin Voltmer (London: Routledge, 2006).

65. Luigi Manca, "Journalism, Advocacy, and a Communication Model for Democracy," in Communication for and Against Democracy, ed. Marc Raboy and Peter Bruck (Montréal/NewYork: Black Red Rose Books, 1989).
66. Katrin Voltmer and Mansur Lalljee, "Agree to Disagree: Respect for Political Opponents".
67. Silvio R. Waisbord, "In Journalism We Trust? Credibility and Fragmented Journalism in Latin America".
68. Katrin Voltmer, "Building Media Systems in the Western Balkans Lost between Models and Realities", 28.
69. Katrin Voltmer, "Building Media Systems", Ibid., 25.
70. Andrew Milton, The Rational Politician: Exploiting the Media in New Democracies (Aldershot: Ashgate, 2000), 23.
71. Interview with author, Tunis, May 2015.
72. Ibid.
73. See Hallin and Mancini media systems.
74. Katrin Voltmer, "Building Media Systems in the Western Balkans Lost between Models and Realities".
75. Ibid.
76. Judith Lichtenberg, "In Defence of Objectivity Revisited," in Mass Media and Society, ed. James Curran and Michael Gurevitch (London, New York, Sydney, Auckland: Arnold, 1996), 225.
77. Kaarle Nordenstreng, 'The Journalist: a Walking Paradox', in The Democratization of Communication, ed. Philip Lee, (Cardiff: University of Wales Press, 1995), 115.
78. Johan Galtung, Peace by Peaceful Means: Peace and Conflict, Development and Civilization (London: Sage, 1996); Hemant Shah, "Modernization, Marginalization and Emancipation: Toward a Normative Model of Journalism and National Development," Communication Theory 2 (1996).
79. Jan. Servaes, Communication for Development. One World, Multiple Cultures (Cresskill, NJ: Hampton Press, 1999).
80. Katrin Voltmer, "Building Media Systems in the Western Balkans: Lost between Models and Realities", 13.
81. Katrin Voltmer, "Comparing Media Systems in New Democracies: East Meets South Meets West", 37.
82. Stuart Hall, "The Determination of News Photographs," in The Manufacture of News: Social Problems, Deviance and the Mass Media, ed. Stanley Cohen and Jock Young, (London: Constable, 1973).
83. Fatima El Issawi, "The Role of Egyptian Media in the Coup," in IEMed Mediterranean Yearbook 2014, ed. European Institute of the Mediterranean (Barcelona: European Institute of the Mediterranean, 2014).

84. Interview with author, Tunis, May 2015.
85. Ishak Ibrahim, "Three Years After the Mapero Massacre: Where is the Justice?," *The Tahrir Institute for Middle East Policy*, September 10, 2014, accessed November 10, 2015, http://timep.org/commentary/three-years-maspero-massacre-justice/.
86. Sherif Younis, "The Maspero Massacre: The Military, the Media, and the 1952 Cairo Fire as Historical Blueprint," *Jadaliya*, October 17, 2012, accessed October 10, 2013, http://www.jadaliyya.com/pages/index/2882/-the-maspero-massacre_the-military-the-mediaand-t.
87. Mohammed Dhia Hammami, "Essebsi and Tunisia: The Nostalgia for Past Glories," *Al-Araby Al-Jadeed*, December 15, 2014, accessed September 10, 2015, https://www.alaraby.co.uk/english/politics/2014/12/20/essebsi-and-tunisia-the-nostalgia-for-past-glories.
88. Lance W. Bennett, "The Media and Democratic Development: The Social Basis of Political Communication," in Communicating Democracy, The Media and Political Transitions, ed. Patrick H. O'Neil (Boulder: Lynne Rienner, 1998), 201.
89. Arthur Charity, Doing Public Journalism (New York: Guildford, 1995), 144.
90. Katrin Voltmer, "Building Media Systems in the Western Balkans", 15.

Conclusions

In a commentary published in October 2015 by an Egyptian newspaper,[1] a young Egyptian journalist, Mohamed el Khawli, struggles to explain the reasons behind the current degradation in ethical practices within the Egyptian journalistic community. Ultimately he blames his senior colleagues, framing them as insufficient role models for his generations, writing, "we were educated at the hands of half journalists who were half in everything: in talents, in generosity, even in ethics, we watched them giving everything for money, for fame, for a meeting with a president, for a trip with a businessman in his private jet". He concludes by attempting to take at least some responsibility: "The profession was lost because no one was looking to find it".

The example of "half journalists" described by this young journalist in his perception of senior colleagues reflects the dichotomies detailed in this book between the many conflicting roles and identities journalists embed simultaneously in their perceptions of their professional duties: the reporter, the watchdog, the activist, the mouthpiece, the preacher of the public opinion, the persona, among others. Their restless swings between conflicting missions make them—senior staff and novices and everyone in between—a collection of many halves trying to reconcile with not much success.

The journalists I interviewed about their practices reporting on the political transitions taking place throughout the Arab world revealed multiple layers of struggle in the quest of independence: endemic obsolete structures, lack of agreement on editorial standards, and imbalanced relationships with the political sphere. They described diffuse barriers—blurred lines between facts and opinions, informing and advocating, television stars and reporters—and seemingly impassable gulfs, like the wide gap between leading and junior journalists, and deep divisions driven by socio-economic and gender inequalities. In her book *Transformations in Egyptian Journalism,* written after the 2011 uprising, Naomi Sakr describes "many long suppressed rifts between opposing traditions"[2] within the Egyptian journalistic community, spanning various fields such as accuracy, relationship to the security apparatus, and opinions versus facts. However, these rifts, which are not specific to Egyptian journalists, are neither sustainable within newsrooms nor conducive to in-depth debate on how to resolve conflicts between opposing traditions. With revolutionary zeal fading, journalists are back to their old traditions of obedience, with the value of "patriotism" having the upper hand over that of investigating regimes' wrongdoing and factual reporting. A large number of journalists interviewed perceive their identity as citizens first and professionals second: The call of the "national duty" is stronger than the demand for the professional discipline.

After the uprisings, media democratization did not garner the support of new regimes or journalists themselves. My field research indicates that the engagement of the media community in the process of media democratization is somehow limited. It was largely perceived by journalists as a unrealistic goal, and also a less pressing battle than the power struggle over shaping new regimes. A large number of journalists interviewed were suspicious of media democratization successfully preceding the building of a political democracy; their doubts are echoed by scholars and researchers who have yet to reach consensus on this issue. As Jakubowicz stresses, "whether mass media lead or follow change, whether they mirror or mold society, and whether they should be conceptualized as agents of change or of the status quo have yet to be resolved".[3]

During political transitions, we expect the national media to be at the centre of the struggle over what values should be promoted in the new society. How to achieve goals like national unity, political stability, economic development, and others is not necessarily a matter of consensus between new political parties and civil forces, assuming they can agree on these goals in the first place. The use of national media post-uprising(s) as a tool for promoting political forces' agendas exacerbated a fragmented and adversarial media landscape.[4] The national media frequently framed transitional dilemmas and divisions as a struggle between good and bad citizens, those who fit with the perceived definition of national identity and those who did not, making it difficult for consensus to triumph over conflict.

I would like to stress here again the crucial importance of agonistic public spaces in transitional contexts, in both political and media cultures. As professor of political theory Chantal Mouffe[5] contends, the main role of a democracy should be to revert antagonistic conflicts (whereby the ideological other is considered as an enemy that can be legitimately destroyed) into agonistic conflicts (whereby the other is seen as an adversary with the legitimacy to exist, but also to disagree with). Political transitions in the so-called Arab Spring countries are rife with antagonism, voiced but also fuelled by a politically charged and biased media discourse. Many of the journalists I interviewed arrived at the same question (and shared the same concern): Is it realistic to expect media to provide an agonistic discourse with the aim of fostering critical practices needed for a thriving democracy, when the political arena is rejecting the "other" through all available tools and tactics? Can we expect media to assume its "ideal" role in stable democracies, namely, encouraging informed decisions and fostering debate, in the context of emerging democracies, where navigating choppy transitional waters is a risky and unpredictable exercise? Is this "ideal" role for national media realistic even in established democracies?

The answer from journalists' experiences was a discordant one: While they had to cope with particularity fluid and complex transitional itineraries, journalists were deeply engaged in supporting parochial interests, threatening to erode nascent democratic institutions instead of consolidating them. The excessive collusion between journalists and political elites both new and old had a contradictory impact on journalists' status. Journalists individually felt empowered via their political activism in the service of ideological camps, but their involvement with these camps reduced them again to political mouthpieces, a role to which they are accustomed through decades of submission to political power. It is also a role they rebelled against in the initial phases following the uprising(s), when they managed to attain some professional dignity and public recognition.

Mouffe's notion of the agonistic public space does not negate the conflictual and passionate nature of the political. On the contrary, conflicts should be allowed to take shape in society without being eliminated in favour of consensus. In that sense, "pacification is not repressing conflict but it is giving conflict the possibility to take shape in a legitimate way without destroying the political association".[6] The role of media is essential in allowing dissension to take place and to gain visibility without leading to destructive antagonism.

After the uprisings, national traditional media managed for a limited time to become a "site of contestation"[7], allowing diverse and conflicting views and accounts of the transition to coexist while avoiding destructive antagonisms. This was heralded as indicative of authentic change in media practices and values amongst these journalists. However, we now see this change is best defined as temporary momentum that could not solidify into new traditions. We can recognize these journalists as examples of what Hallin and Mancini call the "polarized pluralist"[8] model, with their bias in favour of their political and ideological friends represented by the feature Hallin and Mancini refer to as "political parallelism". However, as Voltmer rightly observes, the crucial feature of this model "is not the existence of political parallelism, but a degree of polarisation that leads to a dominance of centrifugal forces over the ability to maintain common grounds for a shared sense of citizenship".[9] It is that extremely high level of polarization that took national media hostage, leading to the erosion of diversity and the triumph of a blunt, unilateral narrative in support of new rulers.

In the immediate aftermath of the uprisings, the community of journalists and media development agents were eager to implement a "watchdog" model for national media, identifying journalists as the monitors of governments and society.[10] The experiences of journalists interviewed demonstrate that the shift towards investigative reporting was largely unsuccessful. Many factors impeded the success of such a transformation: poor journalistic skills and the reluctance of media owners and managers to invest in professional training, the shaky working conditions for journalists frequently facing physical attacks and legal intimidation, lack of job security, the weakness or absence of professional syndicates, the divide between the elite and junior staff, and finally the excessive dependency on social media feeds in breaking news stories, often without verification. While a sudden and rapid shift from a controlled, obedient media to a "watchdog" media proved unrealistic, a gradual approach, defining quality and acceptable standards of partisan reporting, could have been more successful.[11] Instead of struggling to implement models that cannot fit with the local particularities and the nature of a tumultuous political transition, it would be more efficient to encourage debate regarding the quality standards that media should be held to, in order to accommodate both political bias and the core values of the Western model, such as accuracy and fairness in representing conflicting views.[12]

The model of external pluralism has effectively secured a diversity of views on media platforms; however, it is not the only pathway effective in achieving this goal, and it wasn't particularly successful in this region. While private media contributed to the diversification of media content, these new ventures fall strictly into two camps: media conglomerations owned by wealthy businessmen linked to political agendas, or poorly staffed and funded small media outlets struggling to sustain their operations. The endemic wealth inequalities, a reality which was not addressed by post-uprising(s) regimes, perpetuated this situation in which media is concentrated in the hands of powerful economic players who often support the rulers and benefit from their support in various forms like receiving advertising revenue and state subsidies. While Libya was praised for relinquishing state control over media, this was not effective media liberalization. Rather, it left the media vulnerable to political and tribal groups using tactics similar to those used by the Gaddafi regime.

The immense obstacles that hinder the process of transforming the redundant state-owned media into a provider of quality public service information gave weight to voices calling for postponing this project or even selling the redundant structures to private stakeholders. However, opening up the private media sector cannot replace the pivotal role played by an independent and efficient public media in providing a non-market-driven output and assuring a fair representation of various voices in the public realm. Public media contributes to creating social cohesion and counter-balances the excesses of private media; these contributions are even more necessary during tumultuous times of political transition. The relative success of the process of reforming Tunisian state media supports this thesis. However, the lack of an institutional framework to protect this reform and embed it in practice, independent from journalists' personal choices or the impact of the political environment, leaves it in a state of extreme fragility.

For media reforms to be sustainable, they need to be embedded in collective deliberations and legitimized by the public as a gradual process, instead of a temporary cosmetic change.[13] This collective deliberation was lacking from the media reform process in Egypt and Libya, processes that remained largely isolated and missing popular legitimacy. The Tunisian media reform is indicative of the positive contributions of civil society groups in providing legitimacy for this process and protecting it from government attempts to stall and re-impose control over national media. Where the reform process managed to take some institutional shape by involving civil forces, the media's dependency on politics declined or at least lessened, leaving a more balanced relationship between the media and political actors. However, this institutionalisation could not operate as a safety valve to protect independent media practices; the excessive misuse of the judiciary as a prominent tool to muzzle critics, and the heavy arsenal of anti-terror laws with opaque definitions and scopes, threaten to erode hard-won gains in freedom of the press.[14] Journalists in the three countries covered by this research still work in the confines of restrictive regulatory and structural frameworks. As demonstrated by my interviews with journalists, regulatory reform—when it happened at all—did not positively impact media practices, as these reforms were negated by the political and judicial treatment of critical reporting along with militias' hegemony (Libya) and the surge of influence of security services and the Ministry of the Interior in media dictates (Egypt).

Journalists I interviewed struggled to perceive themselves as a community independent from the political sphere, with specific interests and needs that can conflict with those of political and ideological camps. However, it is hard to talk about a unified community of journalists. The divisions amongst the members of this community are multi-layered, and professional syndicates and representative groups seem unable to assume an effective leading role in fostering cohesion and establishing professional standards. The large disparity of financial privilege and editorial power between the "elite" journalists (often enjoying solid connections with political and economic elites,) and the rest (facing vulnerable working conditions,) exacerbates the weakness of journalists' struggle for independence from the political sphere and for the trust of their audience. These media "stars", having allowed their political loyalties to subsume professional ethics, are causing serious professional setbacks.

Gunther and Mughan have described mass media as being the "connective tissue of democracy".[15] While the debate on whether media reform can precede political reform remains unresolved, it is hard to imagine a sustainable process of institutional building taking place while national media is demonising any dissent. Questions on whether the process of media reform should start from professional training and awareness or from regulatory and structural change neglect the fact that both are equally and crucially needed in order to achieve meaningful progress. Neglecting one field while waiting to achieve progress in another has thus far proved ineffective.

As this study demonstrates, effective media reform requires inclusive cultural change, encompassing media practices, newsrooms dynamics, regulatory and structural frameworks, and political and judicial traditions regarding critical media. In her definition of media reform, Rozumilowicz[16] talks about legal and institutional as well as social-cultural support. The first set of supports include passing relevant laws, such as those guaranteeing free access to information and organizing ownership and licensing. The second set involves professional training and values awareness, not only for media professionals but also for the politicians dealing with them.

Lessons from the experiences of the media democratization of the so-called Arab Spring countries indicate that constitutional and regulatory change is not effective without both a change in practices and a response to existing traditions dealing with critical media. These lessons also prove that professional training based on imported models is not efficient unless it is tailored to answer the particular needs of the journalistic community. Training must take into consideration the national context, the inherited media system, and the historical circumstances of the political transition, which is often tumultuous and not immune to a surge in autocratic practices. The reform process will fall short of its goals if it neglects the crucial task of empowering the journalistic community to craft a new identity, encouraging a gradual move towards monitoring regimes' policies in the name of the public's right to accurate, inclusive, and diverse information.

The current degradation of media ethics, witnessed especially in the cases of Libya and Egypt, should be a wake-up call to the journalistic community. With the extreme instrumentalization of media platforms, it is not only the culture of diversity and fairness that is severely threatened, but also the profession itself, which is in danger of being hijacked in the name of "patriotism" by fuelling destructive populism. As el Khawli, the young journalist to whom I referred at the beginning of this chapter, described, the profession indeed needs to be found. For that to happen, journalists and all related stakeholders must recognize the crucial need to find it and to redefine it, not only for the sake of creating democratic media and state building but also for the future of the journalistic profession itself.

Notes

1. Mohamed el Khawli, "On the 'Usurped' Profession," *Tahrir Newspaper*, October 21, 2015, accessed October 30, 2015 http://www.tahrirnews.com/posts/323686/%D8%B9%D9%86-%D8%A7%D9%84%D9%85%D9%87%D9%86%D8%A9-%C2%AB%D8%A7%D9%84%D9%85%D8%BA%D8%AA%D8%B5%D8%A8%D8%A9%C2%BB. (Arabic)
2. Naomi Sakr, Transformations in Egyptian Journalism (London: I.B. Tauris, 2013), 89.
3. Karl Jakubowicz, "Media in Transition: The Case of Poland," in Media Reform: Democratizing the Media, Democratizing the State, ed. Monroe E. Price, Beata Rozumilowicz and Stefaan G. Verhulst (London: Routledge, 2002).
4. See Katrin Voltmer, "Comparing Media Systems in New Democracies: East Meets South Meets West," Central European Journal of Communication 1 (2008).
5. See Chantal Mouffe, On the Political (London: Routledge, 2005).
6. Ibid., 973.
7. Patrick McConnell and Lee Becker, "The Role of the Media in Democratization," Paper presented to the Political Communication Section of the International Association for Media and Communication Research at the Barcelona Conference, July 2002, P2, http://www.grady.uga.edu/coxcenter/activities/Act_2001_to_2002/Materials01-02/DemocratizationIAMCRJuly2002.pdf.
8. Daniel C. Hallin and Paolo Mancini, Comparing Media Systems: Three Models of Media and Politics (Cambridge: Cambridge University Press, 2004).
9. Katrin Voltmer, Building Media Systems in the Western Balkans: Lost between Models and Realities (Sarajevo: Analitika – Center for Social Research, 2013), 18.
10. James Curran, "Rethinking Media as a Public Sphere," in Communication and Citizenship, ed. Peter Dahlgren and Colin Sparks (London: Routledge, 1991).
11. Katrin Voltmer, "Building Media Systems in the Western Balkans: Lost between Models and Realities", 28.
12. Ibid.
13. Laurence Whitehead, Democratization: Theory and Experience (Oxford: Oxford University Press, 2002).
14. See the report by Committee to Protect Journalists on the deterioration of media rights and freedoms in light of anti-terror new legislations in Tunisia, https://www.cpj.org/reports/2015/10/in-tunisia-press-freedom-erodes-amid-security-fear.php.

15. Richard Gunther and Anthony Mughan, Democracy and Media: A Comparative Perspective (Cambridge: Cambridge University Press, 2000).
16. Beate Rozumilowicz, "Democratic Change: A Theoretical Perspective," in Media Reform, ed. Monroe E. Price, Beate Rozumilowicz and Stefaan G. Verhulst (London: Routledge, 2002).

Selected Bibliography

Ayish, Muhammad. "Political Communication on Arab World Television: Evolving Patterns." *Political Communication* 2 (2002): 37–154.

Bayat, Asef. *Life as Politics: How Ordinary People Change the Middle East*. Stanford: Stanford University Press, 2013.

Brown, Nathan. "Can the Colossus Be Salvaged? Egypt's State-Owned Press in a Post-Revolutionary Environment." *Carnegie Endowment for International Peace*, August 22, 2011.

Carpentier, Nico. "Identity, Contingency and Rigidity. The (Counter-) Hegemonic Constructions of the Identity of the Media Professional." *Journalism* 6, no. 2 (2005): 199–219.

Christians, Clifford G., and others. *Normative Theories of the Media, Journalism in Democratic Societies*. Urbana: University of Illinois Press, 2009.

Cottle, Simon. "Media and the Arab Uprisings of 2011: Research Notes." *Journalism* 12, no. 5 (2011): 647–659.

Curran, James. "Mass Media and Democracy: A Reappraisal." In *Mass Media and Society*, edited by James Curran and Michael Gurevitch, 82–117. London: E. Arnold, 1991.

Curran, James. "Rethinking the Media as a Public Sphere." In *Communication and Citizenship: Journalism and the Public Sphere*, edited by Peter Dahlgren and Colin Sparks, 26–58. London: Routledge, 1991.

Eickelman, Dale F., and Jon W. Anderson. *New Media in the Muslim World: The Emerging Public Sphere*. Indiana: Indiana University Press, 2003.

El Issawi, Fatima. "Tunisian Media in Transition." *Carnegie Endowment for International Peace*, Washington, DC, 2012.

El Issawi, Fatima. "Transitional Libyan Media: Free at Last?" *Carnegie Endowment for International Peace*, Washington, DC, 2013a.

El Issawi, Fatima. "Libya Media Transition: Heading to the Unknown." *POLIS*, London School of Economics and Political Science, London, 2013b.

El Issawi, Fatima. "The Role of Egyptian Media in the Coup." In *IEMed Mediterranean Yearbook 2014*, edited by The European Institute of the Mediterranean. Barcelona, Spain, 2014a.

El Issawi, Fatima. "Egyptian Media Under Transition: In the Name of the Regime...In the Name of the People?" *POLIS*, London School of Economics, London, 2014b.

El Issawi, Fatima and Bart Cammaerts. "Shifting Journalistic Roles in Democratic Transitions: Lessons from Egypt." *Journalism* (2016): 1–18.

El-Nawawy, Mohammed and Sahar Khamis. "Cyberactivists Paving the Way for the Arab Spring: Voices from Egypt, Tunisia and Libya." *CyberOrient* 6, no. 2 (2012).

Gunther, Richard and Anthony Mughan. "The Political Impact of the Media: A Reassessment." In *Democracy and the Media: A Comparative Perspective*, edited by Richard Gunter and Anthony Mughan, 402–448. Cambridge: Cambridge University Press, 2000.

Halimi, Serge. *Les nouveaux chiens de garde* [The New Watchdogs]. Paris: Liber-Raisons D'Agir, 1997.

Hallin, Daniel and Paolo Mancini. *Comparing Media Systems: Three Models of Media and Politics*. New York: Cambridge University Press, 2004.

Hollifield, James Frank and Calvin C. Jillson, eds. *Pathways to Democracy: The Political Economy of Democratic Transitions*. London: Routledge, 2000.

Howard, Philipp N. *The Digital Origins of Dictatorship and Democracy: Information Technology and Political Islam*. Oxford: Oxford University Press, 2011.

Hughes, Sallie and Chappell Lawson. "The Barriers to Media Opening in Latin America." *Political Communication* 22, no. 1 (2005): 9–25.

Jakubowicz, Karol. "PSB 3.0: Reinventing European PSB." In *Reinventing Public Service Communication: European Broadcasters and Beyond*, edited by Petros Iosifidis, 9–22. Basingstoke: Palgrave Macmillan, 2010.

Karl, Terry L., and Philipp Schmitter. "Modes of Transition in Latin America, Southern and Eastern Europe." *International Social Science Journal* 128 (1991): 267–282.

Khamis, Sahar. "The Transformative Egyptian Media Landscape: Changes, Challenges and Comparative Perspectives." *International Journal of Communications* 5 (2011): 1159–1177.

Khamis, Sahar and Katherine Vaughn. "Cyberactivism in the Egyptian Revolution: How Civic Engagement and Citizen Journalism Tilted the Balance." *Arab Media & Society* 13 (2011).

Kraidy, Marwan M. "Media Industries in Revolutionary Times." *Media Industries* 1, no. 2 (2014).
Lawson, George. "The Arab Uprisings: Revolution or Protests?" In *After the Arab Spring: Power Shift in the Middle East?* IDEAS series, IDEAS, London School of Economics, 2012.
Lefebvre, Henri. *The Production of Space*. Cambridge, MA: Blackwell, 1991.
Lichter, Robert, Stanley Rothman, and Linda S. Lichter. *The Media Elite*. Chevy Chase, MD: Adler & Adler, 1986.
Martin, Fiona and Gregory Ferrell Lowe. "The Value and Values of Public Service Media." In *The Value of Public Service Media*, edited by Gregory Ferrell Lowe and Fiona Martin, 19–42. Göteborg: Nordicom, 2014.
Mendel, Toby. "Political and Media Transitions in Egypt: A Snapshot of Media Policy and Regulatory Environment." *Internews*, 2011. Accessed September 11, 2015. http://www.internews.org/sites/default/files/resources/Internews_Egypt_MediaLawReview_Aug11.pdf
Milton, Andrew. *The Rational Politician: Exploiting the Media in New Democracies*. Aldershot: Ashgate, 2000.
Mouffe, Chantal. *On the Political*. London: Routledge, 2005.
Mouffe, Chantal and Ernesto Laclau. *Hegemony and Socialist Strategy: Towards a Radical Democratic Politics*. London: Verso, 1985.
O'Donnell, Guillermo and Philippe C. Schmitter. *Transition from Authoritarian Rule: Tentative Conclusions About Uncertain Democracies*. Baltimore, MD: John Hopkins University Press, 1986.
Price Monroe E., and Marc Raboy, eds. *Public Service Broadcasting in Transition: A Documentary Reader*. Oxford: Programme in Comparative Media Law and Policy for the European Institute for the Media, 2001.
Randall, Vicky. "The Media and Democratization in the Third World." *Third World Quarterly* 14, no. 3 (1993): 625–646.
Rieffel, Remy. *L'elite des journalistes: Les herauts de l'information* [Journalists' Elite]. Paris: Sociologie D'Aujourd'hui, 1984.
Rieffel, Remy. *Que sont les médias?* [What Are the Media?]. Paris: Gallimard, 2005.
Rozanova, Julia. "Public Television in the Context of Established and Emerging Democracies: Quo Vadis?" *International Communication Gazette* 69, no. 2 (2007): 129–147.
Sakr, Naomi. *Transformations in Egyptian Journalism*. London: I.B. Tauris, 2013.
Siebert, Fred S., Theodore Peterson, and Wilbur Schramm. *Four Theories of the Press*. Urbana, IL: University of Illinois Press, 1956.
Waisbord, Silvio. "The Mass Media and Consolidation of Democracy in South America." *Research in Political Sociology* 7 (1995): 207–227.
Waisbord, Silvio. "In Journalism We Trust? Credibility and Fragmented Journalism in Latin America." In *Mass Media and Political Communication in New Democracies*, edited by Katrin Voltmer, 76–91. Abingdon: Routledge, 2006.

Waisbord, Silvio. *Reinventing Professionalism: Journalism and News in Global Perspective*. Cambridge: Polity Press, 2013.
Whitehead, Laurence. *Democratization: Theory and Practice*. Oxford: Oxford University Press, 2002.
Voltmer, Katrin. "Comparing Media Systems in New Democracies: East Meets South Meets West." *Central European Journal of Communication* 1 (2008): 23–40.
Voltmer, Katrin. "The Media, Government Accountability, and Citizen Engagement." In *Public Sentinel: News Media & Governance Reform*, edited by Pippa Norris, 137–159. Washington, DC: The World Bank, 2010.
Voltmer, Katrin. *The Media in Transitional Democracies*. Cambridge: Polity, 2013.
Voltmer, Katrin. *Building Media Systems in the Western Balkans: Lost Between Models and Realities*. Sarajevo: Analitika—Center for Social Research, 2013.
Zayani, Mohamed. *The Al Jazeera Phenomenon: Critical Perspectives on New Arab Media*. London: Pluto Press, 2005.

INDEX

A
activism
 cyber activism, 129–46
 journalism and, 60
 patriotic activism, 62, 140
advocacy journalism, 59. *See also*
 journalism
Agency for External Communications,
 15, 16
Ahram Online, 134
al Assema (TV network), 56
"Al Gad" project (Libya), 32
al-Jazeera network, 76, 141
al-Libiyya (TV network), 32, 105,
 117, 118
al-Masry al-Yom newspaper, 74, 75,
 134, 141, 145
Almond, Gabriel, 173n6
al-Rasmiya (TV network), 105, 117
Al-Shams (newspaper), 137
al-Wafd (newspaper), 91
al-Wataniya (TV network),
 105, 113, 118
Amamou, Slim, 133
Amer, Sherif, 82, 91

Amin, Tamer, 60, 82
Amir, Issam el, 62
An-Nahar (TV network), 86, 87,
 89, 165
Annashra al Ekhbariyya news bulletin,
 116 (*see also* Muslim
 Brotherhood)
anti-terror laws, 14, 21–3, 31,
 37, 161, 186
Arab Spring, 2, 3, 9n1, 48, 50, 57,
 99, 101, 121, 141, 145, 147n1,
 160, 163, 164, 166, 169, 170,
 172, 173, 183, 187
Arfawi, Amira, 58, 111, 115
Assabah (newspaper), 106, 133
autocracy, 2, 8, 72, 74, 89, 90,
 122, 132
Ayari, Yassin, 134
Ayish, Muhammad, 11n20, 69n57,
 93n24, 132

B
Bahgat, Hossam, 31, 44n90, 143
Baio, Mohamed, 109

Bani Walid, 55, 67n31, 142, 150n55
Barrera, Carlos, 174n20
BBC network, 113, 141
Beaumont, Peter, 147n7
Beckett, Charlie, 147n8
Ben Abdullah, Rafic, 106, 133
Ben Ali, Zine El Abidine, 14–16, 23, 39n3, 54, 102, 109–11, 115, 120, 131, 133, 135, 161
Ben Hamida, Sofian, 53, 110
Ben Letaief, Mustapha, 112, 113
Ben Mhenni, Lina, 148n27
Berger, Miriam, 150n57, 177n57
Berger, Peter, 66n15
bias, 2, 52, 60, 136, 138, 167–70, 184
bloggers, 8, 34, 130, 132–5, 137, 145, 149n30. *See also* journalism; social media
Boose, Jason William, 175n29
Bosnia, 167
Bourguiba, Habib, 171
Bour, Hamida el, 112, 113
Bulgaria, 101, 160
Bunce, Valerie, 174n13

C
Carpentier, Nico, 65n7
CBC (TV network), 59, 81, 84, 90
censorship
   self-censorship, 5–7, 13, 32, 34, 48, 55, 62, 99, 132, 140, 143, 144, 161
   state, 119
Chadwick, Andrew, 66n13
Chalaby, Jean K., 123n5
Charity, Arthur, 171, 179n90
Chile, 156
Chrisafis, Angelique, 149n30
CNN network, 43n67, 131, 141

collective deliberations, 49, 185
Committee for Supporting and Encouraging the Press (CESP, Libya), 33, 105, 120
constitutional reforms, 21, 155, 162
Coptic Christians, 79
Coronel, Sheila S., 174n19
Cottle, Simon, 9n1, 131, 147n2, 147n11, 148n13
Croatia, 101, 160
Curran, James, 10n12, 10n18, 67n39, 178n77, 188n10
cyber activism, 129–51
cybersecurity, 144

D
Dahl, Robert A., 173n2
Dakhli, Leyla, 147n12
Daley, Suzanne, 67n25
Davidson, Amy, 93n27
Dawoud, Khaled, 68n50, 92n14
Deane, Shelley, 175n30
Deeb, Farid al, 75
democratic corporatist model of journalism, 49. *See also* journalism
democratization
   democracy and, 154–5
   independent media and, 158–60
   media diversity and, 158, 166–8
   overview, 153–4
   privatization of media, 158, 162–6
   professional identity shifts, 158, 169–71
   regulatory reform, 160–2
   role of media and, 156–8
   state-owned media and, 158, 159
Diab, Salah, 74, 75, 92n14
Diftar, Manal el, 59
Dubai, 9n3
Dutton, William, 140

E

Ecuador, 156
Egypt
  centralised control, 24–5
  consitution in theory and practice, 28–31
  Egyptian Radio and Television Union (ERTU), 24, 26, 103, 104
  Egyptian Space Channel (ESC), 25
  General Authority for Investment (GAFI), 26
  Journalists' Syndicate Law, 26, 27
  legal arsenal, 26–8
  media reforms, 23–31
  old media, 24–5
  press, 87
  privatization, 25–6
  regulatory change, 187
  Supreme Press Council, 24, 42n53, 103
  talk shows, 4, 7, 71, 76, 77, 80–8, 171
Eickelman, Dale F., 147n3
elites, media and
  alliance with regimes, 72–4
  French, 72
  Hadidi, Lamees el, 81, 84–5
  Issa, Ibrahim, 87–8
  Moussa, Ahmed, 82–4
  overview, 71–2
  Saad, Mahmoud, 82, 85–7
  talk shows, 74–7
  UK, 92n5
  US, 73
  watchdog/activist identity, 78–80
Emary, Naglaa el, 144, 151n63
Ennahda Movement, 60
Essebsi, Beji Caid, 61
Establishment, The (Jones), 73, 92n4
Ezzat, Ahmed, 150n60

F

Facebook, 77, 130–2, 134, 140–3, 145
Fahita, Abla, 91
Fahmy, Hala, 116
Fahmy, Jamal, 51
Fargali, Riad, 135
Febrayer (newspaper), 111, 136
Field, Nathan, 93n16
Fouati, Yamina, 170
Fouda, Yosri, 78, 81, 94n40, 139
Freedman, Des, 92n8
Freedom House, 34, 35, 43n69, 45n97, 46n113, 67n34, 128n92
freedom of expression, 8, 17, 20, 21, 23, 26, 28, 33, 37, 39n18, 112, 154, 161

G

Gaddafi, Muammar, 32, 55, 58, 105, 109, 136, 142, 153, 160
Gaddafi, Saif al-Islam, 32
Gafsa mining basin revolts, 131
General Authority for Investment (GAFI), 26
Ghidawi, Hamady, 112, 113
Ghonim, Wael, 77, 130, 147n6
Ghourab, Hazem, 143
Gingsley, Patrick, 147n6
Great Fateh Revolution, 34
Gresh, Alain, 91, 98n81
Guerfali, Riad, 133
Gunther, Richard, 173n1, 174n17, 174n21, 174n23, 186, 189n15

H

Habbas, Zeinab al, 111
Hackett, Robert A., 175n28
Haddad, Khaled, 133

Hadidi, Lamees el, , 81, 84–5, 95n56, 96n57
HAICA, 16, 18–21, 38, 40n24, 61, 63, 102, 127n67, 165, 168, 177n58
Hajjaji, Mariyam al, 119, 135
Halimi, Serge, 72, 92n1
Hallin, Daniel C., 11n28, 49, 57, 66n9, 73, 92n10, 157, 174n16, 174n24, 184, 188n8
Hamdy, Ahmad, 52, 110
Hamdy, Naila Nabil, 69n63, 131, 148n15
Hamida, Sofian Ben, 53, 110
Hammi, Emma el, 149n29
Hargreaves, Heap, 123n2
Hassan, Mostapha, 124n28
Hawari, Mohamed, 141, 142, 145
Henawy, Azza el, 90
Hendawi, Hamza, 97n77
Herzegovina, 167
Hinnebusch, Raymond, 69n66
Howard, Phillipp N., 147n4, 148n19
Hughes, Sallie, 69n68, 162, 176n43
Human Rights Watch, 41n49, 43n79, 44n86, 170
Huna el Assima (talk show), 84

I
Ibrashi, Wael al, 82
impartiality, 20, 36, 57, 60, 100, 101, 160
"institutional traces", 167
interdependency, 66n10, 73, 134
International Covenant on Civil and Political Rights (ICCPR), 37
International Federation of Journalists, 112
Internet, 15, 32, 132, 145. *See also* social media
ISIS, 88
Islamism,

Issa, Ibrahim, 87–8, 97n69
Issawi, Fatima el, 10n16, 11n21, 39n1, 39n4, 39n10, 39n19, 40n25, 43n71, 43n76, 43n83, 45n96, 45n103, 66n19, 66n23, 67n24, 67n27, 67n29, 67n30, 68n41, 68n44, 68n45, 68n48, 68n51, 69n61, 69n70, 93n26, 93n29, 94n42, 96n61, 97n75, 97n79, 124n20, 125n30, 125n32, 125n39, 125n44, 126n50, 126n54, 127n73, 127n79, 128n90, 149n42, 150n52, 150n56, 177n59, 179n84

J
Jakubowicz, Karol, 123n1, 123n4, 124n12
Jasmine revolution, 14, 22
Jebril, Nael, 148n16, 174n22
Jeune Afrique (magazine), 84
Jones, Owen, 73, 92n4
journalism. *See also* bloggers; media; press
  activism and, 60
  advocacy journalism, 59
  behavioral patterns of journalists, 49
  causes and, 137–40
  collaborative, 91
  democratic corporatist model of, 49
  Facebook and, 140
  liberal model of, 49, 169
  monitorial role of, 48
  neutral *vs.* engaged, 56–9
  oppositional, 91
  polarized pluralist model, 49, 184
  professional legitimacy, 8, 134–7
journalist advocate, 137–40. *See also* advocacy
Journalists' Syndicate Law, 26, 27
judiciary system, 18, 21

K

Kahki, Amer al, 165
Kahlaoui, Tarek, 133
Kamal, Abdallah, 141
Kamel, Buthaina, 116
Karoui, Nabil, 22, 53, 67n28, 165, 166
Khamis, Sahar, 10n10, 131, 141n5, 147n10, 175n33
Kheir, Mohamed, 58
Kingsly, Patrick, 94n37
Kirkpatrick, David, 95n49
Koubaa, Khaled, 130
Kraidy, Marwan M., 76, 93n17, 93n21

L

Laabid, Kamel, 112, 168
Laclau, Ernesto, 10n17, 74, 92n12
LaMay, Craig L., 66n12
Lamloum, Mehdi, 133
Lawson, Chappell, 69n68, 162, 176n43, 177n56
Lawson, George, 174n14
Lefebvre, Henri, 61, 69n58
legitimacy, 3, 8, 16–20, 49, 61, 71, 74, 80, 91, 99, 105, 113, 116, 118, 119, 121, 122, 134, 137, 156, 183, 185
L'Elite des journalists (Rieffel), 72
liberal model of journalism, 169. *See also* journalism
liberal theory, 163
Libya
  "Al Gad" project, 32
  Committee for Supporting and Encouraging the Press (CESP), 33, 105, 120
  Great Fateh Revolution, 34
  media reforms, 31–6, 172
  new media landscape, 35–6
  press, 32
  propaganda, 32–3
  television stations, 33, 35

Lichter, Robert, 92n7
Luckmann, Thomas, 66n15

M

Maatook, Abdel Hakim, 137
Maged, Reem, 1, 57, 60, 68n40, 68n50, 78, 79, 89, 138, 139, 149n43
Mahlab, Ibrahim, 144
Mahmoud, Mohamad, 110
Makni, Nouriddine al, 107
Manca, Enrico,
Mancini, Paolo, 10n19, 11n28, 49, 57, 66n9, 73, 92n10, 157, 174n16, 174n24, 184, 188n8
Mansoura, 83
Mansour, Adly, 24, 103
marketisation, 163
"marketplace of ideas", 50, 51, 163
Martin, Deborah, 61, 69n60
Martin, Marc, 92n3
Marzouki, Moncef, 40n33, 61, 110
Maspero demonstrations, 170
Matariya, 83, 95n46
Materi, Sakhr al, 102
Mbarki, Nour Edine, 22
media. *See also* journalism; press; state media
  democracy and, 3
  diversification of content, 77, 185
  elite and, 72–4
  Islamism and, 59, 115
  partisanship, 56, 57
  as platform for exclusion, 61–3
  plurality, 18, 29, 50, 166
  polarization, 21, 32, 53
  political elites and, 72–4
  political power of, 81, 82, 90, 108
  reforms, 7, 13–47, 49, 64, 99, 111–13, 117, 121, 122, 153, 154, 157, 160, 162, 168, 172, 185–7

media. *See also* journalism; press; state media (*cont.*)
  rise of private media, 52–6
  secularism and, 54, 59, 115
  state control of, 130, 158, 185
  systems reform, 50
  unilateral storytelling, 50–2
Meherzi, Mourad, 22
Mezwoghi, Ibrahim el, 55
military regimes, 55, 146
Miller, Byron, 61, 69n60
Mismari, Idris al, 107
Misr 25 (TV station), 143
Misrata, 35, 55, 142
Moameri, Mohamed, 126n57, 126n59
Momani, Bessma, 92n13
Moon, Ban Ki, 143
Morsi, Mohamed, 54, 79, 80, 85, 96n62
Mouffe, Chantal, 10n17, 11n27, 74, 92n12, 183, 188n5
Mounir, Safiaa, 124n29
Moussa, Ahmed, 82–4, 95n48, 95n54
Mubarak, Hosni, 74, 78, 81, 83, 87
Muslim Brotherhood, 1, 30, 47, 60, 62, 65, 76, 84, 85, 91, 96n57 116, 138, 144, 159, 167

N
Naqqash, Soha el, 51
Nasser, Gamal Abdel, 80, 103
National Authority for the Reform of Information and Communication (INRIC, Tunisia), 16, 17, 39n12
nationalism, 76, 91
National Union for Tunisian Journalists, 21
Nawat (blog), 135
Nawawy, Mohamed, 131
Nessma TV (Tunisia), 53
Nidaa Tunis party, 53, 165, 166
niqab, 53
Noaman, Riham, 137

nongovernmental organizations (NGOs), 8, 30, 103, 124n18
Nouaimi, Tibr, 109

O
Oaurda, Bechir, 120
Obama, Barack, 91
O'Donnell, Guillermo, 173n3, 174n16
ONT (TV network), 78
Ostini, Jennifer, 66n8

P
Passini, Stefano, 147n9
People TV channel, 88
Philipp, Abby, 95n53
pluralist objectivity, 166
polarized pluralist model, 49, 184
political parallelism, 49, 73, 184
press. *See also* journalism
  four theories of, 48
  independence of, 25, 51
  newspapers, 120
  television stations, 16, 20, 25, 26, 33–5, 53, 61, 138, 166
Press Code (Tunisia), 17, 37, 161
Price, Monroe E., 123n2, 176n39, 188n3, 189n16
privatization, 5, 25–6, 63, 172
protests, 23, 83–5, 118, 130, 131, 134, 174n14
public service media, 100, 101, 108–13, 121, 122, 166
public sphere, 10n12, 50, 57, 77, 132, 155, 163, 188n10
public welfare, 159

Q
Qaddafi, Muammar, 32. *See also* Gaddafi, Muammar
Qatar, 80, 84, 95n56, 151n67
Q-Soft, 80

R

Radcliffe, Damian, 151n66
Ramaprasad, Jyotika, 69n63
Rateb, Hassan, 89
reforms
   media, 7, 13–47, 49, 64, 99,
      111–13, 117, 121, 122, 153,
      154, 157, 160, 162, 168, 172,
      185–7
   political, 64, 158, 186
   regulatory, 4, 5, 8, 16–19,
      160–2, 186
Reporters Without Borders, 22, 36,
   65, 69n69, 124n18
Rieffel, Remy, 11n22, 72, 92n2
Rozanova, Julia, 101, 123n11,
   175n37
Roz el Youssef (newspaper), 107, 141
Russia, 88, 101, 160, 163, 177n53

S

Saad, Mahmood, 82, 85–7
Saad, Ragab, 151n64
Sabbagh, Dan, 92n5
Sabbagh, Shaimaa el, 83, 95n49
Sadat, Anwar, 25, 27
Sadi, Mahmoud R. Al, 93n22
Saghir, Mohamed, 58
Said, Khaled, 130
Salafi, 53, 78
Saraya, Osama, 106, 108
Sarikakis, Katharine, 123n7
Sarjani, Khaled, 106
satellite television, 2, 6, 25, 26, 34,
   78, 131
Sawiress, Naguib, 78
Sayyad, Ibrahim, 117
Sayyad, Nezar Al, 9n1, 147n1
Schedler, Andreas, 173n4
Schumpeter, Joseph A., 173n5
Searle, John R., 66n14
secularism,

self-criticism, 109
Shafik, Ahmed, 78
Sharkasy, Mahmoud al, 32, 56
Sheils, Conor, 128n87, 149n31
Shinnawy, Somaya el, 117, 120
Shukrallah, Hani, 134
Sisiin, Abdel Fattah al, 31
Snnousi, Hicham, 168
Snoussi, Hisham, 63
social constructivism, 49
social media. *See also* Facebook;
   Twitter
   as platform for political dissent,
      143–5
Soviet Union, 155
spaces
   conceived, 61, 69n59
   lived, 61
   perceived, 61, 69n59
state media. *See also* media
   Arab Spring and, 99, 101
   Egypt, 103–4
   Libya, 104–5
   media of shame, 115
   Muslim Brotherhood and, 116
   new identity, 108–11
   overview, 99
   patriotism and, 120, 122
   politics and, 114–19
   as public service, 100–5
   reforms, 7, 99, 111–13, 121, 122
   self-censorship, 99, 119
   theoretical discussion of, 100–1
   transition of, 108–13
   Tunisia, 101–3
State Nile TV (Egypt), 51, 110
Stephen, Chris, 67n31, 150n55
Stepka, Pawel, 123n10, 175n38
student protests, 85
Supreme Council of the Armed Forces
   (SCAF, Egypt), 28, 86, 138
Supreme Press Council, 24, 42n53, 103
Syria, 84, 95n53

T

Tahrir Square, 60, 79
talk shows. *See also* elites, media and
   blurred identity of, 78–80
   case studies, 80–8
   rise of, 77
terrorism, 8, 18, 23, 27, 61, 87, 91, 120, 144, 145
Thabti, Adel, 53
Tuchman, Gaye, 92n9
Tunis Africa news agency (TAP), 102, 112, 124n14
Tunisia
   Agency for External Communications, 15, 16
   decrees, 17
   HAICA, 38
   Internet Agency, 15
   legal uncertainty and anti-terror laws, 21–3
   media reforms, 14–23
   Office National de Télédiffusion (ONT), 15
   old media, 14–16
   Press Code, 17, 161
   Reform of Information and Communication (INRIC), 16, 17
   regulatory reforms, 16–19
   state media reform, 111–13, 122
Tunis, Nidaa, 53, 61, 165, 166, 171
Twitter, 130, 132, 147n7, 147n9, 148n20

U

Ukraine, 101, 160
unilateral storytelling, 50–2
United Nations (UN), 30, 32
Uruguay, 162

V

veils, 53. *See also niqab*
Venezuela, 156
Viber, 144
Voltmer, Katrin, 8, 9n5, 11n26, 36, 46n120, 46n122, 66n11, 66n16, 66n18, 67n36, 67n38, 69n65, 97n78, 155, 167, 172, 173n8, 173n10, 174n15, 175n26, 175n27, 175n31, 176n47, 178n64, 178n67, 178n69, 178n75, 179n81, 179n82, 179n91, 184, 188n4, 188n9, 188n11

W

Waisbord, Silvio, 10n9, 10n13, 11n24, 57, 67n37, 92n11, 94n33, 162, 164, 176n45, 177n55, 178n65
watchdog function of media, 48
WhatsApp, 144, 145, 151n67
Whitehead, Laurence, 172, 173n7, 188n13
World Bank, 10n13, 15, 97n78, 173n10, 177n55

Y

Yahyaoui, Amira, 133
Youssef, Bassemc, 1, 80, 90, 94n36

Z

Zaagar, Hussam, 135
Zaiddi, Zeinab, 129
Zakariya, Issam, 107
Zbeiss, Hanen, 57, 58
Zoghbiya, Bechir, 121
Zohbiya, Bashir, 160
Zugasti, Ricardo, 174n20

GPSR Compliance
The European Union's (EU) General Product Safety Regulation (GPSR) is a set of rules that requires consumer products to be safe and our obligations to ensure this.

If you have any concerns about our products, you can contact us on

ProductSafety@springernature.com

In case Publisher is established outside the EU, the EU authorized representative is:

Springer Nature Customer Service Center GmbH
Europaplatz 3
69115 Heidelberg, Germany

www.ingramcontent.com/pod-product-compliance
Lightning Source LLC
LaVergne TN
LVHW012101070526
838200LV00074BA/3881